Twilight over Burma

Twilight over Burma

MY LIFE AS A SHAN PRINCESS

Inge Sargent

With a foreword by
Bertil Lintner

A Kolowalu Book
University of Hawaii Press
Honolulu

08 07 06 05 04 03   9 8 7 6 5 4

Library of Congress
Cataloging-in-Publication Data
Sargent, Inge.
    Twilight over Burma : my life as a Shan
princess / Inge Sargent ; with a foreword by
Bertil Lintner.
        p.   cm.
    ISBN 0–8248–1623–4. —
    ISBN 0–8248–1628–5 (pbk.)
    1. Kya Seng, Sao. 2. Shans (Asian
people)—Kings and rulers—Biography.
3. Sargent, Inge. 4. Shan State (Burma)
—Politics and government. I. Title.
DS530.8.S45K937 1994
959.105'092—dc20
    [B]   94-17047
                                       CIP

Designed by Paula Newcomb

Printed by
The Maple-Vail Book Manufacturing Group

www.uhpress.hawaii.edu

This book is dedicated to the memory of Sao Kya Seng, the Prince of Hsipaw

(Arthur Lord Lee photo)

ACKNOWLEDGMENTS

I COULD NOT HAVE WRITTEN THIS book without the loving support of my family: my husband, Tad, whose gentle insistence and encouragement kept the project from faltering; my daughters, Mayari and Kennari, who with my son-in-law, Andrew, strengthened my resolve to tell the story of their father, Sao Kya Seng, and of his people. My heartfelt thanks go to them.

I am grateful to my mother, Elfriede Eberhard, for saving my letters from Hsipaw, which helped to refresh my memory. I wish to thank the members of my writer's group, Kirby, Kay, and Robert, for their constructive comments as the work progressed. Kate Clanchie provided helpful editorial comments at an early stage, and I am grateful to her.

This publication would not have been possible without the invaluable help of Bob Pritzker and Charles Goodman; I shall always be indebted to them. I also wish to thank Bill Hamilton of the University of Hawaii Press for his interest in my story.

Last but not least, I must express my gratitude to the brave men and women in various parts of Burma, and to compassionate people elsewhere, who rendered assistance in our most desperate hours. It would not be prudent to name many of them here, but they know who they are. I shall never forget them.

KEY PERSONS APPEARING IN THIS BOOK

A FEW NAMES HAVE BEEN CHANGED TO PROTECT PEOPLE STILL LIVING.

SAO KYA SENG (sao-cha-SENG). Saophalong, Prince of Hsipaw, hereditary ruler of the Shan state of Hsipaw. Often referred to as Sao.

THUSANDI (TOO-sahn-dee). Austrian-born wife of Sao Kya Seng; Mahadevi of Hsipaw, also referred to by her Austrian name, Inge, or Sao Mae (Royal Mother).

MAYARI (MY-uhr-ree) AND KENNARI (KAY-nuhr-ree). The daughters of Sao and Thusandi.

MOEI (MWAY). Shan maid and confidante of Thusandi.

NAI NAI (NIGH-NIGH) AND PA SAW. Shan nannies.

KAWLIN. Shan butler.

BUKONG (boo-KONG), MEHTA (MAY-ta), ZINNA, AI TSENG, AND BA AYE. Shan employees at the East Haw.

NANDA. Shan cousin of Sao Kya Seng; Mahadevi of previous prince.

U HTAN (oo-TAHN). Chief minister of Hsipaw State.

SAO KHUN LONG. Brother of Sao Kya Seng.

NANG LAO. Wife of Sao Khun Long.

AMBASSADOR AND MRS. KOLB OF AUSTRIA. Headquartered in Karachi.

PROFESSOR HANS HOFF. Austrian psychiatrist.

U KHANT. Burmese friend; brother of UN Secretary-General U Thant.

BO SETKYA (Boh-SET-cha). Burmese politician and businessman. One of the Thirty Comrades.

U NU (oo-NOO). Prime minister of the Union of Burma. Deposed and imprisoned by Ne Win in 1962.

MABEL. British-born wife of Sao Hkun Hkio (sao-kuhn-CHOH); Maha-devi of Mongmit State.

PAULA AND BETTAN. Helpful friends in Rangoon.

NE WIN (nay-WIN). Burmese Army general; leader of 1962 coup d'état and dictator of Burma since 1962.

MAUNG SHWE (Mawng-SHWAY). Burmese Army colonel in charge of Eastern Command (Shan states).

TUN OUNG. Burmese Army colonel in charge of Hsipaw State.

COLONEL LWIN. Head of Military Intelligence (MIS).

BURMA

Showing cities, towns, and locations mentioned in the text

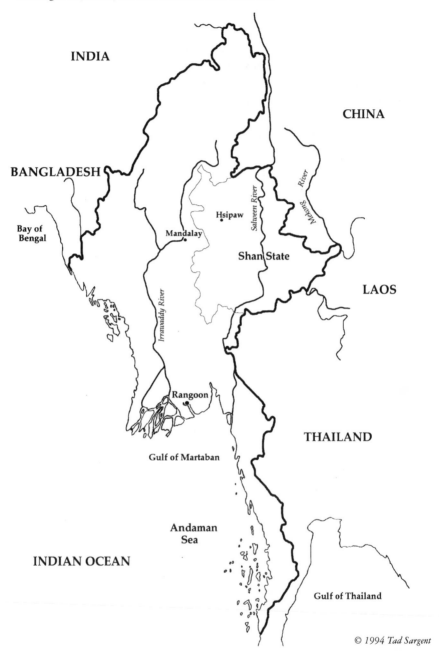

INDIA

CHINA

BANGLADESH

Bay of
Bengal

Hsipaw

Mandalay

Saltween River

Mekong River

Shan State

LAOS

Irrawaddy River

Rangoon

THAILAND

Gulf of Martaban

Andaman
Sea

INDIAN OCEAN

Gulf of Thailand

© 1994 Tad Sargent

FOREWORD

On a sunny summer afternoon in June 1966, a small Volkswagen Beetle made its way toward Schloss Laudon, a baroque castle operated privately as a luxury hotel in the 15th Bezirk, or district, of Austria's capital, Vienna. The iron gates to the estate were closely guarded by the Austrian police, who let the vehicle pass, since it carried official diplomatic identification from the Royal Thai Embassy in Vienna.

The Beetle chugged along the gravel road through the neatly trimmed garden that surrounded the castle and came to a halt right outside the building. A young European woman, her hair tied in a bun in Southeast Asian fashion, got out of the car and climbed the marble steps to the castle's main entrance. Two Eurasian girls, ten and seven years old, clutched her hands. They boldly entered the castle's round entry hall, which was furnished as an elegant lobby with rococo furniture and dark wooden panels.

The hotel guests, all of whom were Asians, stared in round-eyed wonder at the intruders. Still holding her two daughters by the hand, the lady quickly surveyed the hotel guests, spotted her target, and approached a woman in the party whom she addressed in fluent Burmese. "I want to see the general."

The Burmese lady glanced up a flight of stairs leading to a balcony on the second floor. The European lady's eyes followed hers, and she saw a tall Asian man on the balcony, hurriedly turning behind the balustrade and disappearing through one of the doors, which he resolutely shut behind him.

"Please be seated and have a cup of tea," the Burmese lady nervously suggested.

"No thank you. I have come here to discuss personal matters with the general," the other lady replied, holding her head high as the two little girls clung shyly to her hands.

"Er, he's resting. He's not so well, you see," the Burmese lady replied hesitantly.

"Not well? He seemed perfectly fit to me when he ran into that room upstairs," the European lady fired back.

The tall man who had vanished into the room on the second floor was, in fact, Burma's then military dictator, General Ne Win, who had seized power in a coup d'état four years before. The Asian lady was his wife, Khin May Than, who was also known as Kitty Ba Than, and they were on a visit to Vienna, where the general was receiving treatment for an undisclosed mental disorder. Accompanied by an entourage of nearly fifty high-ranking army officers and military intelligence agents, they had rented the entire Schloss Laudon while Ne Win went for daily consultations with one of Austria's most noted and respected psychiatrists, Dr. Hans Hoff.

The stalwart European lady who so boldly confronted the top echelons of Burma's ruling elite was Inge Eberhard. She was better known as Sao Nang Thusandi by the subjects of one of the most prosperous of the Shan states of northeastern Burma, in the valley of Hsipaw along the old Burma railway from Mandalay to Lashio. Her husband, Sao Kya Seng, had been the last *saopha*, or prince, of Hsipaw, and the two girls who were with their mother in Schloss Laudon in June 1966 were the young princely couple's daughters, Mayari and Kennari.

Inge first met Sao Kya Seng in Denver, Colorado, where both of them attended university in the early fifties. Throughout their period of courtship, Inge was unaware that Sao was anything other than just a student. They fell in love and got married in March of 1953.

Sao Kya Seng had assumed the title of Saophalong (Great-Lord-of-the-Sky) in Burma in January 1947, before he went to study in the United States. Inge was officially installed as Mahadevi (Celestial Princess) of Hsipaw on November 2, 1957, at the palace in Hsipaw. They became one of the most popular princely couples of the thirty or so Shan states, which together constituted a semiautonomous region within the Union of Burma.

Aage Krarup-Nielsen, a Danish writer who visited Hsipaw in the late 1950s, wrote in his book *The Land of the Golden Pagodas* that "it was at first somewhat of a shock for the local people to get a young European lady as their princess and in the beginning many were apprehensive. But before long, their reserve melted and the Mahadevi today is admired and loved by the entire people of Hsipaw who regard her as one of them."

Soon after his return to Hsipaw, Sao Kya Seng, with his Western, American education, introduced new ideas to the old feudal system of his state. Perhaps the most radical idea he took back was to give all the princely family's paddy fields to the farmers who cultivated them. In addition, he bought tractors and agricultural implements that the farmers used free of charge, cleared land to experiment with new crops, and began mineral exploration in the resource-rich valley. He plowed the profits back into research and development, as he wanted all to share in the valley's wealth. Old Hsipaw hands still talk with nostalgia about the days of their young prince. Their living standard then was far higher than it is today, under the mismanagement of successive totalitarian, military regimes.

"He had the same spirit as the present king of Thailand," an old native of Hsipaw, now in exile in Thailand, recollects. "He worked hard and he was incorruptible and honest. In those days we always had good rice to eat. Not like now, when the people of Hsipaw have to eat low-grade rice from central Burma because the government demands the local crops for their own use."

So highly regarded were the princely couple that when my wife grew up in Hsipaw in the 1960s, it was still common in many homes to place the official wedding picture of Sao Kya Seng and Sao Thusandi beside Buddha images on the family altar.

Over the centuries, the Shans of the hill country in northern Burma enjoyed a large degree of autonomy. Their autonomy was abolished when the military, led by General Ne Win, seized power in 1962. He immediately replaced the country's old federal system of government with a highly centralized political structure. The new political structure gave no special rights or status to the non-Burman nationalities, such as the Shans.

Burman writers, and some Western writers as well, usually accuse

SHAN STATE

Showing cities, towns, and locations mentioned in the text

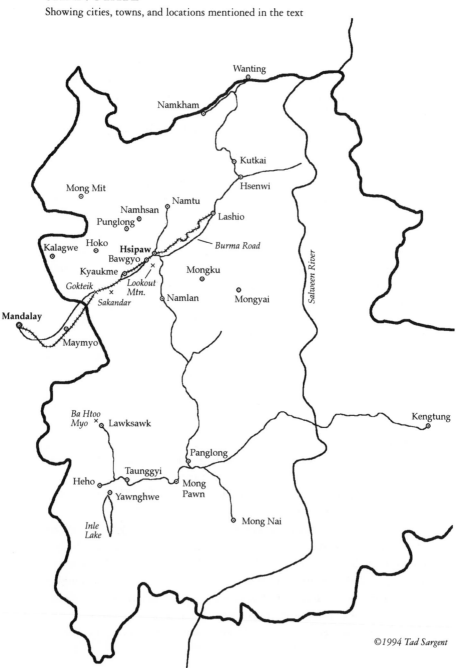

©1994 Tad Sargent

the British during their period of rule of having conducted "divide-and-rule" tactics by deliberately isolating the Shans and other minorities from mainstream Burmese politics. While that may be true, it is also true that the various hill peoples in central Burma's periphery have throughout history tended to perceive the Burmans as arch-enemies and untrustworthy. The British did little more than take advantage of this already existing, centuries-old animosity.

Burma is a country where many different nationalities reside— Kachins, Karens, Kayahs (or Karennis), Chins, Pa-Os, Palaungs, Mons, Myanmars, Rakhines, and Shans. Burma, as we know it with its present boundaries, is a British creation rife with internal contradictions and divisions. Northern Burma has experienced civil wars among the multitude of ethnic nationalities. It has suffered invasions by the British, the Japanese, and Chinese warlords, causing dislocation and the growth of insurgent militia throughout the hill country. Every Burma leader over the past two centuries has been confronted with but unable to control the various conflicting forces in Burmese society that constantly challenged its authority.

The Rakhine (or Arakanese), the Chins, the Kachins, the Lahus, the Lisus, the Akhas, and some smaller groups are of Tibeto-Burman stock. The origin of the Karens, the Karennis, and the Pa-Os is disputed, while the Mons, the Was, and Palaungs speak Mon-Khmer languages. Sao Kya Seng's people, the Shans, on the other hand, are not related to any other ethnic group in the country. They comprise 7 percent of the population according to the 1931 census, the last proper census taken in Burma. The word *Shan* is actually a corruption of Siam or Syam, and is the name given to them by the Burmans. The Shans call themselves "Dtai" (sometimes spelled "Tai" or, across the border in southwestern China, "Dai"), and they are related to the Thais and the Laotians, whose borders they share.

The origin of the Thai peoples, as they are collectively called, is still a question of academic controversy, but according to the most reliable and scientifically documented theories, the cradle of their race is to be found in Yunnan and Sichuan in southern China. Chinese historians mention a Thai tribe called "Great Mung," which inhabited the western part of Sichuan around 2000 B.C. Thai historian Luang Vichitra Vadhakarn states that the Thais began migrating toward Southeast Asia in 69 B.C. to escape harassment by the northern Chinese.

The last unified Thai state in southern China was the kingdom of

Nanchao, which covered large areas of southern Yunnan in the seventh century. This kingdom gradually declined and ended with its conquest by Kublai Khan in 1253. The movement south that had begun more than a thousand years earlier led to the setting up of Thai kingdoms, principalities, and cities all over Southeast Asia.

A western group, later referred to as the Shans, descended from southern China along the Salween River into the vast high plateau of northeastern present-day Burma. They settled in the valleys between the ridges on both sides of the river and established an abundance of principalities that varied in size and importance. The smallest, Namtok, measured 35 square kilometers (14 square miles) and was inhabited by a few hundred peasants scattered in two or three tiny villages. The largest principality, Kengtung, encompassed 32,000 square kilometers (12,000 square miles), larger than the state of Maryland. With 11,890 square kilometers (4,591 square miles), Hsipaw was one of the largest states, roughly the size of Connecticut. Most Shans were hard working, relatively prosperous cultivators who grew rice, soybeans, vegetables, and fruit.

Politically, however, the Shans were never effectively united, but for a short while after the fall of the Burman Pagan dynasty in 1287, the Shans overran most of upper Burma and established rule over the other ethnic groups. According to U.S. Burma scholar Josef Silverstein, "The Shans were direct political rivals of the Burmans for control over the entire area from that period until 1604, when they ceased resisting and accepted indirect rule by the Burmans."

But despite increasing pressure from the Burman kingdoms in the central plains, as well as the Burman military presence in some of the Shan principalities, the Shan hereditary chiefs, or saophas (*sawbwa* in Burmese), managed to retain a large degree of sovereignty. Neither Burma nor China was ever able to achieve effective conquest of the fiercely independent Shan princes and their states. Like their Thai and Laotian cousins, the Shans were Theravada Buddhists, with their own script, history, and centuries-old literature.

Their political status, however, underwent drastic changes in the nineteenth century, when Southeast Asia became an arena of competition between the two main colonial powers at that time: the French and the British. While Burma was being conquered by the British, the French had extended their sphere of influence over present-day Laos in the east. In between French-controlled Laos and British-controlled lower Burma lay the wild and rugged Shan hill country, with its abundance of principalities and local rulers. Sir Charles Crosthwaite, British chief commissioner of Burma from 1887 to 1890, described the situation in this manner:

> Looking at the character of the country lying between the Salween and the Mekong, it was certain to be the refuge for all the discontent and outlawry of Burma. Unless it was ruled by a government not only loyal and friendly to us, but thoroughly strong and efficient, this region would become a base for the operations of every brigand leader or pretender where they might muster their followers and hatch their plots. . . . To those responsible for the peace of Burma, such a prospect was not pleasant.

To avoid the possible emergence of an uncontrollable buffer zone between the two colonial powers of the time, the British extended their area of conquest in Burma to include the Shan states, which were "pacified," with the considerable expenditure of Shan lives, over the years 1885 to 1890. Another reason why the British decided to preempt the French and keep them at bay on the other side of the Mekong was that the trans-Burma trade routes to China passed through the northeastern border areas of the Shan territory. Several envoys sent by the East India Company to Burma during the period 1700–1824 had reported on the extensive and profitable China trade from upper Burma and the Shan states.

The present boundaries of northeastern Burma are, in other words, a direct outcome of nineteenth-century rivalry between the French and the British and the struggle for control of the lucrative China trade. The Shan people, and the numerous hill tribes who inhabit the mountains surrounding their valleys, are today found on all sides of the borders in the region—in all parts of Burma, Thailand, Laos, China, and even in northwestern Vietnam.

The thirty or so Shan states of the northeastern Shan plateau achieved a status different from that of Burma proper, which was a directly administered British colony. They became protectorates and the British recognised the authority of the Shan saophas, who enjoyed a status somewhat similar to that of the rulers of the Indian princely states. Each saopha was responsible for administration and law enforcement in his state; he had his own armed police force, civil servants, magistrates, and judges.

In 1922, the British created the Federated Shan States, and for the first time the Shan area gained a governing body common to all the principalities. The Federated Shan States' Council was established, comprising all the ruling princes and the British governor in Rangoon. The council dealt with such common concerns as education, health, public works, and construction. Due to the efforts of this political body, peace and order were established in the Shan states for the first time in many centuries.

Partly because of their separate administrative status, the Shan states were never affected by the pre-war nationalist movement, the Dohbama and other organisations, that swept central Burma at the time. The colonial machinery was also tenuous in the Shan states: The British presence was confined to a chief commissioner in the administrative center of Taunggyi, and a few political officers in the more important key states. On the other hand, very little was done to exploit the rich natural resources of the area and uplift it economically. The major preoccupation of the British in Burma was to develop the lowlands into a granary and rice exporter for India, its prize possession. For the Shan states, the colonial epoch meant peace and stability—but it was also a period of economic and political standstill. Even the China trade had plummeted following the anarchy that broke out in Yunnan in the 1930s as rival Chinese warlords battled each other for control of their own fiefdoms—and more lucrative undertakings such as the opium trade. Yunnan, not Burma, was the world's most important source of illicit opium before World War II.

The sleepy and stagnant Pax Britannica in the Shan states came to an abrupt end when the Japanese overran and occupied most of Southeast Asia in 1942. In the Shan Hills, fierce battles were fought between the Japanese Imperial Army and Nationalist Chinese (Kuomintang) units, invited by the British and dispatched by Chiang Kai-shek's warlord commanders in Yunnan. The Allies and the Japanese each in turn bombed Shan towns, leaving the hill country destroyed and in chaos.

After creating the nominally independent Burma on September 25, 1943, the Japanese ceded all but two Shan states. Kengtung and Möng Pan were transferred to the new puppet government of Siam (now Thailand). By 1944, branches of the East Asiatic Youth League and other nationalist associations were established in the Shan states. The institutional change of linking the frontier areas with Burma proper also resulted in a political change. It was from this period that the awakening of the various peoples of the Shan states can be measured.

When British rule was restored after the war, Burmese nationalists continued their struggle for independence. Although more politicized than ever before, frontier minorities nevertheless developed a movement that differed considerably from mainstream Burmese politics. In November 1946, the leaders of the Shans, the Kachins, and the Chins initiated a conference at Panglong, a small market town north of Loilem. The first Panglong conference decided on a common plan for the reconstruction of the war-devastated frontier areas. In addition, the Supreme Council of the United Hill Peoples was founded to safeguard the interests of the frontier peoples.

The decision to join Burma and ask for independence from Britain was taken at the second Panglong conference in February 1947. The leader of the Burmese nationalists, General Aung San, and the leaders of the frontier peoples (except the Karens and the Karennis, who later resorted to armed struggle) signed the historic Panglong Agreement. This is the key document in post-war relations between the frontier peoples and the central Burmese authorities in Rangoon. The day on which it was signed, February 12, has since then officially been celebrated in Burma as Union Day, a national holiday.

The Shan saophas also asked for, and were granted, the right to secede from the proposed Union of Burma after a ten-year period of independence (that is, in 1958), should they be dissatisfied with the new federation. This right was also ensured under the first Burmese constitution.

On paper, everything was ready for the declaration of Burma's independence from Britain—which was to take place on January 4, 1948—when an event occurred that was as unexpected as it was tragic. On July 19, 1947, the Burmese nation was shocked by the news that Aung San had been assassinated, along with several other state leaders, among them Sao Sam Htun, the Shan saopha of Möng Pawn.

The state of affairs in Burma when it achieved its independence in 1948 could hardly have been worse. The country had suffered some of the most severe air strikes in Asia during the war; the countryside was ravaged and the political infrastructure was almost destroyed. Burma's inner circle of competent political leaders had been murdered even before independence had been proclaimed. The new leader and independent Burma's first prime minister, U Nu, was a talented, intellectual politician, but he was heavily criticized for not being the strong statesman Burma desperately needed during its first difficult years of independence. With a central government perceived as weak, army units rose in mutiny; the Karens, the Karennis, and the Mons took up arms; and the powerful Communist Party of Burma (CPB) went underground to organize guerrilla forces.

In an attempt to forge national unity, Shan leader Sao Shwe Thaike had been given the ceremonial post of first president of the Union of Burma. But events along the Chinese border in the Shan states thwarted further attempts to placate possible opposition. In late 1949, Kuomintang (KMT) forces from southern Yunnan, unable to withstand the attack of the victorious Chinese Communist army, crossed the international frontier into Shan territory. Led by wartime hero General Li Mi, they invaded Kengtung state and sought refuge in the Shan hills.

The KMT recruited soldiers from the border areas, and the number of KMT soldiers swelled from about 1,700 in early 1950 to 4,000 by April 1951. The Burmese Army was sent to the Shan states to rid the country of its uninvited guests, but was unsuccessful. U Nu then raised the question in the United Nations General Assembly, which on April 22, 1953, adopted a resolution demanding that the KMT lay down their arms and leave the country. Ignoring the UN resolution, the number of KMT soldiers in the Shan states increased to 12,000 by the end of 1953—and civil war was raging across the Shan states.

It was at this pivotal time in modern Burmese history that Inge and her Shan husband arrived in Burma. Hsipaw was not directly affected by the KMT incursion, but the situation was becoming tense in other parts of the Shan states. The traditional way of life in the peaceful, fertile Shan valleys was being changed by the distant turmoil along the Yunnan frontier.

The KMT was conducting a reign of terror from its strongholds in the Shan hills. On the other hand, the years up to 1955 saw a great influx of Burmese troops into the Shan states to rid the country of the uninvited intruders. The southern Shan states had been placed under military administration in September 1952 with the aim of suppressing KMT activities there—but the outcome was that the Shans saw their autonomy undermined. For many Shan peasants, it was the first time in history that they had come in direct contact with any Burmans, and their encounters were, in most instances, frightening, and often deadly.

The KMT invasion, combined with the government's inability to repel the intruders, meant that the Shans became squeezed between two forces, both of which were perceived as foreign. The result was a strong Shan nationalist movement. The central government viewed this development with uneasiness, due to the constitutional right of the Shan states to secede from the Union in 1958.

Authorities tried to suppress the fledgling movement by using the army and its Military Intelligence Service, but the outcome was counter-productive: Groups of young people moved into the jungle, where they organized guerrilla units. By 1959, bands of Shan guerrillas were ambushing Burmese Army camps and raiding isolated outposts in search of arms. The guerrillas even managed to capture the garrison town of Tang-yan and hold it for a few days.

While these violent activities were going on in remote frontier areas, members of the Shan State Council in Rangoon initiated a legal movement to preserve the Union by strengthening its federal character. On April 24, 1959, all thirty-four saophas formally gave up their positions at a grand ceremony in the Shan states' capital of Taunggyi. The Shan states became Shan State, administered by an elected state government. Rangoon, at that time controlled by a military caretaker government, probably viewed it as a victory over the "feudal chiefs" who had "surrendered their powers," while the Shans saw it as the formal finalization of a movement that had begun several years before: The saophas did not hand over power to Rangoon, but to the elected Shan State government. Many of the more modern saophas, including Sao Kya Seng, also stayed on in politics, usually as members of the Shan State Council and the House of Nationalities, or Upper House, of the then bicameral Burmese Parliament.

The war, and the massive concentration of government forces in the border areas as a direct outcome of the KMT intervention, had effectively undermined efforts to create a more democratic system in Shan State. The Shan insurrection, small and insignificant as it might be, was another concern. Several Shan leaders were caught in a dilemma when many of their subjects were rising in rebellion against the central government in Rangoon. Hsipaw, especially, supplied the ranks of the Shan rebel army with many fighters and cadres, most of whom at that time were separatists.

It is said that one of the early Shan rebel leaders, Hsö Hten, who also was a native of Hsipaw, secretly visited Rangoon in 1961 to contact Sao Kya Seng. The intermediary, a Shan student in the capital, asked the Hsipaw prince whether he would like to meet a representative from the rebels. Sao Kya Seng then brought out the Union Constitution and read out the oath of loyalty he had sworn as a member of the House of Nationalities.

Sao Shwe Thaike, Sao Kya Seng, and other Shans began to organize more concerted efforts to solve the widespread rebellion by political means. They reasoned that by restructuring the federal system, the Union would survive, and the fledgling insurgency would be undermined. In 1960, a democratically elected government, again headed by U Nu, had returned to power in Rangoon, and the prime minister was sympathetic to these ideas.

IN 1961, ANOTHER REBELLION broke out in northern Burma: The predominantly Christian Kachins rose up in arms to protest the decision to make Buddhism the state religion of Burma. There were other grievances, and taken aback by the sudden outburst of violence, U Nu's government in 1962 convened the Nationalities' Seminar in Rangoon in order to discuss the future status of the frontier areas (or the Constituent States, as they now were called) and, if necessary, loosen the federal structure of the constitution. All the government ministers, members of Parliament, heads of the Constituent States, and their state ministers attended this seminar.

On March 2, 1962, before any decision had been taken, the commander in chief of the Burmese Army, General Ne Win, staged a coup d'état and detained all the participants of the meeting. Sao Shwe Thaike was among those arrested, and his seventeen-year-old son was gunned down on the night of the coup when, according to the official version, he "resisted arrest." The former president himself died in jail eight months later, presumed extrajudicially executed.

The army claimed that it had to intervene to "prevent the disintegration of the Union." Other analysts argued that the army had grown in strength because of the civil war, and especially because of the fight against the KMT. It had been an uncontrollable state within the state, and became the state itself, with General Ne Win in power.

Sao Kya Seng had attended the Parliament in Rangoon the day before the coup and then flown to Taunggyi to visit his terminally ill sister. Unaware of what had taken place in Rangoon, he left early that morning to catch the plane to Lashio, the airport serving Hsipaw. But at Taunggyi gate, on the road to Heho, the military had already put up a roadblock, and Sao Kya Seng was stopped. He was last seen being led away into captivity by armed soldiers.

Inge was left alone in Hsipaw to deal with the complexities of Burmese politics. She tried desperately to find out what had happened to Sao Kya Seng—but all she got was a mingle of conflicting statements, prevarications, and outright lies from the new military government in Rangoon and its representatives in Taunggyi. Subsequent events forced Inge, Mayari, and Kennari to leave their homeland in May 1964. They went to Austria, where she managed to get a job at the Thai Embassy in Vienna—and where she also continued her relentless efforts to shed light on the fate of her husband.

During the brief encounter Inge had with Kitty Ba Than in Schloss Laudon in June 1966, she was told nothing more than that her husband was "well and treated as a detainee in Rangoon." Earlier, however, military authorities had said that Sao Kya Seng had never been arrested. All this had actually been contradicted in 1964 in Rangoon, shortly before Inge left the country. Bo Setkya, a veteran Burmese politician with solid high-level connections, had told her that Sao Kya Seng had been executed by the army in Ba Htoo Myo camp north of Taunggyi soon after his arrest.

Inge, Mayari, and Kennari left for the United States later in 1966, where they settled down as private citizens. Family tragedies of this nature are not isolated cases in military-ruled Burma, where thousands of people have vanished without a trace over the past three decades. The story of the Hsipaw prince, here told beautifully by Inge herself, is an unusually well-documented one. It is a story of human bravery and courage. It also relates the brutality of a military regime that has tried to control the country by forcefully suppressing the population, and by eliminating even in a physical sense any prominent opponent to its rule, without realizing how ineffective these methods are. With the coup, the 1947 Constitution was abrogated, and the right to secede from the Union was declared null and void. Predictably, the outcome was utterly counterproductive: Rebellions flared anew in Shan and Kachin states, as thousands of young people took to the hills. Hsipaw has continued to supply the Shan resistance armies with young fighters ever since the military takeover in 1962.

INGE STILL WEARS HER WAIST-length hair braided in the traditional Shan fashion and has not forgotten her years in the fertile valley in the northern Shan states. She has shared these happy memories with her daughters over the years as they grew up in the United States. Each year Mayari and Kennari still write to the military authorities in Rangoon, inquiring about what happened to their father. There has never been a reply.

                                                            Bertil Lintner

BERTIL LINTNER is a freelance journalist based in Thailand who has written extensively on insurgency in Burma. He is a regular contributor to *The Far Eastern Economic Review* and other publications throughout Asia and Europe. Married to a Shan woman born in Hsipaw, the foreword to this book is based on a feature story Lintner wrote for the *Bangkok Post* in 1988 that brought Inge Sargent's story to the public. He is author of four books on Burma, *Outrage: Burma's Struggle for Democracy* (1989), *Land of Jade: A Journey through Insurgent Burma* (1990), *The Rise and Fall of the Communist Party of Burma* (1990), and *Burma in Revolt* (forthcoming). Lintner received a MacArthur Foundation Grant in 1992.

One

THUSANDI KNEW BY THE strange sounds that broke the silence of the tropical morning that their dream was over, that the moment they had expected for years had come. She carefully opened the screen door to the balcony, making sure not to awaken their daughters, who were asleep on her husband's side of the bed.

From the balcony she saw that the compound of their residence, the East Haw, was surrounded by hundreds of armed Burmese soldiers. The massive stone wall enclosing the Haw grounds had turned into a living monster. Rows of men in green helmets and uniforms jutted out from behind the stark wall. The sound of rustling boots in the dry underbrush seemed to follow short orders barked into the solitude of this early morning. For a few seconds, Thusandi felt disbelief and utter loneliness. She straightened up and took a few deep breaths before she was ready to meet her followers and her enemies. Thusandi had to be strong and optimistic to safeguard the lives of her husband, the prince, of their two young children, and of their Shan people.

Bukong, the head of their trusted bodyguards, and two dozen followers were in the foyer when Thusandi went downstairs. He confirmed what she instinctively knew: The Burmese Army had taken over the country, and their troops wanted her permission to search the East Haw. Her people were now waiting for her decision, and she was deeply moved by their faith in her. For a split second, the idea of an armed response appealed to her inner rage, but she had to act honorably, in the spirit of her husband. It was clear to Thusandi that from now on she alone, the foreign-born princess, would have to provide strength, support, and comfort for the Shan people of Hsipaw. Above all, she had to protect her two little daughters and wait for their father. She hoped desperately that he had gotten away; maybe he had left Rangoon early and was on the way home.

Thusandi prepared herself to face the Burmese colonel and his troops. With her Shan followers standing behind her, she stepped outside the East Haw and took charge. Dozens of green-clad soldiers stood next to and behind their officers. Their stance was threatening, and they appeared ready to use the Sten guns in their hands. With authority Thusandi demanded an explanation for the intrusion. When she received none, she lectured the officers on the impropriety of using military force against a woman and her children. The colonel and his men were speechless. They had expected tears and desperation from a foreign-born woman, not a tirade in fluent Burmese.

Once the children were in the care of their nannies and sheltered from most of the upheaval, Thusandi had no choice but to give the Burmese officers permission to search the residence. She did not let the searchers out of her sight as they went from room to room, and she became more agitated as the hours passed. They paid special attention to her large bedroom suite on the second floor, emptying the carved teak wardrobes, rolling up the silk carpets, and knocking on the teak parquet floor as they moved back and forth on their knees. In the marble bathrooms, they examined every tile, apparently looking for loose ones. What could they possibly hope to find? Bukong had already handed guns and ammunition over to them, and they did not show any interest in the contents of the private office. They looked under beds, in closets, on balconies, behind bookcases, even inside mattresses. A zealous sergeant poked a four-foot metal rod into every mattress. In the children's room, he thrust his metal stick into every stuffed animal perched on the shelves. His comrades found it humorous when the children's giant teddy bear split open and spilled its stuffing over the other wounded toys.

Finally, Thusandi understood why they were there. The colonel's question at the end of this first of eight searches confirmed her suspicion and the hope she had not dared to nurture: "Can you tell us where we can find Sao Kya Seng, the prince?"

Thusandi folded her arms, looked straight at the colonel, and slowly counted to ten before she answered, "My husband is in Rangoon attending Parliament."

"He is not there. Our troops could not find him," the colonel said angrily.

"Well, you ought to be convinced by now that he is not hiding here either," she said as she walked away, a sense of superiority mingling with her relief.

Thusandi looked for her children. In their company she could express her joy at what she had heard. He was free, not in the hands of his adversary, General Ne Win, and he was alive. That meant everything would be all right again; they would be able to continue their lives and their work together. Some of Sao's responsibilities that needed immediate attention flashed through her mind: The Tai Mining Company expected its first major shipment of machinery, the salt production in Bawgyo was ready to start, the experimental coffee plantation in Loikaw had to be expanded, and the Hsipaw Sawbwa Foundation had to select more students for studies abroad. Thusandi herself was needed to administer the trilingual Foundation School, the Hsipaw Maternity Home, and the Child Welfare Society, as she had for years. She cared for the development and welfare of the Shan people of Hsipaw State and hoped all these projects would continue. She was Mother-in-the-Land to so many, and Mother pure and simple to her own little girls.

It was only eight o'clock in the morning, but this day in March 1962 already seemed endless. The dawn trauma had passed, and things seemed quiet and normal—almost. The Shan bodyguards who used to guard the gate had been replaced by a Burmese contingent. The uniforms of the gatekeepers had changed from khaki to olive green, and the faces of the new men were two shades darker. When the cook returned from the bazaar on his bicycle, the soldiers at the gate searched his basket and indicated that members of the household were discouraged from leaving the East Haw. Thusandi considered this development irritating rather than alarming. She turned on the radio, only to hear the regular morning program of contemporary Burmese tunes. No special news bulletins came over the air, and the daily newspaper had not yet arrived. Thusandi tried the phone. It worked and the operator connected her with friends in Rangoon who hosted Sao whenever he attended Parliament. Their friend Jimmy's voice came through faintly, and it seemed rather shaken when he said, "Our house was thoroughly searched this morning. Burmese soldiers turned everything upside down trying to find Sao."

"What did you tell them, Jimmy?" Thusandi shouted into the receiver as the phone connection got worse.

"I told them that Sao left the city yesterday, but they just didn't believe me." Then the connection was lost.

That was all Thusandi needed to hear. She knew that Sao had planned to visit his dying sister in Taunggyi on his way home. He was still four hundred miles away, probably having breakfast at his brother's house. There was no phone connection with Taunggyi, the capital of the Federated Shan States, and Thusandi decided to drive to Lashio and meet the Tuesday plane from Rangoon, which came via Taunggyi and Mandalay. Perhaps he or somebody with news of him, possibly his secretary, would be on it. She did not need to leave for the airstrip for another three hours; the biweekly plane was not due until one o'clock.

Thusandi planned to have breakfast, walk the children to school, and spend some time there. Her daughters were oblivious to the events of the early morning; she smiled, for the first time that day, as she watched them. Their dark hair, graceful movements, and smiling black eyes reminded her of their father. They also resembled her with their light skin and European features. Carefree and happy, the girls were busy chasing the puppies around the tamarind trees; they did not seem to notice that the uniforms of the gatekeepers had changed.

With Sao away, breakfast in the formal dining room was a lonely affair. The french windows invited rays of the morning sun to dance on the polished table, which was large enough to seat twenty. Thusandi sat down at the oval table by herself, acknowledging the attentive service of the butler, Kawlin, with a grateful nod. He wanted her to eat and smile and not be discouraged by this morning's events. After all, his lord was protected by birth and office; he was invincible and nothing harmful could ever befall him. Kawlin himself was tattooed from scalp to ankle in order to ward off evil spirits. Only the skin of his face, his throat, and the palms of his hands was not covered with black bands of circles, wavy lines, and other symmetric designs. Kawlin's faith was contagious, and Thusandi managed to nibble from the fruit plate. She was about to spread guava jelly on her toast when she heard several jeeps pull up in front of the East Haw. Sao couldn't possibly be home yet, and her secretary had only one jeep. Thusandi's internal alarm system struck a note of shrill warning. They must have come again.

She was right. The circular driveway in front of the residence was teeming with heavily armed Burmese soldiers. Three officers ordered Bukong to assemble all bodyguards and drivers. Thusandi quickly ordered the nannies to walk the children to school, a building just outside the gate. Then she had to witness the soldiers handcuffing her bodyguards and drivers, and brutally hitting them with their rifle butts. Although her men endured these blows without flinching, Thusandi could not bear to witness such brutality any longer.

"Stop that! You can't do that to my people!" she shouted. In response, the captain said in his most authoritative voice, "I have orders to take these suspects into protective custody. We are also taking most Hsipaw State officials, your secretary, and your mechanic to headquarters for questioning."

Thusandi did not dignify this pronouncement with a response. Instead, she turned to her followers and said, "Do not worry about your wives and children. I will take care of your families as if they were my own."

But the captain had not finished with his orders. Thusandi ignored him, until he started speaking again.

"It is my duty, Mahadevi, to read you the following restrictions, which my highest commander has ordered for you."

She stared at him and waited without uttering a sound.

"You may not leave the East Haw without special permission from the colonel. You are not permitted to receive any visitors, or make phone calls. And all your mail must go through the local army unit."

"Anything else?" she asked in a chilly voice.

"No, Madam," the captain said meekly. Thusandi walked into the East Haw with her head held higher than usual, already planning to break every one of these ludicrous rules. Only when she was alone, in the privacy of her bedroom, did she allow the tears to flow freely.

IF SAO DID NOT SEE THE GUARDS through the bamboo matting of his hut, he heard them. They were posted at all four corners of the one-room prison, pacing back and forth. He knew he could not get away; any such attempt would give his captors a perfect excuse for murder. Yet he had to find a way to freedom, a way to return to his wife and children. The morning would bring hope and maybe his release. By then the prime minister would have heard about his illegal arrest and would insist that the army abide by the law of the land.

It was night now, a time to gain strength for tomorrow. He stretched out on the bamboo mat, but sleep did not come. Mosquitoes were buzzing around his head, and Sao wished he had not given up smoking awhile back. He tried to meditate, which had always released his stress before. Tonight was different; meditation did not work. He was imprisoned, without charges, without even knowing why. Over the years Sao had had a few collisions with the Burmese Army, always on matters of principle, but that was not enough to explain soldiers stopping his car today and forcefully taking him to this desolate army camp in Ba Htoo Myo. He knew he would find no answer that night, not from the unresponsive guards outside the bamboo walls.

His thoughts turned to Thusandi. She had followed him to the Shan hills from her native Austria and had been his wife for ten years. She was probably asleep now, with their two daughters on his side of the bed. He could picture her tall and slender body nestled in damask sheets, and her knee-length chestnut-brown hair braided for the night. He was sure that nobody would bother her. He felt satisfaction when he imagined the contempt and fury with which she would receive the news of his arrest. He loved her for so many reasons, but at that moment, he loved her most for that strong will, that determination to do what was right. For the first time on this horrible day, he felt a smile spreading over his face.

He remembered her most recent crusade to rescue a fish. The cook had resigned when a local salmon, intended for the dinner table, ended up thrashing back and forth in the blue waters of the swimming pool. Thusandi closed the pool until the captive fish had recovered its strength and could be returned to the folds of the Namtu River. The children were upset but she had prevailed in her rescue effort, and he loved her for it.

Sao felt strongly that she was safe, but he was not sure if he would ever see her again. He wondered if they would again trek through the jungle together, he in search of minerals, she on the lookout for orchids and wildlife. They had slept in bamboo huts then, not unlike the one confining him now. Their huts had been surrounded by their own bodyguards, to keep tigers out, not to keep him inside. And they had been sheltered by a mosquito net that kept away buzzing insects and gave them an extra sense of privacy in their togetherness. How he missed her physical presence, how he longed for her laughter and her warmth. He wondered if she would find a way to cheer him now; he knew that she never failed him when it counted.

He sat up, startled; somebody was inside the hut, right next to the mat, where he must have gone to sleep a few hours ago. Otherwise the night was still—he could not hear the guards any more. The presence next to him belonged to a man in uniform, that much he could perceive in the dark hut. Was it someone trying to hurt or to help him? He had to keep still and remain very alert.

"I am one of your guards, sir, but I belong to the Kachin tribe. My uncle was in your police force many years ago," whispered the man in Burmese with a noticeable accent.

"Why are you telling me this?" Sao asked suspiciously.

"My comrades have fallen asleep, and I want to help you, sir."

"Can you get me out of here?" Sao asked.

"No, sir, that is impossible. But I can deliver a letter to your Mahadevi in Hsipaw."

There was no doubt in Sao's mind that he should take this chance. He felt quite certain that nobody knew where he was, and a message from him could be the key to freedom. And if this was a setup, he did not have much to lose. On a page torn from his pocket calendar, he wrote a message to his wife, dated March 2, 1962. It read: "Liebling, I am in the army lockup at Ba Htoo Myo. I am still OK."

The Kachin guard lit a cheroot, a fat Burmese cigar, which provided a flicker of light. He also offered to supply an envelope and somehow get the note to the East Haw in Hsipaw. The soldier refused to accept the 100-kyat note Sao offered him; he said he took the risk not for money but because he too belonged to an oppressed hill tribe.

After the soldier stole away, Sao was alone again. This episode had raised his spirits and given him more hope than he had felt since he was ordered to step out of his brother's car at the Taunggyi gate and taken into the army checkpoint station. He was wide awake again and his mind was racing, going over the day that had started with a routine breakfast at his brother's and ended in an army lockup.

His sister-in-law had mentioned that his brother had been called away at four that morning to a meeting of the Shan Security Council.

Despite the unusual hour, nobody had felt alarmed. After breakfast, Sao and his driver had started off to Heho airstrip in his brother's car. There had been a lot of military personnel on the streets of Taunggyi that morning, but it had not interfered with traffic until they had arrived at Taunggyi gate, where all vehicles were stopped at an army roadblock. Several Burmese officers had rushed up to the car and asked if the Saophalong of Hsipaw State was present.

"Yes, I am Sao Kya Seng—what is this all about?"

"Please step into our guardhouse for a few minutes, sir," one of the officers had said and opened the car door for Sao. As he entered the guardhouse, Sao had turned around and seen an officer motioning to the driver to head back to Taunggyi, with his master's luggage but without his master.

Now, sixteen hours later, he was confined within Ba Htoo Myo Military Academy grounds in the southern Shan states, knowing no more than he did when all this had started. Whatever had happened to the Constitution of the Union of Burma if the army could detain a member of Parliament, even for a day? The day's events did not bode well for the Constitution's future.

Sao could not allow himself to dwell on this subject any longer. Some additional sleep was necessary before he faced a new day, which would bring more stress and more danger, and maybe more hope. He directed his thoughts to his wife and children—to their laughter and to the happiness he felt when he was with them. He had to overcome this nightmare and find a way back to freedom.

SAO AWOKE TO A CONCERT OF jungle fowl greeting the very early morning. It was four-thirty, and the nightmare was still with him: the same army camp, the same bamboo hut, no windows, a door barricaded from the outside. He was still at the mercy of his jailers.

At that moment Sao had one overriding desire: to go home, pack up his family, and move to the little mining town in the United States where he had spent the most carefree years of his life.

When he got out of this predicament, he would immediately search his files for the job offers that now and then still reached him from the placement office of the Colorado School of Mines. He was now ready to pursue what his friends had long advised for his own personal safety and what his enemies had tried to promote for their own advantage: his departure from Hsipaw, even though it meant leaving the people who wanted and needed his leadership.

The sound of boots approaching his miserable hut brought Sao Kya Seng back to reality. The door was opened cautiously, finally allowing the first light of day to enter his dark room. A Burmese officer of the dreaded Military Intelligence unit, a smirk on his face, appeared inside the door. Sao knew he had seen him before, a year ago, after four village headmen from the Hsipaw area had died while being tortured with electric current. When the commanding officer had explained to outraged local leaders that the rebellious Shans had to be taught a lesson, this officer had been present.

"I am Captain San Lwin, and I would like to ask you a few questions, sir," he said as he stood with his legs squarely planted on the matted floor to assume an intimidating posture.

"As a member of Parliament, I demand to see Colonel Maung Shwe, the officer in charge of the army's Eastern Command," Sao said calmly.

After an awkward moment of silence, the Military Intelligence captain said, "That won't be possible until you answer some of my questions. I want to help you. Please trust me. But first, you must give me the information we need."

"I have made my request and do not plan to make any further statements," Sao said, turning his back to the captain, who was visibly annoyed. Having to return to his superiors without any answers guaranteed a loss of face.

"You will regret this," said the captain as he turned around, swinging the bamboo door shut. It was dark again save for some thin rays of light that broke through the matted walls here and there. Sao heard footsteps disappearing into the distance.

Sao sat down on the mat that had served as his bed and made a serious attempt to meditate. He shut his eyes and concentrated on his breath as it streamed through his nostrils—on the cold sensations as he inhaled it, and the warmth as it was forced out again. His efforts must have been successful, as he was startled when he heard a male voice next to him saying, "Sir, I am alone on duty till our replacements arrive in a few minutes. As I told you during the night, I am a Kachin soldier and I am loyal to my people, not to the Burmese in whose army I serve. We Kachins respect you very much, and I wish I could help you."

The door was a few inches ajar, so that Sao could clearly see the man, squatting on the floor next to him. He had taken off his boots, apparently in keeping with the tradition of showing respect, and his gun was nowhere in sight. His features, especially his long, sharply defined nose, confirmed his claim that he belonged to the hill tribe.

"What do you think you can do for me?" Sao asked.

"I could forward another letter to your Mahadevi by a different route than the note you gave me in the night," the soldier said. "She must be anxious to have news of you."

Without hesitation, Sao wrote a more detailed message on one of the pieces of paper he found in his pocket: "Liebling, I am writing this secretly. I am being locked up in the Army lockup at Ba Htoo Myo at Lawksawk. Please ask Khin Mg Chone to request Tommy Clift to use his influence to get me out. There is also Ko Hla Moe. Millie can help here. Miss you all. Conditions here are not clean. Hope to see you all again soon. Cheer up yourself! I am still OK. Love, Sao Kya Seng."

On another piece of paper, Sao hurriedly wrote a similar message to his friend Jimmy Yang in Rangoon, asking him to contact Prime Minister U Nu with a request for help.

"Will you have these two letters delivered for me?" he asked the soldier as he handed him the addresses, scribbled on a page torn from his pocket calendar.

"I give you my word of honor, sir. And one more thing, sir. Please be careful. Do not trust your captors. They are evil." With that, the Kachin soldier quietly backed out of the bamboo jail, shutting the door behind him.

A few minutes later, Sao heard that his guards were changed. One soldier, marching away, carried with him the only hope Sao had of communicating to the outside world what had happened to him after he left his brother's house twenty-four hours ago. He had no choice but to wait, meditate, and see if this mission would succeed.

Two

ONLY HOURS HAD PASSED SINCE life in the East Haw had changed in a way that was incredible, yet horribly easy to believe. Thusandi needed to be alone to work through her emotions and consider her future course of action. She chose the east terrace as her refuge. From there, she could see the jungle-clad hill she liked to call Lookout Mountain, the green Namtu River now and then allowing a dugout canoe to disturb its mirror surface, and a sea of wild yellow sunflowers insisting on their right to bloom in the company of hundreds of red poinsettia bushes. A large flock of parrots had just descended on the sunflowers, filling the air with such loud chatter that any attempt at conversation would have been futile. They drowned out the ever-present chirping of crickets and the shrill chitchat of the resident mynahs. The disruption provided by these messengers of nature had the unlikely effect of calming her.

Eight years ago, when Sao had brought Thusandi home to Hsipaw as his bride, this terrace had been decorated with thousands of fragrant blossoms. The welcome at the East Haw had been the culmination of a week of celebrations that had commenced in the port of Rangoon with a shocking discovery for Thusandi.

IN EARLY JANUARY OF 1954, THE SS *Warwickshire* was gliding toward Rangoon, ready to deliver its load of cargo and the two dozen passengers who were assembled on deck, eager for arrival. They were under the spell of the symbol of Rangoon, the Shwe Dagon Pagoda, whose golden rays had caught their eye when they were still thirty miles downstream. Most of the passengers, including Sao and Inge, his Austrian bride, were mesmerized by the brilliant splendor of this 326-foot bell-shaped *stupa,* which was plated with solid gold and tipped with diamonds, rubies, sapphires, and a huge emerald to catch the rays of the sun.

As the ship approached Rangoon harbor, Inge's excitement grew. She liked the low white buildings framed by swaying coconut palms that lined the right-hand side of the river. Somewhere around the next bend, she expected to see tall buildings of a harbor front not like New York, she thought, but perhaps like Genoa or Lisbon. But the ship did not go around another bend; it prepared to dock next to two freighters that were loading rice. The pace seemed casual and unhurried, and Inge noted the absence of loud thumps and shrill whistles that she remembered from the large ports

Sao and Inge were married on March 7, 1953, in Denver, Colorado. (Arthur Lord Lee photo)

in the West. Only her ship's own loud horn disrupted the tranquillity of its arrival in the harbor.

The expected skyline of the city of Rangoon did not materialize; even the golden Shwe Dagon Pagoda was no longer visible. Instead, a number of small boats caught her attention. As they approached the SS *Warwickshire,* Inge saw that they were filled with people dressed in brilliantly colored garments: red, blue, yellow, pink, green. She had never seen so many colors in clothing before, and she stretched to see more. A light breeze playfully twisted colorful parasols and large banners saying "Welcome Home," and smiling black-haired women were tossing flowers into the glistening river. These boats with their exotic passengers approached as if to welcome someone important on the SS *Warwickshire.* Everyone on deck seemed delighted, if puzzled as to who on the ship warranted such an unusual welcome. Everyone, that is, except Sao Kya Seng.

"I wonder what this is all about," said Inge to her husband as she marveled at the spectacle. "Somebody very important must be on board."

Looking very uncomfortable, Sao said, "There is something I have to tell you, my dear."

"Can't it wait? I'd really like to watch the welcome," she said, peering over the side at the decorated boats as they came closer.

"No, it can't, believe me!" Sao said emphatically, catching her hand and drawing her away from the railing.

An unusual urgency in his voice alarmed her. "If it's that important, go ahead, dear," she said.

Sao took his wife by the hand and led her into the deserted dining room. He waited a moment as if unsure where to begin. When he removed his wire-rim glasses to polish them with his handkerchief, Inge knew that he was nervous. But as she took a critical look at her husband, she could not see why. He looked very elegant, impeccably dressed in a beige suit that complemented his brown skin and black hair. Although he was slender and of the same height as she, Sao stood out by his regal bearing and always appeared tall and distinct. Putting his glasses on again, he looked at her with his kind and lively eyes, which always seemed to see beyond the surface. With a glint of apprehension he began, "I neglected to tell you something about myself."

"Don't tell me you've got a girl waiting for you here," she said, half joking, half alarmed.

"Oh no." He laughed. "But I've kept something from you. I hope you will forgive me."

"What is it? Please don't keep me waiting."

"The welcome out there is meant for us," he said, nodding his head in support of this statement.

"Oh, very funny," Inge said. "Why would they welcome a mining engineer like that?" By now she was beginning to suspect that Sao had been keeping some major secret from her, and she found herself breathing rapidly.

"I am much more than that here." He paused. "I'm the Saophalong —the prince—of a whole state, a Shan state."

Her eyes were wide. She was shocked.

"It's a big place, Liebling—the size of Connecticut, or four times the size of Luxembourg, if that makes more sense to you. Those people out there, they're my people. They've come all the way from Hsipaw, eight hundred miles. You'll have to get used to it. There'll be a lot of celebrations when we get back to the Shan states."

Inge stared at her husband in disbelief; then she lowered her eyes to inspect the handwoven Austrian dress she was wearing. She muttered desperately, "You should have told me . . . I'm not dressed right . . . I could have changed my dress."

"Please forgive me," he said again, putting his arms around her and pulling her close to him. Sao felt awful. He had always prided himself on being fair, but he had not been considerate of her. He admitted to himself that he was wrong to wait this long to tell her.

"Why didn't you tell me before we were married?" she demanded, twisting away from him.

"I wanted to be absolutely certain that you married me for the right reasons. But it was stupid of me—I'm sorry."

She did not respond right away and avoided looking at him. She was hurt that he had lacked the absolute trust in her that she had always felt for him. But she realized this was not the time or the place to make it an issue.

"Let's go and enjoy the welcome," she said. She reached out to him as he heaved a deep sigh of relief.

They went on deck, hand in hand, and waved to those Shans and Burmese who had ventured out in the brightly decorated boats. The ship docked, the gangway was lowered, and a group of officials rushed on board to extend a warm, yet respectful welcome to Sao and his bride. Inge tried to appear calm and collected, although she felt anxious and insecure. She wished she had been able to prepare herself for the role awaiting her at the other end of the gangway. For the first time since they were married, she felt resentful toward her husband.

The honored couple was immediately escorted past the immigration and customs stations, away from their stunned fellow passengers. On the pier, hundreds of cheerful and enthusiastic relatives, students, and officials from the Shan states celebrated their arrival, accompanied by rhythmic music from a small band of gongs, drums, and cymbals. Inge was charmed by the beautiful women, who presented her with bouquets of exquisite flowers: fleshy red lilies, perfumed white jasmine, and many delicate blossoms she could not name. Through the flowers in her hand she took a close look at the young woman next to her: a slim and graceful figure, clad in a colorful silk *longyi* and a crisp white *aingyi,* which was held together by five dazzling jewelry buttons set in gold. Her face bore a radiant smile, and her jet-black hair was pulled back into a knot and framed a delicate light brown face. Inge had seen a few female students from Burma in the United States, but they bore little semblance to these beautiful women in Rangoon harbor. In American universities they were disconnected from their surrounding, struggling to keep warm in heavy overcoats and leather boots. Now, for the first time, she saw women of Burma in their own land, competing in beauty with the tropical blossoms they wore in their hair. Many men also wore sarongs of muted colors and designs; a few were dressed in wide, flowing Shan trousers. Their "bath-towel" turbans distinguished the Shan men from the Burmese, who wore a *gawngbawng,* a form of molded headgear.

Overwhelmed and confused, Inge tried to prevent tears from blurring her vision. The intense midday heat and emotional strain combined in making her feel very uncomfortable. She cast a grudging glance at Sao, wishing she was dressed more appropriately. This was her first encounter with the people who would be her family, friends, and, perhaps, enemies. They looked so much more foreign and mysterious than she had imagined, and she wondered if she would ever be able to understand what lay behind their smiles, let alone understand the melodious language they were speaking.

A distinguished-looking lady, a foot shorter than Inge, stepped out of the crowd and presented her with a bouquet of flowers, saying, "Welcome, my little sister. I am Nanda and I will look after you until you feel comfortable on your own."

This surprised Inge. She knew her husband's only surviving sister by a different name, and there was no resemblance between this lady and the photos she had seen. But she appreciated Nanda's warmth and her flawless English. She would not have to rely on the few phrases of Burmese she had learned while crossing the Indian Ocean. Later, as well as Burmese, she would also have to tackle the Shan language for life in bilingual Hsipaw. Next to her, Sao was speaking one or the other of these languages with half a dozen important-looking men. Despite feeling excluded from the conversation, she was reassured by their happy laughter.

Nanda caught Inge's attention as she ushered up three teenage girls, who were fair-skinned and shy. "These are your little sisters Daisy, Grace, and Ruby," she said as the girls giggled. "You must teach them English and good manners."

Inge's interest was aroused and she was about to try to find out how many sisters she now had when Sao gently tugged at her arm.

"We have to move on and get out of the hot sun," he said. "I have invited our welcoming committee to meet with us at the Strand Hotel. There I will introduce everyone to you." He took her hand and led her to a waiting car.

"What about our luggage?" she asked, suddenly remembering the responsibilities of traveling.

"We don't need to worry about such things any more. The secretary will take care of everything."

Inge was startled. Throughout her life, traveling had meant lugging suitcases onto trains, buses, and ships, worrying about baggage claim and customs inspection.

They had barely settled into the back seat, drawing close to each other, when he said, "One more thing, Liebling. You can't call me 'Sao' in public any more. You see . . . it's not respectful enough."

"So, what do you want me to call you?"

"It's not what I want you to call me, it's what my people consider proper."

"Okay, just tell me what I should call you." Her exasperation was beginning to show.

"You'll have to call me 'Saopyipha' when others are around."

"Saopyipha? What does that mean?"

"It means 'older-brother-who-is-the-ruling-prince,'" he said as they both burst out laughing.

"And I can't call you 'Inge' anymore," he continued. "The Shan name given to you by our astrologer is 'Thusandi.'"

She wanted to ask what that meant, but the excitement and the heat had exhausted her so much that she decided to postpone asking any of the many questions on her mind. She was hoping that the Strand Hotel was very far away so that she could rest her eyes and her overwrought emotions. Her wish was not granted; the drive took only a few minutes. Foreign street scenes filtered through Inge's half-closed eyes: bicycle-drawn passenger carts, orange-robed Buddhist monks, buses constructed of wood, women carrying huge baskets on their heads. In their midst a white-coated policeman was attempting to bring order to the traffic melee.

The Strand Hotel, a white colonial building, exuded the splendor of a time past. It was an island of cool, British tranquillity amid the gay, bustling life of Rangoon. Some of that teeming Asian life was invading this sacrosanct space as they arrived with their entourage. Barefoot Indian attendants ushered them into a meeting room, where at least fifty people were already assembled. Thusandi sat through three incomprehensible speeches, feeling that every pair of eyes was subjecting her to a thorough inspection.

Confused and apprehensive, she wondered if she had made the right decision in leaving her family and her friends. She doubted if she would feel at home in this sunny, unfamiliar land. She wondered if she would be able to fully believe Sao after today's surprises. But her doubts were not fears, and she was determined to give her new life a chance.

The next five days in Rangoon were filled with an endless process of introductions, receptions, informal social calls, and lessons from life about a new culture and its sensitive politics. Thusandi enjoyed the whirlwind of activities and postponed any serious soul searching. The first morning in Rangoon included breakfast with Sao Hkun Hkio, foreign minister and head of the Shan State central government, at his residence; shopping at Rowe and Company, the most exclusive English department store in Rangoon, for hundreds of yards of curtain material, Wedgwood china, and lamps for the new home Thusandi had not yet seen; a reception at the

Strand Hotel for all students from Hsipaw State currently studying at Rangoon University; and a short visit to a woman astrologer at Sule Pagoda in the center of the city. She was one of several astrologers whom Sao had consulted before he went to the United States, and Thusandi wanted to meet her.

Although Ba Maung, the English-speaking secretary, accompanied Thusandi everywhere she went, she felt most comfortable when Nanda joined her. She was actually Sao's first cousin, not a sister by European definition. Thusandi learned on her first day in Burma that different standards applied, and absolutely everybody they met was addressed as a member of the family; younger people were sisters and brothers, older ones were uncles, aunties, grandfathers, and grandmothers.

Nanda had been the Mahadevi of Sao's predecessor until she left him and his court in Hsipaw for a man in Mandalay. After she had endured hardships and official banishment from Hsipaw, Sao had brought her back to the family. She was now in a unique position to help introduce Thusandi to her new life. Nanda knew proper etiquette, she could interpret from Shan and Burmese into English and vice versa, and she was invaluable in suggesting what to purchase for the East Haw, the residence in Hsipaw State.

The three teenage girls, Daisy, Grace, and Ruby, turned out to be Sao's half-sisters. They giggled a lot and were enjoying their first visit to Rangoon. They had been given their English names by the nuns at the convent school they attended in Maymyo.

"YOU WILL LIKE LIVING IN THE Shan states," many people in Rangoon said to Thusandi. But the Burmese seamstress who sewed the first longyis and aingyis for her warned of witchcraft, powerful spirits or *nats,* and headhunters descending to the Shan valleys. She sighed as she adjusted the length of a sky-blue silk longyi on Thusandi, finally giving her new look a wink of approval; the longyi, a long wraparound skirt, accented Thusandi's shapely figure; the sleeveless white aingyi appeared crisp and cool. For the sake of completeness, the seamstress had even managed to find a pair of Burmese velvet slippers—in a men's size. Thusandi beamed at her mirror image. She liked what she saw and how she felt in her new clothing.

"Poor lady," the seamstress sighed. "So young and so pretty and going to the Shan states!" She continued in Burmese, according to Nanda, with a Buddhist prayer for Thusandi's safety.

"I'll come and see you next time I'm in Rangoon," Thusandi said with carefree laughter. "I think it's safer in the Shan states than in the city. I'll prove it to you." But her comments had not convinced the seamstress, who did not laugh.

Most Burmese she met acted as if the Shan states were a foreign country; some even considered it a dangerous place beyond civilization. They alluded to fierce hill people in pursuit of lowlanders, to headhunters in search of well-fed victims, and to Shan maidens who bewitched and destroyed their hapless suitors. Very few bearers of such news had ever been there or indeed planned to see this mysterious Shan land for themselves.

Thusandi was puzzled that people so close to the Shan states knew practically nothing about life there. Her source of information was Sao, and she trusted him implicitly. His honesty had always disarmed her, and his failure to disclose his princely position to her had not shaken her faith in him. When he laughed heartily about the rumors she had heard, she dismissed those too.

While in Rangoon, Thusandi's curiosity about the Shan states grew by the hour. She believed she would be happy there with Sao, even though it sounded like the end of the world. It pleased her to share with the people she met what she had learned about that part of the Union of Burma.

The Shan states covered approximately one-fourth of the country's hills in the northeast, bordering China, Laos, and Thailand. The three million Shans living in that area, together with dozens of hill tribes, were much more like the Thais than the Burmese. They had originally come from China and migrated south to conquer Thailand and Burma after the Tartars destroyed their kingdom, which was called Nanchao. But their conquest of Burma did not last, and three centuries later the Shans were driven back into the hills. Unlike the Burmese, they had no king. Instead, the Shans were ruled by hereditary princes and chiefs who, at times, were forced to pay tribute to the Burmese. When Britain annexed Burma, the Shan states had become part of the British Empire, though they enjoyed special status. Burma's monarchy had come to an end, but the Shan princes retained their feudal powers and a large measure of independence.

Thusandi remembered that Sao had told her about his land and his people when they were hiking in the Rocky Mountains. Nothing he had said alarmed her, and she expected no difficulties in adjusting to life in such a distant culture. However, when Thusandi was lying sleepless in their luxurious suite in Rangoon's Strand Hotel, she began to wonder if she had made the right decision. She wondered if she would ever see her home in Austria again. Hanni, a girl from her hometown, had ended up a virtual prisoner in a Middle Eastern harem, and she considered for a moment that the same fate could await her. She remembered how secure she had always felt in Austria, even when bombs destroyed their home during World War II. And how privileged she had considered herself when she wore her first ball gown made out of old curtains, or when she had slept in a youth hostel on her first trip to Salzburg. Now here she was in the most exclusive hotel in Rangoon, surrounded by the luxuries of opulent silk, shiny silver, and attentive servants, and she found herself longing for that secure and confident feeling of her growing years in Austria.

Three

ON A CLOUDLESS JANUARY
morning, it was at long last time for Sao Kya Seng and Thusandi to proceed to their home in Hsipaw, northeast of Mandalay. A motorcade took
them to Mingaladon Airport and to the DC-3 that made a biweekly haul
of passengers and cargo to Lashio, the only airfield in the northern Shan
states.

"These are the most reliable planes in existence," Sao said to calm his
bride's nerves. The two engines roared and the plane shook vehemently
during take-off. She was white as a sheet, and her hands trembled as she
clasped the arm rests of the flimsy seat of the converted cargo plane. Barely
acknowledging his concern with a faint smile, she closed her eyes as if to
shut out the potential danger. The noise level in the nonpressurized cabin
was so high that Sao made no further attempts at conversation. When they
were airborne, Thusandi relaxed somewhat, and Sao pointed at the sights
below, anxious for her to get a bird's-eye view of the plains of Burma
proper. The paddy fields, sustained by big, winding rivers, gave way to the
mountain chain of the Shan plateau, and they had their first glimpse of
the thick green jungle. From a distance, it seemed uninhabited and mysterious.

Once the plane left Mandalay, on the banks of the mighty Irrawaddy
River, Sao became restless, eagerly peering out the small window for clues
that they had finally reached his land. The DC-3 immediately climbed to a
few thousand feet to clear the hills around Maymyo, the former summer
retreat for British colonists. Sao saw first the railway track, then he spotted
the road from Mandalay to Hsipaw that he had so often traveled. He kept

his eyes on that thin black line until he spotted what he was looking for. There it was, the gate between Burma and his state.

"Look, now we are over Hsipaw State!" Sao shouted, excited enough to make himself heard over the plane's engines.

"This is it. We are back where we belong," he said in a low voice, doubting that she was able to hear him. As he looked at his ancestral land below him, his emotions ran the whole gamut of joy, relief, and happiness to anxious anticipation of what lay ahead. He removed his wire-rim glasses to wipe a few tears from his eyes. He needed all his self-discipline to hold back a flood of tears. Sao reached over and put as much of his arm around Thusandi as his seatbelt permitted; he needed to touch and hold her. He had achieved a goal he had set himself four years ago and was returning home as a mining engineer. He was returning to help his people benefit from the wealth buried under their soil. He was going to "earn" his hereditary title as their ruler. Moreover, he was bringing home the wife of his own choice, one who would love and support him in whatever it took to fulfill his destiny.

They were now directly over Nawnghkio, the small town closest to the Burma border. Sao was taken aback when he saw how such an insignificant trading center and railway link had grown since he last flew over it. He quickly traded seats with Thusandi, wanting to get a closer look. With concern, he spotted new army barracks, more Burmese troops, and military equipment. Although the defense of the Union of Burma was controlled by the central government, he was alarmed and disconcerted to see such a troop buildup in a peaceful town in Hsipaw State, far away from the Chinese border.

At the northern edge of the high plateau, behind wide-open fields, Sao caught a glimpse of the village where he had hidden during the Japanese occupation while his father and brother collaborated with the occupying forces. Sao started to fidget with his fingers when memories of those days surfaced; memories of flight and fear, and of final triumph. It was during his stay there that an astrologer had first predicted what had just become true: that he would travel to a distant land and return with a wife who was neither from that country nor from his, but from somewhere in between. Sao smiled about his lingering belief in astrology and fortune telling. He had been warned; he had never told his bride that not only happiness and success but also great troubles and possibly a violent death at an early age lay ahead of him. It was surprising that he had not put these unscientific aspects of his Shan upbringing in proper perspective while at engineering school.

The plane landed smoothly at Lashio airstrip and coasted toward a solitary wooden shed. Although Sao had told Thusandi to expect a big welcome, he noticed that she started to bite her lower lip when the huge crowd came into view. The secretary asked the handful of passengers to get off the plane first so that the official reception of the Saophalong and Mahadevi of Hsipaw State could proceed without interruption. Sao led his bride toward the door of the DC-3, and as they descended the steps to the red carpet, the police band struck up a cheerful march. A troop of Hsipaw State's police force presented arms as Sao took their salute, making sure that Thusandi was beside, not behind, him. They both walked tall and proud, aware of the hundreds of pairs of eyes fixed upon them. Sao greeted ministers of state, dignitaries, and elders, introducing them to his bride. He noticed the warmth with which she shook hands and tried to repeat the names of his men. They stared at her with unabashed curiosity, but Sao perceived their welcome of her as genuine and friendly. He did not detect a resentful face among the crowd, even though he knew that some of their daughters had hoped to be in Thusandi's place. He had, after all, been the most eligible bachelor in the Shan states.

The motorcade of fifty vehicles wound its way from the airfield through the town of Lashio and onto the main road leading toward Hsipaw. Preceded by several jeep loads of bodyguards, Sao and his bride relaxed in the back seat of their car. "We have twenty minutes before the strenuous part begins," Sao said to her. "Once we cross our state's border, we'll be welcomed by tens of thousands of people from all over. They'll be lined up along the road. And they'll all want to catch a glimpse of you."

Thusandi drew closer to Sao and put her hand in his. He held her hand tight, and she thought back to their honeymoon in Denver, Colorado. As she talked, she was pleased to see a relaxed smile on his handsome face. She became acutely aware that he was the only person in that entire country who cared about her. He held her fate in his hands. As they reminisced about their first weeks together, Thusandi realized that she could depend on him as strongly as when they lived on the other side of the world.

When they crossed the bridge over the Namtu River at Se En, it was obvious that they had arrived in Hsipaw State. Hundreds of villagers had set up a colorful roadblock on the Burma Road of World War II fame, transforming it into a stage. A dozen little girls in bright longyis were dancing, a Shan ensemble was playing drums and gongs, two tattooed youths performed a daring sword dance, and a masked dancer in the costume of a mythical bird, the Kenaya, twisted and turned to a rhythmic beat. All activities came to a halt when Sao and Thusandi stepped out of their car. The village headman of Se En was a tall man with a kind brown face, a salt-and-pepper mustache. He approached, said something in Shan, and presented Thusandi with a huge bouquet. She picked one radiant blossom and pinned it in her hair, just like the Shan women in the crowd. That spontaneous gesture broke the ice. There was laughter, women and children crowded around her, and the music and dancing resumed. The headman offered Sao a silver cup filled with water, a traditional offering to the weary traveler. Thusandi was spellbound by the welcomers and their performances, but Sao pressed on, saying there was much more to come.

After a few minutes on the road, she understood what he meant. The welcoming scene presented itself again: Another village hidden in the teak forest had emptied its schoolchildren, its elders, its beautiful women onto the road. There were more dancers, more music, more flowers, and another endearing headman. The dances, the decorated bamboo gates, the roadside stands, and the people's fineries had been carefully prepared, but their expressions of joy and excitement were spontaneous and catching. Sao and Thusandi were swept up in this whirlwind of happiness; laughing and delighted, they celebrated with the crowds at each of the countless welcoming stations along the twenty-five-mile stretch. Thusandi stuffed one Chevrolet completely full with bouquets of intoxicating flowers.

Three-and-a-half hours later, the motorcade arrived at the gate of Hsipaw town. A huge banner proclaimed "Welcome at Home," the slogan that eight hundred schoolchildren chanted in English as Sao and Thusandi passed underneath. All fifteen thousand inhabitants, young and old, must have lined the streets of the town, with bands playing nonstop, between the eight major welcome stations. The buildings, most of them wooden structures one and two stories high, provided a backdrop for the colorful crowds.

Finally, they reached the northern section of town, reserved for Sao and those relatives he chose as neighbors. A white two-story manor house appeared around a bend in the road. Thusandi knew at once that this was the East Haw, their residence. Her imagination had been unable to come close to what she saw at this moment: a beautiful white brick building with a tiled roof, large french windows and doors, and balconies and terraces, surrounded by well-kept gardens, lawns, and exotic trees. When Sao glanced at his wife, her eyes told him she would feel at home here. The guards stationed by the moat presented arms, the staff of servants lined the driveway, and dozens of relatives stood in front of the entrance to this Shan version of an English country house.

The gracious people along the road had already captured Thusandi's heart, but now she felt that she had come home.

THE LAST OF THE RELATIVES left, collecting their slippers from the marble steps outside the massive teak door. Sao and Thusandi were home alone except for the maid, the valet, the butler, the cook, his kitchen boy, and half a dozen other servants whose functions were not yet evident to their new mistress. Thusandi was

Entrance to the East Haw, residence of the Prince and Princess of Hsipaw and their daughters.

exhausted, having spent the past two hours in drawn-out family introductions. She was bewildered by the unusual circumstances of many of the people she met; her father-in-law was in the robes of a Buddhist hermit, yet was living with a young wife and fathering children rather than leading the contemplative life of a hermit in seclusion; seven of Sao's young half-siblings, two of whom were in infancy; eight old aunties, all widowed wives of one uncle who at one time had had forty wives; a cousin banished from Hsipaw until recently for a major indiscretion; a formidable aunt who talked about her experiences at Queen Victoria's court; and countless cousins whose personal stories Thusandi could not remember. Sao's only full brother and sister were conspicuously absent; the explanation given was that they lived in another town.

Thusandi wanted nothing more than to find a bed—any bed—and sleep. She would be happy to learn more about this unusual family, about her house, her servants, and her duties, on the following day. But her duties did not wait. The boom of a gong almost lifted her out of the soft chair in the drawing room where her eyelids were heavy with sleep. She was alone and she looked around the huge room. The vast audience hall was divided by slender pillars into three distinct sections, and each area was given its own character. Thusandi had settled down in the east section, with a tall, oversized bay window and contemporary European sitting room furniture. Soft sunlight flooded through the lace curtains and was reflected in two enormous silver bowls decorating pedestals on either side of the french doors, which opened onto the marble terrace. The middle section set an example in simplicity and served as a reception area for Shan visitors, who traditionally sat on the floor. A thick Chinese silk carpet covered the entire area. The only piece of furniture, a low platform sofa, stood across from the large fireplace. The third section on the west side had at some time housed a large book collection, judging from rows of empty teak shelves, cabinets, and intricately carved small tables. Heavy curtains over the large windows and over a second terrace door lent an air of privacy and formality.

"It is suppertime, darling," she heard Sao say as he came to take her through the foyer to the dining room. He put his arm around her waist and whispered in her ear how much he loved her. As they entered the exquisitely furnished dining room, the butler, Kawlin, again struck the huge dinner gong, which was held by two tall carved elephants. Thusandi could not remember ever having seen table and chairs of such beautiful mahogany; their gracefully curved legs lent lightness to the long, glossy table.

"I feel kind of lost at this huge table," Thusandi said as Sao helped her into her chair. She wondered if Sao could hear how loudly her heart was beating. She was overwhelmed by the stately surroundings and the realization that, from now on, all meals would be served by a butler.

"We'll have lots of company and at least four children," Sao said as he checked the polished silver and sparkling china. He was looking forward to this, their first dinner at home.

The butler was silently gliding back and forth from the kitchen, preparing to serve a meal over which the cook had labored for days.

"I want to taste real Shan cooking!" Thusandi said, just before Kawlin served an English appetizer. It tasted spicy. They ate a bland consommé, which did not inspire, but neither one of them commented. When the main course appeared, however, both of them looked at each other in dismay. They had not expected tough-looking mutton, watery potatoes, and colorless vegetables.

Sao took one bite and said, "I can't eat this stuff, it tastes terrible."

"This isn't exactly what I had expected either," Thusandi said, "but the cook tried his best, so I'm going to eat it." As she sampled each and every dish, Sao called in the cook and gave him a lecture in Shan.

"When you're finished with the cook, I would also like to say something to him. Will you please translate?" she asked.

"Well, of course I will; he'll then get to hear from both of us what a disappointment his first supper turned out to be."

Her message to the cook caught Sao unaware: "Thank you very much for working so hard on this meal."

Sao translated unenthusiastically as the cook perked up.

Thusandi continued, "I do appreciate that you wanted to make me feel at home with the menu you chose. But I've come here wanting to become one of you. And to do that I must learn about Shan cooking. Will you please cook all your best Shan dishes for me from now on?"

On hearing the translation, the cook's smile spread from ear to ear. He said that he would start doing so tomorrow. Thusandi acquired two loyal followers that evening; the cook and the butler had both seen that she understood and cared. Ready or not, she also demonstrated to Sao that she had just taken charge of the household.

Sao found himself in a new role. His word had been the final one in this house until today, but he liked the way she had handled the cook. He had often worried how this independent but unsophisticated girl from Austria would adjust to life in the East Haw—how she would manage the large household and preside over all the people who depended on them.

Before they were married, he had announced that no relatives would live with them under the same roof. This was a break with tradition that had upset many who had been planning to participate in his immediate family life, just as they had in the past. Sao knew that he had nothing to worry about. His wife had shown him on the first day that she needed no help.

After supper, Sao had plans for this first night under their own roof. He gave Thusandi a more detailed tour of their private wing on the second floor: the cozy sitting room, the luxurious bath, the screened verandah, and a bedroom large enough to be a gymnasium. It was decorated with an interesting mixture of colonial, contemporary American, and Burmese styles. Thusandi expected to add her personal touch to their very private quarters. She had been accustomed to large rooms and high ceilings in Austria, but they could not measure up to these dimensions.

Their bed was already made up, with the mosquito net tucked in carefully under the mattress. Malaria was so prevalent and deadly that it was inadvisable to let the net hang down decoratively to the floor, even though all doors and windows were equipped with screens.

Sao had tea served on the verandah, and he asked the valet to rearrange the candles. It was the first of the many happy evenings he had so often anticipated—holding Thusandi in his arms, smelling her hair and the faint scent of perfume behind her ears. They would talk about the events of this day, about their hopes and concerns. And then they would make love, for the first time in their own bed.

The candles were finally arranged to please him, and the aroma of the fragrant tea, grown in the hills nearby, filled the air. Sao pulled his bride down on the sofa and kissed her as she nestled up to him. Neither one of them felt like breaking the stillness of the evening. They quietly watched the silvery reflection of the rising moon on the water, and they breathed the earthy smell of the nearby riverbank.

Sao removed his glasses and closed his eyes. He was wide awake, filled with a range of deep emotions impossible to ignore.

"I'm so happy, darling—I must be the happiest man in the world right now. Do you realize that I've come back home with all I've set out to accomplish and more? I have done it. Yes, I have."

But, strangely, there was no response from her. He looked and realized that Thusandi was sound asleep. Her cheeks were rosier than they had been all day, and strands of her long, dark brown hair fell over her mouth. This hectic day filled with too many ceremonies and too many people had finally caught up with her. That did not matter to Sao as long as she was by his side, with him in Hsipaw.

Sao remembered a cold February day in 1952, at Mario's Restaurant in Denver. He was nervously wining and dining his Austrian girlfriend on her birthday, unable to take his eyes off her. From the day they had met at a foreign students' party, this attractive and unusual girl had constantly been on his mind. Her warmth, her cheerfulness, and her poise made him long for her company. After four months of courtship, he could not imagine life without Inge. He had big plans for the evening, wondering when the right moment would come for him to ask her to marry him. Should he wait for appropriate background music, a cue in their conversation, dessert? He could not eat much, and the waiter's rendition of "O Sole Mio" did nothing to calm his nerves. Inge was the right one, he knew that, but he did not know if her plans for the future included him. He was not sure if he could ask her to give up her family for his faraway land. And if she accepted his proposal; he was worried that they might not be able to overcome the many obstacles facing their union.

They were in love, they were friends, and they had enjoyed every moment together. On Saturdays, when they picnicked in the mountains and looked out over the endless Western prairies, they had talked and shared their most intimate thoughts and aspirations. On bad-weather days, they explored the museums and theaters of Denver, eager to discover new cultural experiences together. Now and then they overheard offending remarks by persons who objected to a "nice white girl" holding hands with a "colored" man. While they had spent many happy hours and days together, they had never touched upon the subject of marriage.

It was before dessert; he could not contain himself any longer and pulled out a small velvet ring box from his pocket. He opened it and laid a sparkling ring on the white tablecloth in front of her. Inge held her breath as she stared at the pigeon-blood ruby set in diamonds; it was as though the ruby had drawn the color out of her usually pink cheeks.

"Inge . . . with this ring I want to ask you to marry me," Sao said nervously, reaching to hold her hands, which all of a sudden were cold and moist.

"Please try it on, wear it, and give me your answer when you are ready," he continued. "The ruby is a symbol of my love for you."

Sao had imagined all kinds of reactions from her when he rehearsed his marriage proposal; however, he had not counted on the tears that started to roll down her cheeks. Confused and helpless, he could think of nothing better than to pull out his handkerchief and offer it to her.

After regaining her composure, she said, "I've thought a lot about my answer in case you'd ever ask me. Yes, I want to marry you—but I'm also scared."

"What are you scared about, my darling?" he asked as he again reached to hold her trembling hands.

"I believe we are meant to be together . . . but I don't know if I could fit in, if I would be accepted by your people." More tears welled in her eyes.

"I've spent nights thinking about that too. And I'm sure that my people will accept and love you. You'll fit in, believe me!"

She replied by slowly slipping the ruby ring on her finger.

He could not remember their conversation over the spumoni dessert, except that they were both bubbling over with happiness and confidence. But he recalled her sudden cry of desperation: "Sao, my curfew!" They had to rush back to campus, and he delivered her to Mrs. Smith, the house-mother of the dormitory, two minutes before the nine o'clock curfew. He had become used to these dormitory rules, although he did not like them.

Sao felt very lonely after leaving her that night, not knowing when or where they would be married. The drive back to Golden in his convert-ible Nash Rambler, the only luxury he had permitted himself during those student years, took him through the city of Denver past fields of greening winter wheat and past the Wheatridge Dairy. He decided to stop there for a big, soothing vanilla milk shake. He was uncomfortable about having proposed to Inge without telling her the truth about himself. To her, and to everybody else who had met him in Colorado, he was a student from the Shan states of Burma who was planning to return to his homeland to be a mining engineer. Only the president of the Colorado School of Mines had been informed of his status as the ruling prince of Hsipaw, with the request to keep this information strictly confidential. And it had worked.

He was able to lead the life of an average foreign student, sharing the same worries and joys as the others. Now, however, he felt he was deceiving Inge, who trusted him unequivocally, putting her future into his hands. Yet he could not bring himself to reveal his background to her at this time and place. Their relationship would have to grow and withstand the test of time, distance, and cultural differences before he could confess. More than that, he wanted Inge to marry him for the right reasons.

From the day of their engagement, Sao felt a new energy, an added purpose, and a stronger sense of self-confidence. In spite of the daily telephone marathons and extended weekend dates, his grade point average soared to new heights, his correspondence with Hsipaw State was done expeditiously, and life seemed to be a succession of happy events.

One day he surprised Inge with the news that he was learning German.

"Why would you do a thing like that?" she asked curiously. After all, they spoke English to each other.

"I want to be able to speak with your parents without an interpreter when I pass through Austria this summer. Remember, I have to ask them for their daughter's hand in marriage."

He preferred not to think of the many months they would have to be apart. Inge was committed to returning to her Austrian university after a year as an exchange student, and he had to spend the summer in Burma making arrangements to bring his foreign-born bride to Hsipaw after his graduation. On his way back to Colorado for his senior year, he would at least see Inge in her home environment, among her family and friends.

CAREFUL NOT TO AWAKEN Thusandi, Sao took a sip of tea and thought of his work, which would begin tomorrow. He was not sure that he was ready to assume his duties as the legislative, judicial, and administrative head of Hsipaw State, as a member of the Shan State Council and the House of Nationalities of the Union of Burma. But he certainly was ready to bring about agricultural improvements and the beginnings of a Shan mining industry. And above all, he was determined to work hard for a political change from feudalism to democracy. He had always felt burdened by his status and by the absolute power he held over his subjects. After four years in the United States, it weighed more heavily on his mind than ever. Returning to this residence with servants kowtowing and approaching him on their knees depressed him. He thought of the years in his rented room in Golden, Colorado, where he had enjoyed the freedom of being one of the students, the pleasure of being equal. His people had a right to be heard and to participate in decisions affecting their lives. And he was determined to give them this opportunity.

As he turned to look at his sleeping wife, he noticed how a breeze from the river caused the candlelight to dance and throw mysterious shadow images onto the wall behind her. Sao thought he recognized an endless chain of soldiers marching toward him.

Four

SAO WASTED NO TIME IN TAKING charge of Hsipaw State. Some of his officials were pleased and others were worried when he decided to work out of an office in the administrative headquarters. It would have been more convenient had he followed his predecessor's example and run the affairs of state from his private office in the East Haw. But he wanted to be among those he served. Sao was concerned that traditions and his long absence had isolated him from the people who, after World War II, had voted for him rather than for his elder brother to succeed cousin Sao Ohn Kya. The latter had died in 1938, childless, while his two nephews, in line for succession, had been underage. The administration of Hsipaw State had then been entrusted to a British administrator until 1947, except for the years of Japanese occupation.

Now back home at last, Sao Kya Seng was determined to honor the trust his people had placed in him. He cared deeply about his subjects. After the ravages of war, their economic plight was uppermost on his mind. The orange groves in the valley needed replanting, irrigation canals feeding paddy fields were in disrepair, roads had deteriorated, and most cottage industries had shut down.

Moreover, although he was their feudal ruler, he was responsible for upholding their democratic rights at village and district levels. Decisions made by villagers and townspeople at informal meetings had to be respected and seriously considered. It was Sao's duty to keep informed about popular opinions and demands.

One of Sao's first administrative decisions caught the attention of every state employee. He dismissed two top officials for corruption and misuse of power while he had been abroad. Word spread quickly that he would not tolerate the corrupt practices that had been considered part of public life in the region. Contractors and businessmen were at a loss when their bribes were no longer accepted, and they began to fear for their privileged position. They learned very quickly that things had changed in Hsipaw State; now everyone was expected to adhere strictly to laws and ordinances.

A matter of serious concern to Sao and his conscience were the annual gambling festivals, called *pwe*s, that had been held in all Shan states for centuries. He wished he could put an end to this tradition because of the detrimental effects of gambling on an economically deprived population. But he also understood the people's weaknesses and their need to continue the time-honored festivities of their ancestors. Reluctantly, Sao allowed only two such pwes a year to be held in Hsipaw State, while Hsenwi, a neighboring state, held many more. The income from these gambling festivals had always belonged to the ruling prince, but Sao wanted no part of the money that his poor villagers and hill people gambled away. He established a charitable trust with the income—a precedent not appreciated by his fellow rulers, who attributed his ideas to American influence.

But Sao's value system had been formulated long before that. He was never groomed to be heir-apparent to Hsipaw State as his elder brother was. After the death of both his mother and stepmother, Sao had not had a place he could call home, except for the schools he attended in Mandalay, Taunggyi, and Darjeeling. Books were his best friends, history his favorite subject. He read every book he could find on the American Revolution and the evolution of the United States long before his studies took him there. While he learned about government "by the people, for the people," Sao also developed a strong sense of social responsibility for the injustices he witnessed around him: As a child, he watched his father discard his stepmother and subsequent wives in order to make room for new ones; later, he observed his brother's misuse of power and feudal privilege during the Japanese occupation. Sao was committed to help his people, not exploit them. For him to accept revenue from gambling festivals was sheer exploitation and therefore unacceptable.

One day soon after Sao's return, the chief minister, U Htan, ushered a visitor into the simply furnished office. The man was a representative of the special commissioner, a Shan prince who was the regional representative of the central Shan government responsible for relations between the Shans and the Burmese Army.

"Please have a seat. Tell me, what brings you to my office?" asked Sao in a friendly manner.

The man looked nervous and sat down on the edge of his chair.

"Sir . . . Hom Hpa, the special commissioner, sent me to you with a special request," he said in a high-pitched voice.

Sao pushed his chair back from his large, uncluttered desk, folded his arms, and said, "Well, let me hear what this request is all about."

"Sir . . ." the man hesitated. "The Burmese Army wants to hold a special gambling festival in Hsipaw to raise some funds, and the commissioner requests that you cooperate."

Sao sat straight up in his chair, wondering if he had heard correctly. "Would you repeat what you just said? I'm not sure I understand."

The commissioner's representative became even more nervous and fidgeted with his briefcase. "Well, you see . . . the army needs money, and Hsipaw has the largest attendance at its festivals. So, the colonel in charge of the Northern Command approached the commissioner and felt that . . ."

Sao gestured with his right hand that he had heard enough. He stood up, walked around the desk to the man who had just conveyed this request, and said emphatically, "Go and tell the commissioner that I will not ever let my people gamble for the benefit of the Burmese Army or for anybody else. He knows my position on this matter very well."

The man looked at the chief minister as if he hoped for intervention from him. Instead, U Htan said, "You heard my lord's decision. Take it back to the commissioner. And if you need something in writing, I'll get it for you in my office." With that, the representative bowed several times toward Sao and hurriedly backed out of the office, followed by U Htan.

Sao was upset. He walked slowly to the large window and looked out onto the green Namtu River, the lifeline for the valley. How could the commissioner, his neighboring ruler who was once married to his cousin, endorse this cynical request by the Burmese Army when he knew full well what the response would be. On top of this, the Burmese had forever condemned the Shans for allowing gambling. In Burma proper it was prohibited except for horse racing. Sao foresaw trouble, but he knew the army's request was wrong and that he could never go along with it.

When U Htan knocked and entered the office again, Sao was still standing by the window. The unusually tall Shan waited till Sao turned toward him before starting to say what was on his mind. "Sir, I respect your principles on the gambling issue, but . . ."

"There is no 'but,'" interrupted Sao, shaking his head as he sat down at his desk. He did not feel like talking to U Htan at the moment, but the chief minister ignored his hints.

"I must warn you, sir, that the leadership of the Burmese Army is not used to having their requests turned down," U Htan said.

"That may be so. But that's their problem, not mine," Sao replied.

"I have to contradict you—it will be ours!"

"Don't forget we have our Constitution, and I am willing to die defending it," Sao said heatedly. He opened a file on his desk, indicating that the conversation was over. As U Htan left, Sao thought he heard him muttering something about this not being the United States of America.

There were no other appointments on his schedule for the afternoon, and Sao called for his driver. He headed for the other side of the river, where he had fifty workers digging up the old racetrack. It would become a big orange plantation, a model for the citrus growers of the Hsipaw valley, whose groves had been severely damaged during the war. There, among the men and women working on his favorite agricultural project, he regained his composure after the upsetting episode in the office. He took a jungle knife from one of the workers and began to attack the thick brush covering the black, fertile soil. For a few moments the crew stopped in awe to watch their prince, with a pith helmet on, work in their midst. Then they swung their knives with renewed vigor.

Sao had plans for other agricultural projects—pineapples, coffee, peanuts, ginger, soybeans—but he had to wait for the tractors and bulldozers that he had ordered.

IT WAS THE TWENTY-SECOND OF March, the day before the full moon of Tabaung. Sao and Thusandi were on their way to the biggest pwe in the Shan states, which was in progress near the Bawgyo Pagoda, six miles west of their residence, on the way to Mandalay. Zinna, their driver, navigated the Mercedes along the one-lane highway, an extension of the Burma Road. The narrow strip of pavement did not make driving easy in any kind of traffic. Now, it created a motorist's nightmare as thousands of people streamed toward the biggest event of the year, the Bawgyo Pwe.

Thusandi was excited, happily anticipating an event that for months had commanded the attention of everyone around her. Moei, her maid, had helped her dress in a gold brocade longyi and a white silk aingyi fastened by five ruby buttons set in gold, with rings and bangles to match. Her knee-length hair, tamed in a Shan knot, was adorned with a fragrant garland of jasmine. When Moei had given Thusandi a final inspection, she had said approvingly, "Mahadevi, you look more like a born Shan every day." Then, with a sigh, she had continued, "If only you were a few inches shorter."

"I wish you were looking forward to this event half as much as I am," Thusandi said to her husband.

He responded with a smile and a gentle squeeze of her hands, and said, "You know how I feel about pwes. I wish I could stay away altogether. But I can't disappoint my people."

A large crowd watching Shan dancers at a Pwe festival in Hsipaw State. Pwes were held annually in Hsipaw and other Shan states.

She knew very well how he felt about this issue. She knew that he disliked public functions, large crowds, and having to dress in ceremonial Shan clothing. She had seen him happiest when he was clad in his khakis, inspecting ore deposits, visiting his subjects at work in their villages, and checking up on agricultural projects.

The road became more and more crowded with buses, bullock carts, and groups of pedestrians. Each of the many buses they passed was unique in size, design, and color; the bodies had all been hand-carved by masterful Chinese carpenters, and decorated by the owners with bold designs and clashing coats of paint. As long as the resourceful mechanics could keep the engines running, the appearance of these vehicles could expect to go through several more metamorphoses.

The bullock carts were not nearly as striking—for them, nothing seemed to have changed since the wheel was invented. Two hunchbacked Sindhi oxen pulled a two-wheel cart, complete with thatched roofing and matted sidings to assure privacy and shelter for the family in residence. Most carts had been on the road for days, even weeks, and their owners were preparing to set up camp at the festival grounds. Some children walked along at the side of their cart; they had no problem in catching up with the oxen when the diversions were over.

Thusandi was most interested in the groups of pedestrians, mostly Shans from surrounding villages, dressed in their finest. The women, in brilliantly colored silk longyis and crisp white aingyis, were protecting their light complexions with huge straw hats. Many of them were carrying their wares to market. A bamboo pole resting on one of their shoulders held a basket on each end, making the women's walk an exercise in grace-ful balance. The turbaned men, walking ahead of the women, were not burdened by merchandise. Instead, they carried their Shan swords over their wide, brown cotton jackets and trousers. Woven Shan bags, slung over their shoulders, contained their savings, destined for the gambling tables at the pwe.

Whenever groups of men and women recognized the car of their ruler, they knelt on the roadside, holding their folded hands in front of their faces, the traditional greeting of respect.

Sao and Thusandi's car approached the festival grounds, an area the size of ten football fields in which there was a chain of paddy fields during the growing season. On the left, the Bawgyo Pagoda beckoned pilgrims to stop for a prayer. This white, bell-shaped stupa with its gold jeweled tip, or *htee,* was the reason for these annual festivities. According to legend, Sao Nang Mon, a Shan princess from the ancient Shan empire of Mong Mao (which had its capital on the China border near Namkham), had rested on that very spot on her flight home from Ava, where she had been residing as an unhappy consort to the king of Burma. Deeply grateful to be on Shan soil again, the princess had had a pagoda built there.

The crowds became very thick. Thusandi could hear fragments of conversations conducted in a dozen different languages. The orchestra of the Burmese theater group was rehearsing for its evening performance. She could smell the aroma of different foods being fried and steamed for the hungry crowd. Members of the various hill tribes displayed striking costumes; the Kachin women wore heavy silver ornaments on their black-and-red dress and on their woven bags—only the red woolen leggings were not adorned with silver. The Palaung tea growers from the hills to the north also covered their dark blouses and round hats with heavy silver jewelry. And the Lisu women in their mosaic of colors provided a stark contrast to the Taungthus, who simply wore black. The Burmese women were indistinguishable in their dress from the Shans. Their men were the only males wearing sarongs, though of different color and design from the women. The Nepalis, the Bengalis, the Muslims, and the Chinese all added to the exciting ethnic variety, which was now and then intruded upon by a Caucasian traveler. Three hundred thousand people came to this sparsely populated spot for the festival that year.

After inching forward through the crowd, the car had come to a stop. Sao and Thusandi walked to the building that had been specially erected for the audiences they were to give during the festival. In front, dozens of Shan beauties awaited them, the vanguard of a welcoming committee. The girls, dressed in a rainbow display of silk longyis, blushed as they gracefully presented exquisite bouquets of flowers. With their delicate complexions, smiling dark eyes, and beautiful black hair, they were like exotic blossoms.

The audience hall was constructed of bamboo, like all other temporary buildings on the festival site, and resembled a huge tent. Its bamboo floor was covered with carpets. The only furniture was a raised platform covered with red velvet cushions elaborately embroidered with gold thread. Sao and Thusandi were ushered in to be seated. On the carpet below them sat several hundred people, absolutely quiet, waiting for the short respect-paying ceremony to begin. The most senior *buheng,* or district headman, approached the ruling couple on his knees, bearing a traditional offering of bananas and Shan tea leaves on a red lacquer tray, requesting permission for the assembled subjects to *kadaw.* Sao touched the symbolic offering and granted their request. Hundreds of folded hands went up almost simultaneously as the buheng chanted a short Shan incantation to which Sao responded by bestowing blessings on his subjects.

After that short ceremony, everybody relaxed, and people came forward to chat informally with their prince and princess. The hall was filled with laughter and expressions of joy for being recognized. Many *bumongs*— the elected village headmen—came with requests: Some offered to send their children to the East Haw as servants; others asked for advice on personal and communal matters; many offered invitations to special events in their towns and villages. The bumong of Kutyom came with a problem. His village on the Namlee River grew rice in paddy fields belonging to the estate of the prince. The tenant farmers had been unable to pay their levy for two years due to bad harvests and asked for their debts to be pardoned. While the bumong presented his case, Sao and Thusandi exchanged glances, remembering their long discussions on the morality of owning farmland worked by sharecroppers. Sao wanted no part of this feudal heritage and was planning to give away tens of thousands of acres of paddy lands belonging to him as the Prince of Hsipaw. The people who had been working the land for generations had a right to keep what they produced. This idea was of course not popular with the feudal landowners of neighboring states.

Thusandi decided that this was a good time to slip out and take a walk around the festival grounds. Sao was surrounded by the leaders of the districts and villages, and discussions about this problem could take hours.

Accompanied by two cousins, a secretary, and two bodyguards, Thusandi headed toward rows of bamboo stalls where traders were exhibiting their wares. The Shans and various hill people quietly smiled at prospective buyers, while the Indians and Burmese used more vocal sales methods. The variety and originality of their wares inspired Thusandi to go on a shopping spree. She carried no cash herself and only needed to point at the item of her choice; the secretary took care of payment and delivery. She chose delicately crafted Shan hats—lots of them—water containers made out of dried gourds, handwoven silk longyis, brooms in all shapes and sizes, toys crafted from bamboo, lacquer containers, finely woven mats, and many baskets. The secretary began to look nervous and alarmed when Thusandi's uncontrolled purchases increased with every step she took. Somehow, the ceremonies and pomp surrounding this festival had given her a new awareness of the status and wealth that she had acquired through her marriage to Sao. For the first time in her life, she felt free to buy anything she wanted, to spend money in any way she pleased. For a short while she relished that exhilarating feeling.

Then Thusandi decided on her own that it was time to move on. Special fragrances attracted her to the food stalls, where traders were offering food staples and snacks of every imaginable variety. She had never seen rice grain in so many shades and beans in so many colors. And the spice stalls offered everything from masala to mustard seeds, coriander, cinnamon, dried chilies, and palm sugar, not to mention Shan *thonau* (fermented soybean cake) and Burmese *ngapi* (fermented fish paste). The fruit stands were laden with huge mandarins, juicy pomelos, fragrant custard apples, lichees, fresh strawberries, and at least twelve varieties of bananas. Thusandi had a difficult time withstanding these temptations, but she abided by her husband's request never to buy food in an open market.

Next was a row of restaurants with freshly prepared foods of every ethnic group represented at Bawgyo. Pots of steaming Chinese noodles competed with *panthe khowsoi,* and Shan rice noodles with chicken and coconut curry sauce. The aroma of freshly fried tofu and milk-dough blended with fried papadams. Shan *khowlam,* sticky rice cooked in bamboo, eaten by peeling back the bamboo and eating the inside the same way one would a banana. And, of course, there was a large choice of Burmese curries, Indian curries, vegetarian delights, breads, pancakes, even Chinese doughnuts.

Leaving these mouth-watering temptations behind, Thusandi and her tired entourage toured the entertainment area, which housed a Chinese circus, Indian magicians, an exhibit of domestic animals, two cinemas, and two theaters for live evening performances by Burmese and Shan ensembles. A little hospital was also tucked into this corner. It was staffed by a doctor and two nurses, who had yet to receive their first patient. Nobody seemed to have time to get sick. Behind the hospital, an electric plant, specially installed for the pwe, provided the only electricity many visitors would enjoy all year long.

One area of the pwe that interested Thusandi most was yet to come:

the gambling area, probably the biggest attraction of the festival. Since gambling was permitted only during these Shan pwes, large crowds from everywhere came to try their luck. The entire operation was run by Ah Fatt, a Chinese contractor, who had been the highest bidder when Hsipaw State had auctioned off the festival for that year. The contractor received all the income from the gambling operations and concessions, while he had to provide free facilities and entertainment for all. The state supervised all aspects of the festival, assuring that strict guidelines were followed.

"I don't want you to set a bad example by placing any bets," Sao had said to his wife earlier. Being so strongly opposed to gambling, Sao would have preferred if Thusandi had not gone to the gambling area at all. But she was determined to see for herself what fascination those games held for their servants, their relatives, their guests, and most of their subjects.

The first table she came to was covered with a large cloth depicting four animals: a chicken, a pig, a snake, and a frog. The attendant spun a die with a long pin through it, with the four animals engraved on its four sides. While it was spinning, he covered it with a bowl. People started throwing money on the table, betting on the animal of their choice. When the bets stopped, the attendant uncovered the die, and winners were paid three kyats to one. Men and women of all backgrounds tried their luck on one table after another. The four-animal game seemed to be the most popular. Taller than all women and most men, Thusandi was able to see over those crowding around the gambling tables. She counted more than a dozen gamblers around each table, representing young and old, but no children. Men were in the majority, although a few women placed heavy bets on the four-animal game. Most gamblers were Shans and hill people, who looked as if they carried every penny they owned with them to the tables, intent on risking all. They were too poor for this, Thusandi thought, worried about the hardships their losses would bring to their families.

A sprinkling of well-to-do gamblers came from Mandalay and other parts of Burma proper or from the local Chinese business community. But all of them, rich or poor, men or women, were oblivious to everything around them. With eyes fixed on the dice and smiles expunged from their faces, the gamblers unsettled Thusandi. She wished she had listened to her husband and stayed away from this area of the pwe.

She moved on to learn about the biggest event of the day, the thirty-six animal lottery with a drawing at eleven o'clock that night. Thusandi saw the twenty-foot pole on which the contractor would later hoist a box containing one of thirty-six carved animals. Previously, it had been the ruler who selected the winning animal, but Sao had now assigned that task to the contractor, who had been sworn to secrecy. After the little box with the winning selection was raised, guards kept a watchful eye on the pole. People had from five o'clock to eleven o'clock to place their bets. Everybody hunted for clues, analyzed dreams, and hoped to guess whether the rat, the elephant, the tiger, the peacock, or one of the other thirty-two animals would be the day's winner, returning twenty-seven kyats for each one ventured. For this event, bookies had taken bets in distant towns that could be reached by telephone, like Lashio, Maymyo, Mandalay, and others. Fascinated, Thusandi toyed with the idea of disobeying her husband.

The tour had come to an end, but not before it had presented one more surprise: the shrill sound of a locomotive's whistle announced that the Lashio-Mandalay passenger train was carving its path right through the middle of the festival grounds. It made a special stop right there, spilling out visitors and enabling through passengers and crew to join in the festivities for a little while. The train stood empty, with its locomotive patiently huffing and puffing while the railway engineer, the attendants, and every single person aboard disappeared into the crowd of the Bawgyo Pwe. Another blow of the whistle would signal the train's departure whenever the engineer decided to resume the journey away from the remarkable festivity.

Sao and Thusandi did not stay to attend the stage performances by Burmese and Shan musical groups, which would provide entertainment till dawn. Instead, they returned to their verandah to watch the full moon pour its silvery light over the Namtu River.

"It'll take me a long time to sort out my feelings about all I saw at the pwe today," Thusandi said to Sao.

He did not reply. She turned her eyes away from the glimmering serpent of a river to his face, only to see sadness in his eyes.

"You'll be able to bring about changes in their lives," she said, wanting so much to cheer him.

"I wonder. I just don't know if I can . . . if anybody can."

Five

EVERY DAY PROVIDED NEW
surprises for Thusandi, new impressions to store away to be shared during
those wonderful evenings on the verandah with Sao. They still conversed in
English, the language they had spoken when they first met, although she
made quick progress in learning spoken Shan and in Burmese, the official
language.

Thusandi appreciated Sao's patience in helping her practice the five
standard tones of the Shan language. As the choice of tone determined the
meaning of a word, she always used great caution in addressing elders and
persons deserving of respect. Using the wrong tone could turn a compli-
ment into an insult. The meaning of the word *ma,* for instance, could
change from "come" to "dog" according to the pitch of the voice. After
boldly practicing her Shan on staff and relatives, Thusandi often wondered
how many times she had unknowingly insulted them. They were too kind
to bring her embarrassing mistakes to her attention. Only Sao pointed out
laughingly that she had called him one animal or another by applying the
wrong tone. She had been a student of foreign languages at an Austrian
university before she met Sao, but learning Shan presented the biggest language challenge of all.

The people of Hsipaw were pleased that their foreign-born princess
was serious about learning their language. And no matter how many major
mistakes she made, they never said a discouraging word to or about her.

Sao enjoyed hearing about Thusandi's challenges and how she met
them. She had a knack for finding humor in upsetting situations. When
the pump broke down and left the East Haw without running water, she

placed dozens of floating toys in the huge water jars that were set up near bathtubs and toilets, reminding Sao to smile even though he found the breakdown annoying. When the generator broke and left the East Haw without electricity, she set off sparklers saved for the New Year celebration. And she laughed a lot—at herself, at him, at funny and not-so-funny events. Sao needed these light moments with her. He arranged to have Thusandi by his side for as many official functions as possible. Her cheerfulness made the biweekly audiences, the inspections, the public appearances, and the official visits almost enjoyable for him.

Away from public life, though, he wished Thusandi would not depend so heavily on him as her only companion and friend. Sao wondered what it would have been like if he had not married a foreigner but a Shan girl, with her own circle of confidantes, her own family nearby. Thusandi had nobody other than him to turn to for advice, for conversation, and for support.

A constant stream of local and foreign visitors asked to be received daily. Sao liked to watch Thusandi graciously welcome and entertain their

The Saophalong (with turban) and Mahadevi of Hsipaw performing an official function. Thusandi's mother (center) was visiting from Austria.

guests, and he remembered how uncomfortable he had felt as a bachelor when he had to play host. The most important ambassadors to Burma, those of the United States and Great Britain, came to lunch at the East Haw within a few months of their return. Many other diplomats, Burmese cabinet ministers, and dignitaries followed. Sao hosted tennis tournaments as soon as the courts were repaired from their four years of disuse.

Shan villagers from the remotest areas in the state came in droves. They had a right to see their ruler, pay their respects, and ask for any help they needed. Thusandi never missed an opportunity to join Sao for these sessions. For such occasions, the drawing room—the size of a small movie theater—was covered from wall to wall with carpets. The villagers removed their slippers outside, filed in, and sat on the floor. They sipped roasted Shan tea flavored with salt, nibbled on Petit Beurre biscuits, and smoked sweet-smelling cheroots until Sao and Thusandi entered. They too sat on the floor, facing their guests, instead of using the elevated sofa-platform. While Sao talked, Thusandi studied the wonderful faces under the big Shan turbans. Each and every face had stories to tell: of courage, of survival, of compassion, of pride, of humor, and of humility, as well as an occasional twinkle of mischief. Several mustachioed and tattooed men had risked their lives hiding British and American pilots from the Japanese

Shan village and district headmen from remote areas of Hsipaw State in front of the East Haw, after paying respects to their prince.

conquerors during World War II. The hill tribes and most Shans had remained loyal to the Allies, actively supporting Stilwell's men, while the Burmese had aided the Japanese in occupying the country. Thusandi recognized Sanglu, a lean and tall man who had carried a downed British pilot on his back for four days to reach a safe haven among Palaung tea growers.

ONE DAY SAO'S BROTHER CAME, unannounced and quite unexpected. The bodyguards at the gate waved his jeep through as soon as they recognized him and pointed to the tennis courts where Sao was playing against the northern Shan state champion. Although he was taller and much darker than his brother, Thusandi knew at once who the visitor was. His eyes were similar and yet very different from Sao's. They were cold and piercing and lacked Sao's compassion and warmth.

He walked up to Thusandi, stretched out his hand and said, "So, you are my younger brother's wife! I am pleased to meet you at last."

She shook his hand, expressed her pleasure at meeting him, and invited him to watch the remainder of the set with her. The servants immediately offered him refreshments.

"Hey you," he yelled at one of them, "get me some tea! You ought to remember that I don't like lime juice."

Thusandi did not like the way he treated their servants, and she did not feel comfortable in his company. Sao Khun Long was opposed to their marriage—she knew that.

He soon grew impatient and said, "I'm getting tired of this game. How much longer is it going to last?" He walked off toward the pavilion, where the butler was preparing some snacks. It surprised Thusandi to see the butler kneel in front of Sao's brother, a custom they had abolished on their arrival. All the other servants seemed to be afraid of him, bowing deeply and trying to get out of his way.

Sao appeared pleased to see his brother again and welcomed him with open arms. But Sao Khun Long put some distance between them, grabbing his brother's arm instead of reciprocating with an embrace. The brothers were used to speaking Burmese to each other, but Sao had switched to English for Thusandi's benefit.

"I am going to the United States on a study trip," said Sao Khun Long. He was an employee of the central Shan government. "And I need some help from you, little brother." He did not specify the kind of help, and Thusandi wondered what he meant.

She remembered the bits and pieces she had heard about Sao's brother from her followers. He had collaborated with the Japanese during the occupation, treating his people cruelly, and had not been allowed to live in Hsipaw State when the British returned. The people of the state, for these and other reasons, had refused to accept him—the older of the two brothers in line for succession—as their ruler in 1947, when the country was gaining independence from the British. In the election for succession, Sao had been the winner.

Although the short visit was cordial, Thusandi perceived an underlying tension and distrust between the brothers. She availed herself of the first opportunity to ask Sao about his relationship with his brother, a subject they had never discussed. His almost curt response, "It's fine," was quite out of character and gave Thusandi a clear message that it was best to drop the subject, at least for the time being. She decided not to pursue her question about the help her brother-in-law had come to seek.

HARDLY A DAY PASSED WITHOUT someone from the state coming to Sao with a complaint against the Burmese Army; villagers were intimidated and forced to provide free labor, women were harassed and sometimes raped, and elders who tried to protect their people were arrested and taken away. The army behaved as if it were the enemy and not the protector of this land. Strong protests to the special commissioner and the central government of the Union of Burma went unheeded. Whether the leadership was not in control of its troops or whether these excesses were part of a greater plan against the minorities was not clear. Sao, among other Shan leaders, raised these questions in Shan State Council and Parliament but did not receive a satisfactory reply.

Another matter of concern for the non-Burmese states of the union was the economic policies of the central government. Revenues from border trade, teak, and minerals were channeled to projects in Burma proper, while funds for the constituent states dried up. Students, local leaders, and simple villagers came to Sao suggesting that the Shan states had made a mistake when they had voluntarily joined the Union of Burma in 1947. They also proposed a solution: independence from Burma, as guaranteed by the Constitution, when the ten-year trial period of voluntary union with the Burmese ended in 1958.

"I understand your frustrations," Sao said. "I am angry too. But I do not believe that secession from the Union of Burma is the answer. We must insist, through the Shan Council and through the House of Nationalities, on our rights to regional autonomy within the Union. The Constitution we helped create guarantees these rights, and we have the proper channels to address our grievances."

This answer disappointed those Shans who hoped Sao would lead them in a growing separatist movement. On the other hand, pro-Union advocates suspected Sao of being a secessionist due to his open criticism of Burmese politics and of the army's misconduct. It did not concern Sao that he was misunderstood by both sides. The only thing that mattered to him was standing firm on his principles and on his commitment to all the people who had faith in his leadership.

One day, the colonel in charge of the Northern Command in Lashio called on Sao to inform him that General Ne Win, the supreme commander of the armed forces, would be passing through Hsipaw in a few days. Sao listened to this news and said to the colonel, "I will be pleased to invite the general and his party to lunch at the East Haw."

"I must decline your invitation, sir. The general won't be able to spend much time in Hsipaw," the colonel responded.

"In that case, we could make it tea," Sao said politely.

"I'm sorry, sir, but that won't be possible either," said the colonel without further explanation.

"How unfortunate. That means I won't get to see the general. I do appreciate, though, that you informed me of his itinerary through my state," Sao said with a noncommittal smile.

"The general does want to meet with you when he passes through," the colonel replied quickly.

"Well, he is, of course, welcome in my office for a short stopover, if he has time only for that."

"That won't be convenient either. What we suggest is that you, sir, come and wait by the roadside for the general's motorcade next Wednesday. We'll give you his approximate time of arrival at the Hsipaw junction by Tuesday evening."

Sao could not believe what he was hearing, and he looked at the colonel in utter amazement: He could not believe that this man was really suggesting such a breach of protocol. In a calm and deliberate voice he said, "If I were a private citizen, I would not hesitate to wait along the road for General Ne Win. But as long as I am the ruler of Hsipaw State, I must follow the procedures expected of me by the people I represent. Visitors owe the head of this state the courtesy to call on him if they wish to meet him."

The colonel took his leave, promising to convey the message. He must have done so; on Wednesday, the general's convoy passed through Hsipaw without stopping. When Sao attended the next parliamentary session in Rangoon, he saw two letters to Prime Minister U Nu denouncing Sao for snubbing a hero like General Ne Win. The letters were from the colonel and Hom Hpa, the special commissioner. The prime minister supported Sao's decision, but Ne Win and the army were of a different opinion. They let it be known that they considered Sao Kya Seng their enemy.

ON A CRISP AND BEAUTIFUL DAY in June, after the rains had cleared the haze created by the slash-and-burn agriculture, Sao took his wife to Lookout Mountain. Conditions for the outing were perfect: The air was light and clear, and the ground had dried out enough for their car not to get stuck in the mud. They took the Land Rover, filling it with attendants and also some offerings for the hermit who lived on top of the hill.

From time to time, the attendants had to get out and clear the Land Rover's path with their jungle knives. Vines and foliage crept from one tree to another, and tender tree shoots sprouted everywhere. Waves of sweet and heavy scent from white citrus blossoms drifted from a cluster of wild bushes across their path. An audible silence lay over the jungle. Only the car's motor and the swishing sound of the jungle knives disturbed the peace. They had no problems with the six-mile ascent, except that it took

an exceptional amount of time. Half a mile from the summit, Sao asked
the driver to stop and said, "We'll have to hike the rest of the way. We
must not disturb the hermit." Turning to Thusandi, Sao continued, "He
avoids people, but the wild animals join him quite often. The villagers say
they've seen all sorts by his hut—leopards and tigers, a bear, even an elephant."

Thusandi tried to keep up with the trailblazer, hoping to catch a
glimpse of any wildlife. She did not. However, she saw the hermit, a short
ascetic man with a shaved head, wearing the brown robe of his order. He
hastily retreated into the jungle, wishing to avoid human contact. The
attendants left offerings for him in front of his bamboo-mat door: rice,
cooking oil, salt, sugar, and condensed milk to help augment his diet of
roots, leaves, and wild fruit harvested from the jungle. The realization that
this man had chosen to live the past fifteen years of his life in this secluded
spot, away from all human contact and amenities, touched Thusandi
deeply. She had heard of nuns in her native Austria who had never left the
confines of their convent and were cut off from the outside world. But the
setting here was different.

She lagged behind Sao and their attendants as they followed the hermit's path to a clearing. The view took her breath away; below them the
wide Namtu River wound through the rich, green valley, past their white
residence, the East Haw, and the remnants of the old palace, which was
destroyed during World War II. The sleepy town of Hsipaw with its fifteen thousand residents, who lived tucked away in one- and two-story
buildings, was shaded by hundreds of flame trees, some still displaying
their fiercely red blossoms. To the north and west, the valley was covered
with succulent green paddy fields, whose sweet scent filled the air. Where
the bright green expanses stopped, dark teak forests took over, covering the
rolling hills until they peaked in rugged mountains. White pagodas,
shaped like graceful bells, topped dozens of hills, some standing alone,
others in clusters.

The beauty and tranquillity of the valley below affected Thusandi
deeply. She was filled with a sense of complete harmony when all of a sudden she was overwhelmed by a terrifying insight. She sensed that the peace
of the valley below would not last—that her happiness with her husband
and their life together would be short. Overcome by great fear, she felt her
knees weaken and the blood drain from her face. A tree stump saved her

from fainting. Thusandi sat down, trying to control the shakes that possessed her body, when she heard Sao ask, "Has the hike exhausted you, my darling? You look so drained."

"I'm not too fit," was the only response that occurred to her. She could not share her frightening vision with him; she simply had to push it out of her mind. Sao helped her up and led her to the edge of the cliff. From there, the view was even more spectacular and forced her to push her fears aside.

They could see several small villages hugging the banks of the river. Sao pointed out Tapok, the noodle village they had visited recently. She thought she could smell the sourish product from here. The villagers produced fermented rice noodles for the entire area. She had seen how they first ground the rice into flour, then made the dough, let it ferment, and created the fat, round noodles that they took to market. Mixed with a spicy sauce, it was a delicacy.

A little farther downriver, she recognized the Pangsai village where she had witnessed the ancient art—slightly modernized—of Shan paper making. She recalled how four or five women had boiled the bark of the mulberry tree in water over a small fire, stirring until the pulp was thick and smooth. Then three little girls, aged from seven to ten, had taken over. They had giggled nonstop as they spread the sticky mass onto frames of wire mesh. Their skill in spreading the pulp evenly and quickly had met with the approval of the watchful women. The one-foot by three-foot frames had been set up at a steep angle, facing the sun to dry. Depending on the intensity of the sun and the level of humidity, the brownish pulp turned into off-white paper within hours. The resulting sheets of paper were strong and beautiful, displaying an intricate design of natural grain. The girls peeled the dry sheets off the wire-mesh frames with ease, oblivious to the fact that they were producing samples of an ancient art.

"We must leave now if we want to pay the sawmill a visit," Sao said, breaking the harmonious hum of the chirping insects and the chattering of a few inquisitive mynahs.

Thusandi reacted instantly to the word sawmill, turning her back on Hsipaw valley and hurrying down the hill to the Land Rover. They were carried to one of her favorite families: the forty-year-old bull elephant Maha Tsang, his spouse Nang Tsang, and their five-year-old son Sai Leng. As they approached the mill, Sai Leng was ready for them with his own ʾdblock. He was already five-and-a-half feet high and used his height

Encounter on the Burma Road: a convoy of working elephants, outfitted with household goods and thatch for roofing, makes room for the Volkswagen Beetle belonging to the Prince of Hsipaw.

and weight to full advantage. He knew that no vehicle could ignore his presence, and would come to a screeching halt rather than risk a major collision. Sai Leng gave the passengers of the Land Rover a chance to get out of the car before he started a body search with his trunk. He was looking for bananas, melons, papayas, or sugarcane, and he was not disappointed. He also wanted his bananas peeled, and that is what he got from Thusandi. When she handed him a small melon, he shook it to make sure it was ripe. After it met with his approval, the gray teenager munched on it with delight. When the treats were gone, he wanted more.

"Watch out!" Sao shouted as Sai Leng attempted to stamp on Thusandi's feet with his front hoofs. Two attendants diverted him by digging a steel hook into the skin behind his ear. He had no choice but to let them lead him away, though he protested by trumpeting loudly, calling his mother's attention to his woes. Nang Tsang was stacking teak logs nearby, and after depositing the log she carried to the top of the stack, she came to rescue her son. He was consoled only when she allowed him to nurse for a few minutes. He paid no further attention to the visitors but went to play on some teak logs, trying to use them for a balancing act. When he fell off, he called his mother again, but she paid no attention. Her maternal instinct must have helped her distinguish between serious trouble and temper tantrums.

Maha Tsang, the majestic father, showed no interest whatsoever in this family affair. He worked on his logs, deigning only to obey his mahout, or elephant boy. Maha Tsang had lost an eye during the war, due, it was said, to a Japanese bullet. Now he was only interested in his day's work at the little sawmill by the stream. Its wealth lay in the stacks of big, long teak logs, not in the two sheds housing the equipment to process them. There was no shelter for the elephants and only a roof-covered area for the people caring for them and working at the mill.

"It will be eleven o'clock in a few minutes," Sao said.

"Why is that important?" Thusandi asked curiously.

"You will see!"

Indeed, she saw. Exactly at eleven, the two adult elephants dropped the logs they were working on, collected their son, and hurried off into the jungle, nibbling on a tender growth of bamboo as they disappeared behind the thicket. Thusandi learned that the elephants had the right to go off into the jungle, their larder, at that time every morning to find their own meals. No food was provided for them at the sawmill; their internal clock told them when it was time to go and eat.

"Do they come back after they have had their fill?" Thusandi asked.

"Every morning at five, the mahout goes to find them and bring them back to work. He has an idea where the best feeding places are, and that is where he starts calling them. After a routine hide-and-seek game they always return. The chain on their hind legs slows them down so that they travel no farther than ten miles."

On their way back to the East Haw, Thusandi tried to place the morning's experiences into proper perspective. She was grateful for the new impressions she had gained of their valley. She was, however, deeply disturbed by her premonitions of troubled times ahead, especially since she felt strongly that she should not share these worries with anyone.

HER LARGE HOUSEHOLD RAN so smoothly that Thusandi eased into her management responsibilities very naturally. She started daily by filling twenty vases with cut flowers, setting the menu for the day's meals, and trying to figure out which servant was responsible for which duties. During this process, Thusandi began to realize that every servant was at work every single day of the week. For the first few weeks, she had attributed this unusual effort to their recent arrival. However, when months went by without a sign of a fair workweek, Thusandi called a meeting with the secretary and the butler to discuss the issue. Kawlin, the butler, assured Thusandi that the servants did not want time off, that they preferred to come to work in the East Haw every day of the week. Thusandi could not accept that; she refused to exploit her loyal staff. Instead, she designed a monthly schedule, carefully outlining who was on and off duty each day of the week.

The plan looked very impressive and took its place of honor over the table in the servants' dining room. However, Thusandi's bewilderment grew when, day after day, the person who had a scheduled off-day appeared and worked happily all day long. Another meeting clarified the position of the servants; they wanted to have free days according to need, not according to schedule. They preferred to be at work regularly, to take care of their duties, and to ask for personal leave if they wanted to attend a festival,

Kawlin (front left) and Moei (third from left) with some members of the East Haw household staff. Several of the royal family's bodyguards are in the back row.

a family event, or a religious retreat. They made it clear to Thusandi that pursuing this matter along her lines would make the staff feel unimportant and expendable.

Moei, her efficient and cheerful personal maid, was Thusandi's favorite from the day of their arrival. She was one of the few heavy-set women whom Thusandi had encountered among the slim Shans. Partly due to her stature, partly due to her position as the butler's wife, Moei commanded considerable respect among the predominantly male household staff. Her black eyes sparkled with joie de vivre, her round face sported a disarming smile from morning till night, and her resonant voice conveyed authority. Yet she was soft and gentle when she attended Thusandi, combing her long brown hair, applying *tanaka*, a paste of tree bark, to her face, and smoothing the folds of Thusandi's silk longyi. With Moei, Thusandi dared to practice the Shan language from her first days, and Moei proved to be a patient but stern tutor.

One morning, Moei did not appear to help Thusandi get ready for a day of important visitors. Kawlin, the butler, knocked at the bedroom suite with news that Moei had become ill and was receiving medicinal herbs. He did not seem unduly concerned. Moei did not come to work the next morning either, and Thusandi decided that she would pay her maid a visit. Shielded from the intense sun by a bright red silk parasol and followed by a dozen curious children, she made her way to the servants' quarters behind the moat. Thusandi had help in finding the wooden house that belonged to Moei and Kawlin. It was beleaguered by dozens of people camped around the front porch. Some of them sipped Shan tea from tiny cups, others puffed on fat cheroots, while still others concentrated on the prayer beads in their hands. An old lady ushered Thusandi into the house and to Moei's bedside. She lay on a thin mattress on the floor, seemingly oblivious to the crowd around her. When Thusandi touched her, she knew that Moei was burning with a dangerously high fever. Thusandi panicked, but she could not let her people know how worried she was. There was no time to lose. She sent for the driver and told him to fetch the one and only medical doctor in town. Thusandi started to apply cold compresses to Moei's burning head, repeating over and over, "Moei will get well, Moei will get well." The doctor, who had received his medical training in India, did not take long to come to a diagnosis—typhoid, to be treated at the local hospital, not at home.

Moei was critically ill. She became comatose and lost all her hair. For two weeks, there was no sign of improvement. Then, one morning, the headman of Moei's village and fifty of her relatives and friends came to see Thusandi with a request. "We have come to ask that you give Moei permission to die," the headman said to her.

"Why do you ask me such a thing?" Thusandi said, her voice trembling. She bit her lower lip so hard that it hurt. "Moei will get well again—she won't die."

"Permit me to tell you about our Shan custom, our Royal Mother," the village headman said in a calm voice. "Moei has wanted to die for two weeks now, I know that. However, because she is your maid, she can not die until you release her and give her spirit permission to go wherever it wishes. Please free her and let Moei pass on."

Thusandi lowered her head and said nothing. She had to control her inner turmoil, although she felt like screaming and throwing everybody out. She could not believe they could ask such a thing of her and make her the master over life and death. Shan customs or not, she could not accept the responsibility for such a pronouncement, especially as her maid was too young to die.

All eyes were on her. Nobody seemed to breathe. Thusandi raised her head and said with authority and strength in her voice, "I cannot give Moei permission to die—I want her to live." She rose from the floor and left the room without giving anyone a chance to appeal. Losing no time, she summoned the driver and asked to be driven to the hospital. Moei was still in a coma, but Thusandi thought she saw the faintest smile on her lips when she said quietly but firmly to her friend, "Moei, you must live. You may not die!"

And Moei lived. She began to show marked improvement on that same day and recovered rather quickly and completely. Her hair grew back and she came to work again, seven days a week. She often said to Thusandi, "Thank you, Royal Mother, for not allowing me to die."

After that occurrence, Thusandi noticed that her people, her relatives, and the villagers treated her with more reverence, which sometimes even bordered on awe. They sought her opinions and blessings more frequently than before, and it concerned her that she was considered more powerful than in reality she knew she was.

Six

IT WAS APRIL AND THE HEAT IN the Hsipaw valley was oppressive. Weary humans, thirsty animals, and parched plants were longing for the first rains of the monsoon season. Remembering the crisp spring mornings in the Rocky Mountains, Sao disliked breathing the smoke from jungle fires, which had been hanging over the valley for weeks. He planned to teach his people in the nearby hills to replace their traditional slash-and-burn agriculture with new methods that would produce better crops and do less harm. For now though, Sao wished to escape to a hilltop, somewhere reminiscent of cool and clear Colorado.

"Tomorrow, we are going to Sakandar to spend the day," Sao pronounced, setting the sleepy household into motion. Mehta, the cook, rushed to the bazaar on his bicycle after ordering the kitchen boy to prepare for the outing. Ba Aye, the mechanic, put his head under the hoods of assorted vehicles to make sure they were operational. And Bukong, chief of the bodyguards, gave orders for weapons to be cleaned and boots to be polished.

"Go ahead and invite anyone you'd like to take along," Sao said to Thusandi. He was pleased when she sent messengers to half a dozen relatives asking them to join the party. Sao loved to visit Sakandar, the former summer palace, and he preferred to have lots of company. He wanted to be reminded of the bustling life he had enjoyed there until World War II turned his favorite boyhood place into merely a deserted reminder of its former grandeur. Sao wanted Thusandi to be favorably impressed by Sakandar; maybe, in years to come, they would turn it into their main residence. He hoped that one day he would no longer have to rule the state, and he could devote his time entirely to its economic development. Sao was convinced that the time for feudal rule of the Shan states was over, that he and the other princes should waste no time in surrendering their powers to a democratically elected central Shan government within the Union of Burma.

Sao drove the Land Rover himself, with Thusandi at his side, following a jeep load of bodyguards. He no longer needed to convince his wife that travel to anywhere in this part of the world without armed guards was inadvisable. Dacoits, the highway robbers of Burma and India, were still plying their trade on the roads as they had been for centuries. Two weeks ago, the Prince of Tawngpeng and his Mahadevi, neighbors to the north, had been "dacoited" on this very stretch of road. They had arrived in Hsipaw from Maymyo, without guards, to tell the story of how three armed dacoits had relieved them of their cash and jewelry. They had been napping in the back seat of the car when their driver slammed on the brakes and yelled to high heaven. He had come around a curve and almost hit two Shan men in the middle of the road, aiming their muzzle-loading guns at his windshield. A third armed bandit rushed up to the driver and asked for the identity of the two passengers. When the Prince of Tawngpeng, concealing his true identity, said he was a merchant from Lashio, the dacoit spokesman demanded "toll." The prince emptied his wallet and his pockets, hoping that almost 500 kyats in cash would satisfy the dacoits. Then he saw that the sparkling diamonds of his Mahadevi's buttons had caught the eye of their leader. The prince thought they would not embarrass the lady by taking away the buttons holding together her blouse. Unfortunately, they did. The dacoits made one concession: The lady was allowed to remove the five jewelry buttons from the aingyi by herself.

When they stopped at the East Haw half an hour after that ordeal, Thusandi immediately recognized what kind of help her neighbor, who was frantically holding her blouse together, really needed. She sent Moei for the jewelry box and chose her sapphire buttons to lend to the Mahadevi of Tawngpeng for the trip to Namhsan. Khun Pan Sing, the Prince of Tawngpeng, solemnly vowed never to leave his bodyguards at home again.

The rest of the convoy on the way to Sakandar consisted of half a dozen cars and jeeps filled with excited relatives, state officials, and attendants. Sao enjoyed driving the uncrowded, paved road in the direction of Mandalay. Now and then, he hummed a tune to make up for the lack of a station strong enough to be received on the car radio. He stopped in two places along the road, which he had earmarked for agricultural experiments.

"This is the land where we'll grow pineapples," he said to Thusandi, pointing at a rolling hillside near the village of Loikaw. Sao envisioned rows of pineapples as far as his eyes could see. He did not seem discouraged by the dense growth of bushes and vines, now thirsting for rain, that would have to be dug up by dozens of diligent workers. A little farther down the road, Sao showed his wife where he planned to experiment with coffee and ginger.

After they had passed their future plantations and a few sleepy villages, Thusandi turned to Sao. "Tell me a little bit about your Sakandar. Is it Shangri La?"

"It used to be, it really did," Sao said with emphasis, "and it's going to be heaven again, I hope. I used to go there to visit my cousin, Sao Ohn Kya. They were the happiest times I had. He and my uncle, Sir Sao Hke, they followed the British example. The British couldn't take the heat, so they used to move the whole government up to a hill station when it got too hot in the summer. The British station's just near here, actually—Maymyo. It's just sixty miles down the road."

"We flew over Maymyo—I remember," Thusandi said.

"Anyway, my predecessors moved their court too, up out of Hsipaw to Sakandar. It was a great success. Everybody loved it here. The palace was so large and beautiful, people used to come from miles away to stay. It was always full of people, guests."

Sao was so engrossed in memories that he almost missed the turn-off from the paved road. He had to pay full attention to the steep gravel road which had seen better days. It was wide and carefully laid out, and although weeds had spread over the gravel, it still made a crunchy sound under the tires.

The ride was becoming rather bumpy, and before Thusandi could ask, Sao said, "Only five more miles and you'll see why this is all worth it." They were climbing rapidly, and the flora started to change. The air felt much cooler, and Thusandi thought she recognized smells of her childhood, of the evergreen forests she had explored with her father.

"Look, fir trees," Thusandi shouted excitedly. "I haven't seen any since we arrived in Burma."

"I knew you'd like that," Sao said laughingly, "and there'll be more surprises." He knew how much she loved trees. During one of their discussions on the verandah, she had confessed to him her belief that trees had souls and deserved to be respected just like other living beings. At the top of the hill, they entered a terraced park where jacaranda trees kept company with silver oaks, pines, Chinese cherries, and figs. As they slowly passed beneath these majestic trees, Thusandi made Sao promise that they would take a long walk and have a closer look at them later.

At last, the palace came into view and Sao stopped abruptly. The cream-colored neoclassic building looked as though it belonged on a hill in northern Italy. The white marble for the staircase leading to the central section of the palace had actually come from the Mediterranean. Large windows, slim pillars, and ample terraces gave the building an appearance of lightness. Only the central part had its original roof; the right wing was covered with makeshift corrugated sheets. The left wing, devoid of ceilings and roof, bore witness to the senseless destruction of war. In spite of apparent damages, the simple beauty of the palace captivated Sao and his entourage.

Sao wanted to experience to the fullest the happy feelings this sight evoked in him. It had been his safe haven in the thirties, a place where he could forget about the unhappiness of his father's household. Sao remembered the carefree laughter that had filled the spacious halls of Sakandar

Sakandar, the summer palace of the ruling princes of Hsipaw State.

when he returned from school in Darjeeling. Here, he had fallen in love for the first time. He recalled the feeling but not the girl who had been the object of his affection. Sao also knew that the talks he had here with his cousin, Sao Ohn Kya, who had earned an M.A. degree from Oxford, had brought about his own resolve to get a good college education.

When the Land Rover pulled up in front of the grand entrance, the caretakers and their families were waiting with flowers and smiles. They had heard and seen the approaching convoy as it was climbing the hill. Sao felt like a little schoolboy, anxious to show off his playground. However, he restrained himself and gave proper attention to his employees, who had many requests and much to report to their master. Once he had absolved himself of his duty, Sao took Thusandi's hand and led her through the still ornate throne room and adjoining halls. The large rooms were empty save for the intricate patterns of the parquet floor and the elevated podium on which the throne had once stood. It was framed by elaborate wood carvings, resplendent with gold leaf that glittered as if it had been put on yesterday. Large french doors opened onto a terrace with a breathtaking view. Layer upon layer of wooded hills extended into the distance, where a mountain range with jagged peaks put a stop to them. No man-made constructions, no villages or farms disrupted the flow of nature.

"How beautiful and gentle—so different from the Alps or the Rocky Mountains," Thusandi mumbled to herself. She only turned around when Sao took her hand to lead her through the preserved wing of the palace, where the private living quarters used to be. Neither one of them spoke. He seemed to hear the echo of long-past conversations as their footsteps resounded on the parquet floors.

The left wing of the palace, containing reception rooms and offices, had been burned down by the Japanese occupation forces, as were the outlying houses, which had been the homes of state officials, relatives, and servants.

"What a senseless waste," Thusandi said as Sao took her past the burned-out section. "Did the Japanese start the fire deliberately or was it caused by a battle?"

"It wasn't due to fighting. The Japanese fled before it came to that. But nobody knows whether they set the fire intentionally or whether they were just careless. And once the villagers discovered the flames, they had no means of stopping them. They had to let the fire take its course. It's a miracle it stopped short of the throne room."

Sao led his wife to the balustrade surrounding the top tier of the marble terrace, expecting her to become absorbed in the view once more. Instead, she surprised him with a practical question: "This is a beautiful place. Why haven't you rebuilt it?"

"I've thought about it a lot, darling. Things haven't been easy since the Japanese left back in 1945. The British came back, and they had an administrator run Hsipaw for two years. Then I was enthroned, but I had my hands full defending the state, because we were surrounded by Communists. They'd taken over Lashio and Maymyo—we had to fight to keep them out of Hsipaw."

"It's hard to imagine all the fighting going on here—I've never been to a place where I felt such peace," Thusandi said when Sao paused to adjust his glasses.

"Well, things did get better and I went to America. U Lek, the Shan administrator, took care of the state. So you see, rebuilding Sakandar hasn't exactly been a priority. I don't think I could even justify it now—not until my Tai Mining Company brings prosperity to the state."

"I'd like to raise our children here," Thusandi said before Sao took her face in his hands and kissed her gently.

"Come," Sao said as he led her from the terrace. "I still owe you that walk through the park." They strolled through former lawns, rose gardens, and strawberry patches, past the venerable trees that had welcomed them. The air was as crisp and clear as Sao had remembered it. But looking down from their vantage point of more than four thousand feet, they saw the steaming and hazy valley below them.

"I wish we could stay up here for a few days," Thusandi said as she sat down on a stone bench, shaded by a cluster of Chinese cherry trees.

"One day we will," Sao said, happy to see that she liked Sakandar as much as he did. He sat down next to her, feeling as carefree and relaxed as the last time they sat on a park bench together in the City Park of Denver. Neither one of them seemed eager to leave this tranquil hideaway.

"Who decided to build the summer palace here? Was it your grandfather?"

"No. My uncle Sir Sao Hke built Sakandar. I guess he needed space

for the forty wives he married and the dozen children he adopted in addition to his own four."

"I'm glad you're not following in his footsteps," Thusandi said
laughingly. "He must have lived in grand style."

"He had grand ideas—but then, he was brought up in a palace, the
Royal Palace of Mandalay, when King Thibaw was on the throne. He went
to England and Australia too. I wish I could remember him. I was only
four years old when he died. But Auntie Gyipaya told me many stories
about him. You should ask her. She likes to have an audience."

Thusandi was fascinated by what she had heard. "Has anybody written some of these stories down?" she asked.

"Not yet. Maybe, you can do that one day." Sao looked at his watch
and jumped up. "We shouldn't keep our party waiting for the picnic too
much longer."

They slowly made their way back to the palace, passing under dozens
of majestic trees planted some forty years ago. Dark green Norfolk pines
towered over umbrella-shaped jacarandas whose cool lavender-blue blossoms were just beginning to fade. Next to them stood a group of cassia
trees, their branches completely covered with masses of pink flowers. Their
brilliant pink branches emerged from a bed of green leaves, like playful
garlands crowning another masterpiece of Mother Nature. Sao and Thusandi trod lightly, listening to the leaves rustle in the mountain breeze.
They watched the sun's rays filter through the treetops and create their
own version of a shadow play on the dry grasses along their path.

"This is more than a park, it's an arboretum," Sao heard Thusandi
say, when all of a sudden he spotted a leopard, two hundred feet to the left
of them. He put his finger on his lips and stopped abruptly, pointing his
other hand toward the big cat. They both froze and hardly dared breathe
when they saw that the leopard did not flee. He stood motionless, with his
eyes fixed on them. Sao was thrilled that they encountered the magnificent
animal in this setting. They had a clear view of the right side of his sleek,
long body and of his head, which was turned toward them. From his
perked ears to his tucked tail, he resembled a picture of liquid gold,
reflecting the sun from his shining fur. Though motionless, he exuded
energy and strength as if to show that he was master of the territory.

Sao decided caution was in order and signaled the two bodyguards to fire a few warning shots into the air. The leopard heeded the warning and sped away with graceful, mighty leaps.

The caretakers confirmed that leopards and tigers roamed the hills around Sakandar. There had been no incidents of attacks on human beings in the area, and nobody hunted the animals.

The leopard sighting provided the main topic during the picnic, which was served on low, round lacquer tables on the marble terrace. The cook produced a great variety of fragrant dishes and sizable mounds of steaming rice. Tender tamarind leaves, picked in the early morning from the trees around the East Haw, made a delectable salad garnished with ground peanuts, hard-boiled eggs, sweet onions, lime juice, and oil. Pickled ground venison was broiled over an open charcoal fire and served piping hot; it had a sourish yet delicate flavor. A mild chicken curry, several vegetable dishes, and the Shan staple, thonau, completed the menu. Green and red chilies and other sauces provided spice and color, while an assortment of cut-up melons cooled the palate.

"Let's eat Shan style, with our fingers, and not use the silverware," Thusandi suggested. Sao had never approved of it at home, but he agreed that they were in an appropriate setting. He wanted to give Thusandi some practice; besides, eating with his fingers always improved his appetite. Attendants rushed to bring towels and lacquer bowls with water so that everybody could wash their hands before, during, and after the meal. All eyes were on Thusandi as she tried to follow the example of the skilled diners around her. Only their fingertips touched the food, while the rest of the hand stayed clean. Thusandi fared differently: Her fingers, hand, and arm—practically to her elbow—illustrated everything on the menu until bowls of water removed the evidence.

At the foot of the terrace stood two heavy marble blocks that proved very useful for all the picnic supplies. "These blocks weren't meant as picnic tables, were they?" Thusandi asked Sao during the meal. "They must have served some special purpose."

"You are right," Sao replied, "and there are two more facing in other directions. But that is another long story."

"Perfect," Thusandi said. "While I practice eating Shan style, you can tell me."

Sao began, "When my uncle had this summer palace built, he

ordered four bronze statues of guardian spirits to protect the residence from harm."

"Is this a Buddhist tradition?" Thusandi asked.

"Not at all—it has nothing to do with Buddhism. The belief in spirits goes back to a prior religion. People believe that every house is protected by guardians and that they must be looked after. Sakandar had four of them, and the sculptures that housed them were mounted on these marble blocks. My uncle commanded them to do their duty, and in return they were offered a meal of meat once a week. Well, my uncle died and his son, Sao Ohn Kya, stopped feeding the spirits. He'd been educated in England, you see, and he thought all these beliefs were nonsense. But from then on, the spirits turned nasty, and they took revenge on the servants and made them ill."

"What happened to them?" Thusandi put her plate down and listened to Sao intently.

"For instance, if a servant touched any of the statues, his hand would swell and hurt for days. A cook who patted one of the spirits on his head and suggested he come and help in the kitchen became violently ill and ended up in a hospital. The people working here got so frightened that my cousin had to do something about it. He and his Mahadevi were the only ones not affected."

"Why not?"

"Because they were the spirits' superiors, no harm could befall them. My cousin decided that the guardian spirits should be fed again, but in exile. They were removed from here and sent to guard the Bawgyo Pagoda with strict orders never to misbehave again. The four statues have been at Bawgyo ever since, and there have been no complaints."

"Do you really believe all this?" Thusandi asked incredulously.

"I told you only what I heard from eyewitnesses themselves. We can stop at Bawgyo on the way home, and you can have a firsthand look at the culprits."

On the way back to Hsipaw, Sao stopped at the white pagoda of Bawgyo and led Thusandi to the four gates where the bronze figures stood guard. The five-foot-tall spirit by the east gate looked especially mischievous. His eyes followed anyone observing him, and his expression appeared to change to a sneer. Sao confirmed that he was the one suspected of the most serious transgressions when he was on duty in Sakandar.

Guardian spirit at the white pagoda of Bawgyo after being exiled from Sakandar.

A FEW MONTHS LATER, THERE occurred a most unusual phenomenon—a total solar eclipse. Neither Sao nor Thusandi could remember having experienced one before, and they awaited the event with great excitement. Astrologers, who played an important role in Shan society, had alerted people about the upcoming event. They made their predictions according to traditional calculations going back thousands of years. Sao was concerned about eye damage and warned his people not to look at the sun during the eclipse. He called a meeting of all schoolteachers and demonstrated the pinhole method of viewing the eclipse by projection.

Even though the rainy season had officially set in, the day of the eclipse began with a cloudless sky and a bright, hot sun. It was a calm morning, and a special stillness lay in the air. Thusandi expected a gradual dimming of the light, without any fanfare. Sao had set up a shadow box on the terrace so that they could observe the process of the moon blocking the sun's light. He handed the box to Thusandi to see the first dent in the sun, when an enormous racket started: Cannon shots rang out, thousands of drums reverberated, and the clatter of all the pots and pans in Hsipaw town contributed to the deafening noise. Thusandi dropped the box and turned to Sao, completely puzzled. "What's that? World War III?"

"I forgot to tell you about that," Sao shouted in an attempt to be heard in spite of the racket. "Our people are trying to scare away the dragon."

"What dragon?"

"Well, the one who is trying to swallow the sun."

"I see." Thusandi finally understood.

"The same thing will happen with the next lunar eclipse as well. Old legends never die."

As the daylight drew dim, the noise also subsided.

"Are they giving up or running out of steam?" Thusandi asked Sao.

"A bit of each, I guess. They probably didn't expect it to last this long."

Eventually, it became very dark and very quiet. A ten-minute night set in and with it came sleep: sleep for the crickets, the insects, the birds, and most animals. The mynah birds fell silent, and the two tame peacocks settled down for a nap on the front lawn. The sudden absence of daytime noises startled Sao and Thusandi even more than the previous clamor. There was something frightening and ominous about this trick nature was playing on its creatures. They had become helpless observers of a rare alignment of the prescribed courses in the solar system.

Only when the light grew brighter did life begin to stir again. The confidence of the noisemakers returned. They began their campaign with renewed vigor—and they finally succeeded. After having swallowed the sun, the dragon let go of it again and retreated, until next time.

Seven

Another rainy season had
washed the dust from large teak leaves, cleaned the land, and restored life
to agriculture and to the jungle. Once again, the swollen waters of the
Namtu River shared their blessing with the thirsty paddy fields of Hsipaw
valley. After the villagers had planted their crops, they could watch rain
and sun continue the work. The rainy summer months were a time for fast-
ing, for going within. Monasteries were crowded with young and old practicing their meditative techniques and seeking the words of the Buddha.
The temple bells of a village monastery near the East Haw daily invited
the neighborhood to early morning meditation practices.

"I'm going to meditate for the next two weeks," Sao announced to
Thusandi a few days before his birthday. "Would you like to join me? A
special teacher will come to our private chapel every morning."

Thusandi did not reply immediately. She had often expressed interest
in learning how to meditate, yet she was not ready. In her eyes, practicing
meditation meant a commitment to Buddhism that she was not prepared
to make. True, her childhood religion no longer satisfied her spiritual
needs, but she wanted more time to understand what Theravada Buddhism
had to offer.

Surrounded by practicing Buddhists from the day she arrived, Thusandi had seen their faith in action. She had learned much more from
observing the effect of Buddha's teachings on her people's daily lives than
from reading the scholarly Buddhist books that Sao had ordered from a
renowned abbot in Ceylon. Her servants were forever doing good deeds,
giving away things they needed themselves—money, clothing, food—to

those who were needier. They reached out with compassion and kindness to the sick, the helpless, and the distraught before anybody had a chance to ask for support. Therefore no orphanages, old people's homes, or mental institutions existed. And the town of Hsipaw happily supported five hundred Buddhist monks who were sworn to poverty. At daybreak, the saffron-robed monks walked through the streets collecting food in their lacquer bowls. Women of all walks of life prepared it for them at this early hour every morning, year in and year out. The boundless generosity of her people impressed and worried Thusandi at the same time. How could those who had so little ever improve their lot if they gave so much away?

She started again to read Theravada Buddhist texts about the Triple Gem, the Four Noble Truths, the Eightfold Path, the Three Characteristics of Existence, and the Four Sublime States of Consciousness. And she was immediately troubled by the first of the Four Noble Truths. It said: Life is suffering. Thusandi rejected this tenet as pessimistic and negative. The other Noble Truths explain that the root of all suffering was desire and gave instructions on how to become detached. Thusandi was not convinced that detachment was so desirable; what would happen to the community

Buddhist novice monks collect alms (their daily food) in front of the East Haw. All Shan, and Burmese, males become novices for at least one week in their lives.

and to the country if everybody followed the example of the Sangha, the order of Buddhist monks, and practiced detachment? There would be nobody to carry the burden of providing for the needy and for those who had chosen a life of poverty and become ordained. Thusandi realized that she was not yet ready to join in meditative practices.

Finally, she said to Sao, "Thanks for asking me, but I'd rather wait till next year. I hope that you'll tell me about your meditation."

Sao looked disappointed that she wasn't ready to share in this experience so important to him. But Thusandi knew that he would never try to influence her decisions or put any kind of pressure on her. She felt guilty that she could not accept his decisions with the same magnanimity. It had, for example, upset her considerably when Sao decided against holding a Shan ceremony officially recognizing her as his Mahadevi.

THE VILLAGE ELDERS OF HOKO came to invite their prince to a very important cremation. It was the culmination of extensive funeral rites for their revered abbot, who had died six months earlier, after a monastic life of sixty years. His body had been embalmed and was lying in state in a specially erected mortuary chapel near the monastery. The designated time for the three-day cremation ceremonies had finally come, and Sao agreed to attend the funeral rites on the last day, together with his wife.

Thusandi had attended several Shan funerals and had learned that they were lighthearted, almost jovial events. Neither dress nor mood of the attending crowd had anything in common with the gloomy, mournful funerals she had attended in Austria. The Shans rejoiced that the deceased person had completed another life in an infinite cycle of death and rebirth. She wondered if the funeral of an important Buddhist abbot would be more formal and somber.

Contrary to Thusandi's expectations, thousands of cheerful people milled around the special building that housed the coffin; there were no evident expressions of grief or mourning. A constant stream of devotees approached the sarcophagus to pay their final respects to the deceased abbot, just as they had revered him when he had been alive. Flowers in their folded hands, they knelt by the coffin and made their obeisance. Sao and Thusandi joined them while the minister of ceremonies, together with the village elders of Hoko, chanted special prayers from Pali scriptures. The morning breeze seemed to carry these soothing chants over the tree-tops of the nearby jungle, away from the jolly crowds.

After completing this ritual, Sao and Thusandi were escorted to the area where for weeks villagers had been making bamboo ropes to pull the funeral cart. Sao was asked to put the final touch to the last of the four six-hundred-foot bamboo ropes. Each village of the surrounding area had been responsible for producing a section of rope. While their men were work-ing, the village band contributed background music, and the women pre-pared culinary treats. In order to make a sturdy, uniform rope, they had drilled a hole eight inches in diameter in the middle of a tree. Soaked bam-boo shavings had then been fed into the hole and twisted to produce a heavy rope.

As the royal couple watched, the villagers fastened two ropes each on the front and the back end of a sturdy cart with four huge wheels. Then the coffin was lowered with great ceremony from the platform of the mortuary chapel onto the cart for the final journey to the funeral pyre, on a slight hill several hundred feet away. It was an elaborate structure: a platform on a white square fifteen feet high, made of matted bamboo, topped by a seven-roofed spire.

Then the most unbelievable spectacle began to unfold. Dozens of able-bodied men stationed themselves along the ropes. A deafening blast from a homemade cannon announced the beginning of the tug-of-war, and enthusiastic villagers simultaneously tried to pull the cart in opposite directions. At first the forces pulling uphill toward the pyre were ahead, but then the other side gained momentum, dragging the funeral cart back to its starting position. Everybody who had gathered at the funeral grounds became part of the strange contest. Those who could not find space along the ropes waited to take the place of a tired warrior. Women and children provided noisy support. The struggle went on for over an hour until, finally, the funeral cart reached the pyre. Sao explained to Thu-sandi that this rope-pulling contest symbolized the struggle between the worldly and spiritual forces for the karma of the deceased. She wondered what would have happened if the worldly forces had won, but she decided against asking that question.

THUSANDI WAS RETURNING FROM
an inspection tour of the flower garden when she saw a dozen Shan elders
file out of Sao's private office. They looked dejected and disappointed. She
was used to visitors leaving her husband's presence appearing happy and
inspired. She wondered what had gone wrong. She cautiously opened the
big french door to his study to find out firsthand what had happened.

Before she had a chance to ask Sao about his visitors, he said to her
with a big sigh, "They came with the same old request."

"And your answer was 'no' again, wasn't it?" Thusandi settled in a
chair across from him and placed her folded arms squarely on his teak desk.
He reached across the polished desktop for her hands, which cooperated
reluctantly.

"You really want this ceremony, don't you?" Sao asked, searching her
face for the smile he had come to expect.

"Of course I do. You know that!" Thusandi said emphatically. She
was not smiling. "I never wanted a second Shan wedding after we arrived
here, but this ceremony is different."

"But you are my Mahadevi, nobody questions that. Why go through
all the formalities when it isn't necessary?" Sao asked as he pulled back and
looked at his wife with a frown.

"Because the ceremony of bestowing this title is important to the
people of your state and to me," she said. "Your subjects want to be included in the big events of your life—they have a right to be—and I . . .
well, I too, need to be assured, in public, that I belong at your side perma-
nently."

Sao had not expected such a reply. He had always assumed that she
supported his decision to discontinue ceremonies that harked back to the
splendor and pomp of times past. He leaned back in his chair and looked
out the window at the mighty banyan tree resplendent in its new, shiny
leaves. A southern breeze made them come alive with a quiver. He felt perhaps that he had been carrying his commitment to lead a "normal" life too
far. His people had a right to carry on with traditions that linked them
to the past, and it was true that she should have some official public
recognition.

With a sense of urgency, Sao called Zinna, the attendant who was waiting at his assigned place by the door. "Go quickly and tell the elders to return to my office. I wish to speak to them again." Then he turned to Thusandi, whose eyes were large and full of questions.

"I have changed my mind—no—you have changed it for me," he said and saw her radiant smile.

She felt overwhelmed by her husband's surprise decision. At last, she would officially be confirmed by the various levels of government within the Union of Burma and recognized by every citizen of the state as the Mahadevi of Hsipaw State. The reasons for her feelings of inadequacy and insecurity would be removed. She no longer had to fear those nagging sentiments that had kept her awake at night when Sao was away from home. Once she was officially recognized as a leading member of the Hsipaw royal family, she would no longer worry about being an outsider, a white-faced foreigner.

After that day in September, the East Haw began to bustle with excitement. The astrologer, Saya Ba Han, came and determined that the eleventh day after the new moon of the eleventh month would be the most auspicious day for the ceremony. He had consulted Thusandi's horoscope and a chart of significant numbers referring to the exact position of the planets at the time of her birth.

That left only two months for elaborate preparations. Sao decided that it should be a celebration by and for his subjects and that outsiders should be informed rather than invited to the festivities. He entrusted all the arrangements to his minister of ceremonies.

The jeweler, the silk weavers from Mandalay, the caterers, and the dressmaker all converged upon the East Haw to consult with Thusandi. The drawing room began to resemble a colorful arts and crafts exhibition. Burmese artisans spread their samples of lustrous silk and embroidery on the burgundy-colored carpet; the tall Indian jeweler presented his sparkling diamonds and rubies on velvet trays in the most favorable light. With the help of cousin Nanda, Thusandi sorted through gems, patterns, silks, and velvet, choosing only the most exquisite. Mandalay silk was heavier than Shan silk and woven in such a complex design that one weaver could finish only two inches a day. Thusandi chose a broken-patterned design of deep pink and rich yellow on a white background for her traditional court dress. When it arrived from Mandalay for a fitting, Thusandi learned that this was the most extravagant dress that had been created there for decades. It was beautiful but simple: a tight-fitting, long-sleeved top and a slim, long skirt with a train that was tailored from the hand-woven silk she had chosen. When she tried it on, however, Thusandi pan-icked. "Moei, I can't move. I can't walk in this tight *thamein* with its train."

"Of course you can, Royal Mother, it just takes a little practice," her maid Moei said cheerfully as she demonstrated the tiny steps that Thu-sandi had to master. "All the former Mahadevis of Hsipaw and all Burmese queens had to function when they wore these court dresses," Moei added.

"I can't see how they could have done much of anything in these con-fining costumes except sit around," Thusandi said as she attempted to sit down gracefully. When she heard and felt her thamein ripping, she recog-nized the difficulty of this otherwise simple function as well. But Moei took charge and arranged for the dressmakers to sew seams that could withstand an active woman from the West who had not yet mastered the catlike movements of her Shan peers.

When Hkun Htun, the minister of ceremonies, made one of his daily appearances at the East Haw, Thusandi inquired, "How many invitations have you already sent out?"

"Five hundred, Mahadevi," he said with a troubled look on his face as if he expected her next remark.

"You'll have to send out some more," she said with determination. "I heard that dozens of important people have not received their invita-tions yet."

"I beg you, Mahadevi—leave these decisions up to me," Hkun Htun pleaded. "I am already being hounded by thousands of invitation seekers wherever I go. We only have room for five hundred special guests to attend the actual ceremony in the East Haw. But other festivities will continue for an entire week so that everybody can celebrate in some fashion."

"I guess you're right," Thusandi said pensively. "I'd better leave this up to you."

The people of Hsipaw discussed little else at the bazaar, in the tea shops, at the Buddhist monasteries, and at home. They consulted each other on the most important questions: Who would be invited to the ceremony, whether the spirits gave signs of approval, and what would their Mahadevi wear? Most of all though, they were happy and grateful that their Saophalong, their Heavenly Ruler, had given them a reason to celebrate.

Finally, on a clear November morning, the East Haw and its residents were ready for the occasion. The first floor had been cleared of all furniture, save for thick carpets covering the teak parquet floors. The golden throne-platform that had been stored away for decades was set up in the large drawing room. Red velvet cushions, embroidered with heavy gold thread, made the throne look soft and inviting. When Sao inspected the throne, he ordered the attendants to remove the large white umbrellas that were attached to the four corners. He said that they had been appropriate for the old Grand Palace, built by his grandfather Sao Hkun Hseng and destroyed in World War II, but not for the modern East Haw.

Although the ceremony was set for one o'clock in the afternoon, guests began to arrive in the early morning and were welcomed by court music, official greeters, food, and drink. Thusandi started to dress at ten with the help of Moei, several cousins, and the wives of all Hsipaw state ministers. Her large bedroom suite accommodated them all, as they fussed over every detail of her dress, her coiffure, her jewelry. They worked on tightening her bodice as much as possible so that her shape would conform to the flat-chested ideal of a Shan woman. And they twisted and tugged on her knee-length hair until she threatened to cut it off if this painful activity continued much longer.

Finally, three hours later, the transformation from the active modern woman to the picture-book princess was complete. When Thusandi finally confronted herself in the three-panel mirror, she could not believe her eyes. Her tight-fitting pink, yellow, and white court dress, heavily embroidered with a golden peacock emblem, hugged her slim, tall figure. The pink sash repeated the golden peacock emblem, as did her diamond necklace set in heavy gold. Her long brown hair, tamed in the traditional court hairstyle, resembled a natural crown highlighted by a diamond-studded comb and a five-carat solitaire. The glitter of her diamond earrings, bracelets, and rings completed the impression of a fairy-tale princess. Thusandi was stunned, wondering what the exotic mirror image had in common with the simple girl from Austria who climbed mountains and rode her father's bicycle to school.

Thusandi hesitated before stepping outside the safety of her bedroom suite. She needed assurances from herself that the fairy princess in the mirror was not an apparition from another time, that she was very much the determined young woman who had arrived in Rangoon harbor in her Austrian cotton dress. She felt jubilant and humble, happy and more confident than ever that she was meant to be at Sao's side in any situation, including this one. But when Moei returned excitedly from a scouting mission and said to Thusandi, "The prince is waiting in the upstairs hall to escort you to the ceremony," Thusandi felt almost paralyzed with sudden fear at the thought of five hundred pairs of curious eyes focusing on her in a few minutes' time. Her hands and feet were ice-cold, although the room was bathed in warm November sun. "Do I look all right, Moei?" she asked, her voice trembling.

"You look as beautiful as the moon and the stars," Moei said so convincingly that Thusandi allowed herself to relax. Cousin Nanda took Thusandi's hand and led her to the prince. The moment he set eyes on her, he froze. Backing away, Sao stared at his wife, spellbound, as if he had never seen her before. It seemed forever until the spell her appearance had put on him was broken. She heard him say, "You look like a fairy tale—you are my fairy-tale princess!" He took her hand tenderly and led her downstairs to the waiting crowds.

Sao wore a simple white Shan silk suit and a pink silk turban. A single ruby button secured the standing collar of his white shirt. It was Thusandi in her courtly splendor who stunned the assembled guests into admiring exclamations. As Sao led her through the assembled crowd, "oohs" and "ahs" were audible from all directions.

After the royal couple was seated on the throne, the official ceremony began. The sweet sound of festive court music came from four traditional instruments: a boat-shaped harp, a carved box with bamboo keys, a flute, and a violin. The minister of ceremonies raised his right hand, the musicians stopped abruptly, and the crowd grew quiet. In a commanding voice he began to read from a scroll of Shan parchment in his left hand.

> The ruler over land and water of Hsipaw State in the land of the Shans is the ruling prince due to his rights and his royal ancestry. Karma has led him and his royal spouse together, and he has taken her as his spouse according to Buddhist customs. She complements him, makes him perfect, and she equals the rays of the moon which illuminate the earth. Surrounded by his subjects and state officials, the prince declares that he has bestowed upon his spouse the name 'Sao Thusandi,' and that he has elevated her into the royal family in this Haw of Hsipaw. May she, from this day on, be free of all evils and illnesses, and may the five blessings be with her forever.

After this proclamation, three old Shans designated as ceremonial custodians of the prince's private Buddhist chapel blew into their conch-shell horns as if to entrust these words to the winds. Thusandi sat motionless on the left side of her husband, listening to the mellow sound of the horns. Although her eyes were to remain downcast during the ceremony, she could not help but steal a glance at the guests below them. Approval and admiration were written in all the eyes that met hers. She felt jubilant, deeply grateful to her husband, and a bit sad that her parents and all the people who had been part of her early years could not witness this day.

Chief Minister U Htan approached the throne on his knees to read a shorter version of the declaration from a plaque of gold: "The Prince of Hsipaw solemnly declares that his royal spouse has been elevated to be Mahadevi of Hsipaw State as of the day of their marriage, and that her name from then on has been Sao Thusandi. The prince evokes the five blessings on her."

U Htan then placed the gold plaque on a round lacquer stand, handing it to his ruler. The prince turned to his spouse, and with as much of a smile as protocol permitted, he presented the shining plaque to her. As she accepted it with both hands, Thusandi bowed deeply, hoping that her trembling hands would go unnoticed. She took a deep breath and turned to the audience, holding up the gold plaque with a triumphant smile.

After that signal the guests could contain their excitement no longer. They crowded around the throne with their good wishes, their laughter, and their expressions of joy. Twenty photographers tried to take pictures before Sao led his Mahadevi to a huge bamboo tent in the gardens where a tea party gave them the opportunity to mingle with their guests, listen to speeches, and express their own happiness and gratitude.

The monumental day was happy from beginning to end. All along, Thusandi had entertained secret fears of an unwelcome incident, some unexpected discord that would interfere with the ceremony. When the day was over, she was able to put those fears to rest. As she waited for Sao on the verandah, Thusandi gave her emotions free rein. She felt tears streaming down her cheeks, and she tasted their salty flavor on her lips, wondering if she had ever cried so hard out of happiness.

She had never been so overwhelmed, not even at their wedding. The recognition she received that day, in public, finally helped her believe all that Sao had so often expressed in private: that he loved and trusted her,

Official portrait of Sao Kya Seng and Thusandi, the Saophalong and Mahadevi of Hsipaw State.

that she was his equal, and that they belonged together as long as they lived. Her faith in him and her hopes for their future were reaffirmed, leaving no room for doubt or apprehension.

THE FESTIVITIES CONTINUED FOR a week at the annual Hsipaw Pwe. Tens of thousands of people tried to catch at least a glimpse of their royal couple at the festival grounds or at the religious ceremonies. Thousands more came to demonstrate their loyalty and pay their respects at the East Haw. When, in turn, Sao and Thusandi went to pay homage at the big white pagoda near the festival grounds, countless hands reached out, trying to touch their bare feet as they passed the crowds.

The morning after the colorful ceremony, seven senior Buddhist monks were invited for offerings at the East Haw. After the saffron-robed

Royal tea party in a bamboo tent. Sao Kya Seng and Thusandi celebrating her installation as the Mahadevi of Hsipaw.

pongyis took their seats on the carpet, they were served a festive meal by the entire staff, who hoped to gain merit by performing this service. Attentive men and women hurried back and forth with bowl after bowl of fragrant dishes and steaming rice, all served to the monks on six-inch-high tables, decked with fine china. This was a special occasion for the Buddhist monks; they usually had to wander through the streets, collecting food in their lacquer bowls for their one and only meal of the day.

When the meal was over, Sao and Thusandi paid their respects to the monks and offered gifts acceptable to Buddhist pongyis, who had taken a vow to live in poverty, with a minimum of worldly possessions: saffron robes, blankets, slippers, shades for sun and rain, paper and pencils, soap, toothpaste, tea leaves, and conserved food items like sardines, condensed milk, and Ovaltine. Finally, the senior monk recited Buddhist scriptures in Pali and gave his interpretation of those texts in Shan.

"I didn't understand a word he said, either in Pali or in Shan," Thusandi said to Sao afterward. "Did he give his blessings or good advice to us?"

"Yes and no," Sao replied. "Buddhist monks always pronounce their blessings over those who seek their teachings. But they don't concern themselves with worldly matters such as civil ceremonies."

"Then why did we invite them for this event?"

"Because we want to do good deeds and gather merits on this auspicious occasion."

This answer confused Thusandi; she wanted to know whether their charitable deed was motivated only by a selfish desire for spiritual advancement.

"So are we giving only that we may receive?" she asked Sao.

"Oh no, this is not a calculated decision," he said shaking his head. "The act of giving rouses positive forces within us, and they advance us to a higher level—very, very gradually. I didn't mean to say that we are consciously trying to collect merits. Do you understand my point?"

"I suppose so," Thusandi pensively agreed.

"I know you do. I've watched you experience the joy of giving many times."

Thusandi said nothing, but she regretted not participating emotionally in the offerings that were made on her behalf to the seven Buddhist monks. Even though she had been present at many religious events, she had not made deliberate efforts to understand Theravada Buddhism and its teachings. She decided to change from then on.

After the excitement of the festivities, Thusandi settled down to the same routines that had occupied her days before. Nothing much had really changed, and she wondered if Sao was not right when he insisted that this ceremony was unnecessary; except now, when she drove past the guardhouse by herself, the honor guards presented arms to Thusandi in the same precise manner as they had when previously she had passed them in the company of their prince. And all the people seemed to treat her with even more respect than before the day when she was officially recognized as the Mahadevi of Hsipaw State.

Eight

❖ ❖ ❖ ❖ ❖ ❖ ❖ ❖ ❖ ❖ ❖

THE HOT SEASON HAD SETTLED
over Hsipaw valley again, with a vengeance. Man and beast sought shelter
from the merciless rays of the sun under trees and roofs, suspending their
lives until the big red disk disappeared behind the hills to the west. Then
activities resumed, laughter filled the air, and fragrances of evening meals
cooking over charcoal traveled in waves through the neighborhoods. As if
to remind people that the heat would return next day, hundreds of fiery-
red royal flame trees (poinciana) were in full bloom, spreading their striking scarlet umbrellas over the town.

Sao and Thusandi had ventured onto the terrace from the cool interior of the East Haw. It was time for their cocktail hour, when they discussed the day's events and sought counsel from each other. Sao fed cashew
nuts to Senta, their favorite German shepherd, who sat on the marble floor
at their feet.

"I've got lots to tell you, dear," Thusandi said to Sao after taking a
sip of iced fresh lime juice.

"Go ahead, I'd rather forget about my own worries anyway," Sao said
as he stretched his legs and settled in the wicker chair next to her, ready to
listen.

"I was asked to organize the Maternity and Child Welfare Society of
Hsipaw."

"Who asked you?" Sao looked up, surprised.

"A high-powered delegation—Dr. Ba Nyan, Dr. Hkun Saw, and
Chief Minister U Htan."

"And—what did you say?" Sao smiled, obviously pleased by this
development.

"Well, I couldn't say no—the women and children here need help. Can you believe that our hospital doesn't admit women for normal childbirth? They have to call a midwife or go to a place that doesn't even have running water."

"I know, believe me, I know," Sao said with a sigh.

"And many of the babies," Thusandi continued, "don't live very long. Dr. Ba Nyan said as many as three out of four may die before the age of two." Her voice became louder and louder, and her hands did some of the talking. "It just can't go on. I've got to help."

"You'd be wonderful in this capacity," Sao said, stroking her hair. "I can just see you organizing and supervising a top-notch Maternity and Child Welfare Society."

"But I don't have any training." Thusandi's objections didn't sound very convincing. She was pleased by Sao's faith in her, and when his gentle hand stroked her hair, he could have almost anything he wanted. Those tender expressions of his love touched Thusandi beyond all others.

"You have what's needed: common sense, concern for the people, and perseverance. Everything else will come with time."

The next day, she invited the leading women in town to help organize an active and dedicated steering committee. Thirty-seven women of all ages, mostly Shans and Burmese, came to the first meeting. All of them were mothers, but only two had reared every child they had given birth to. Thirty-five of them had experienced the losses this newly formed society was hoping to reduce.

The day after the society's first meeting, Thusandi asked Maggie, its elected secretary, to join her in an inspection of the maternity home. Maggie, an attractive Anglo-Burmese woman, had lived in Hsipaw for many years, but she had never been inside Hsipaw's only delivery home. The two women arrived unobtrusively in an old jeep and entered the modest one-story building quietly, without any followers. Thusandi was determined to keep her presence and her work in this field low-key and personal, separate from her role as the revered Mahadevi. An elderly ward servant, wiping the stone floor of the corridor, dropped her wet cloth and hurriedly disappeared behind a door, only to return with a beautiful young woman. Nang Noom, in a blue cotton longyi and white aingyi, was the nurse-midwife in charge, and she happened to be on duty. She was tiny, maybe four-and-a-half feet tall, yet her demeanor left no doubt about her authority.

Nang Noom, the *sayama,* or nurse, knew who her visitors were and immediately offered to give them a tour. The three rooms contained a total of twelve narrow beds, each with a small crib at its side. Seven beds were occupied, but only six of the cribs held tiny babies, each wrapped in tidy white bundles.

"May I hold one of the babies?" Thusandi asked Nang Noom, who handed her a little baby girl. The warm little bundle with its pink face and mop of black hair touched Thusandi's heart. She could not remember holding a newborn before, and she experienced a surge of maternal feelings. The baby's mother, sitting on her bed fully dressed, folded her hands in front of her face in acknowledgment of the great honor of her child being held by the Mahadevi. Thusandi needed no introduction. Wherever she went, people recognized her; there was only one tall Caucasian woman, wearing native dress and speaking Shan, in the entire country.

"What is your baby's name?" she asked the mother.

"Pihoo, naw." The young woman replied that she didn't know yet, and covered her giggling mouth with her left hand.

Puzzled by this answer, Thusandi turned to Maggie and asked her in English, "Why doesn't this mother know the name of her own child?"

"It takes weeks, often months for us to name our children," Maggie answered. "The name will depend on the day of the week when the baby is born. Also, astrologers and older relatives often make the selection."

Reluctantly, Thusandi returned the baby to the crib.

"Would you like to see the delivery room?" Nang Noom asked as they returned to the corridor.

"Yes, we would, but only if it's not in use at the moment," Thusandi replied.

"It isn't," Nang Noom said. "But we never know when a trishaw or a bullock cart will pull up with a patient in the last stages of labor."

The delivery room was spotless and light, but empty, devoid of modern equipment. Thusandi saw a wooden delivery table, a stand with a wash basin, and a small cabinet containing what looked like a pair of forceps and a pair of scissors. There was no sign of indoor plumbing or electricity, and she wondered how a place like this could function without them.

"How many deliveries do you have a month?" Maggie asked the nurse as they returned to the corridor.

"We average twenty births a month. Most of them happen around the full moon." Nang Noom smiled as she answered the question.

"Why is that?" Thusandi was surprised.

"I don't know. But it's a fact, and we plan our schedules around it." Nang Noom became increasingly relaxed and outgoing as the inspection proceeded.

"How many midwives do you have on your staff?" Thusandi wanted to know.

"We are two nurse-midwives. We really need a third one, but the doctor can't spare any for this building," Nang Noom said with a deep sigh.

"What about pre- and post-natal care?" Thusandi asked. "You don't have time for it, do you?"

"No," Nang Noom mumbled, shaking her head. She looked puzzled, almost as if she didn't quite understand the question.

THE NEXT DAY, THUSANDI ASKED Moei to take her to Namyai, Moei's village by the Namtu River. She wanted to find out firsthand about its women: how they lived, worked, became mothers, and nurtured their children.

By the time their Land Rover stopped in front of the bumong's house, many villagers, young and old, had already made a wide deferential circle around them.

"I've come to talk to your wife and all women in the village who have time," Thusandi said to the mustachioed old headman who was kneeling in front of her. "Women's talk, you know," she added with a smile. Then she followed Pa Leun, the headman's wife, up a few steps into the main room of their bamboo house, which was set on stilts. Wide and airy, it was furnished with finely woven grass mats, a few brown cushions, and two low red lacquer tables. The hostess sent her two daughters to the kitchen, a small structure separate from the house, to bring Shan tea for her guests. The room filled with girls and women of all ages for an afternoon of talk. They were occasionally interrupted by the cry of a baby, which was swiftly quelled by a mother's nipple.

They allowed Thusandi a look into their lives and their daily activities, which revolved around child rearing and childbearing from their own childhood to old age. From the age of four or five, girls took care of their younger siblings while their mothers cooked, washed clothes, and gathered food. Some women and children also worked in the principal industries of the village: basket weaving, papermaking, food production, and farming. Village girls married young and more often than not stayed in the household of one or the other set of parents.

Pa Leun had two daughters-in-law living with her, one pregnant with her first child, the other cradling an infant in one arm and holding a toddler in the other. Her two teenage daughters were not yet married. She had given birth to nine children and felt blessed that four survived. One had died shortly after birth, the other four at various stages of early childhood.

Ae Nawng, her nineteen-year-old daughter-in-law, was a typical representative of the village women. She had married at sixteen, had become pregnant, and delivered her first baby at home ten months later. She had never seen a doctor or a nurse. Pa Leun and the untrained village midwife had assisted in her delivery. Mother and child had then followed long-established practices; Ae Nawng nursed her baby whenever it cried, she bathed it daily, and rarely let it out of her sight. The child received no vaccinations, no medical checkups, and no food or drink other than her mother's milk. Nevertheless, the baby grew and thrived until the mother became pregnant again eight months later. When the mother's milk dried up, the child's diet changed abruptly to soft white rice and little else. Cow's milk was not available, since Shans disliked all dairy products. Fruit and most vegetables were suspected to be the cause of stomach disorders and other diseases; therefore, they were kept from young children. Tiny amounts of a few select vegetables—a spinach-type leaf and a mild pumpkin—were sometimes mixed with rice. The child became malnourished and sickly until the new baby arrived and the mother had some leftover milk to spare. The future well-being of Ae Nawng's two children was questionable; but, without doubt, she would have more.

Thusandi had heard and seen enough. She was determined to turn the delivery home into a modern facility and a center for maternity and child health care. With Maggie and other members of the society, she appealed to her husband and other wealthy members of the community for financial help. The prince, the tea broker, the rice mill owner, the meat contractor, and other businessmen responded very generously. The society also involved the entire town in the project by organizing community events; movie showings, soccer matches, and athletic and musical competitions generated further income.

A ribbon-cutting ceremony, attended by a large crowd, ushered in the era of electricity and running water for the maternity home. It was a true celebration when, for the first time, the faucets in the delivery room were turned on, and hot and cold water poured out into the basin.

The Maternity and Child Welfare Society, under Thusandi's direction, assumed responsibility for the maternity home, paying salaries and all other bills. While the local Indian doctor offered to come and help with complicated cases, he was greatly relieved that he no longer needed to administer the delivery home, for which he had neither time nor interest. To him, normal childbirth was a matter for women, preferably to be conducted at home. Thusandi hired two more of Dr. Seagrave's Namkham-trained nurse-midwives to improve services at the maternity home, and to build an outpatient program for mothers and children.

The response to the new facilities was not immediate. A few women from town came to have a closer look, but the shy and traditional villagers stayed away. Thusandi decided that the society had to take its program on the road, carrying it into the villages.

One early morning, society members and nurse-midwives loaded a dozen jeeps and Land Rovers with gifts of baby clothing, milk powder, vitamins, and lots of goodwill. The colorful convoy made its way to Viengkau village, on the other side of the Namtu River, where more than a hundred people cautiously awaited its visit. After Thusandi acknowledged the headman's welcome, she made a little speech, urging pregnant women and nursing mothers with their babies to come to the headman's house for an examination. There was some hesitation, but once the first woman came forward, a line started to form.

While the nurse-midwives administered pre- and post-natal care in the privacy of the headman's house, Thusandi, Maggie, and the others worked out of their cars. They demonstrated how to give vitamin drops and milk powder to small children who were no longer breast-fed. Since Shans did not boil their drinking water, the customary practice of mixing the milk powder with water was dangerous. Thusandi remembered hearing of tragedy in Mandalay: A group had distributed milk powder to mothers who were anxious to improve the health of their children. Instead of thriving on the new food, many children became ill and died of amoebic dysentery, typhoid, and other intestinal diseases, caused by the contaminated water used in the mixture. Thusandi's society therefore suggested that the milk powder should be sprinkled over cooked rice and eaten. She demonstrated this and tasted some of the mixture herself, much to the delight of everyone present.

After the work was done and the gifts were distributed, the village women of Viengkau did not want their visitors to leave. The younger mothers especially enjoyed the attention they had received and seemed to be at ease with the new procedures. They promised to come to the society's little clinic to consult with the nurses and replenish their supply of vitamins and milk powder. The older women who were past their child-bearing years expressed some doubts about the need for any changes in the practices that had served well for them and their mothers. They were pleased, however, that their Mahadevi cared enough to come to their village.

Word of the visit to Viengkau spread like wildfire, and many other villages had soon invited Thusandi and the society to visit them. There

Thusandi visiting a Shan village meeting with the villagers to discuss her maternity and child welfare program.

were results: Within six months, deliveries at the maternity home doubled, the clinic was always busy, hundreds of children received vaccinations, and thousands of pounds of milk powder were handed out. Women and children who used the services of the Hsipaw Maternity and Child Welfare Society stayed healthier than they had been before, and infant mortality decreased significantly.

THUSANDI'S INVOLVEMENT WITH matters of childbirth and infant care came at a very appropriate time.

Moei had suspected that Thusandi was pregnant long before anybody else did. She discretely informed the entire household of her discovery. "We must look after our Mahadevi so that she may present us with a healthy and happy baby," she said to the others. The cook received special instructions from Moei as to which foods to serve and which to avoid: no squash, no pickles, only one variety of bananas. Rice and chicken were okay and so were spinachlike tender greens.

When the Danish doctor in Namtu confirmed Moei's suspicions, Moei didn't let anyone forget that she was the first to know.

In the evenings, on the verandah, the expecting parents talked about their hopes and dreams for their child. They were awed and happy, believing that nobody else could possibly feel as elated as they did.

"Do you want a son?" Thusandi asked Sao one evening.

"Not necessarily. I just want our child to be healthy," Sao said with the happiest smile she had ever seen.

"But what about the succession if it's a girl?" She thought, with concern, about the universal expectation that men of power produce male heirs.

"What about it?" Sao mused. "There is no reason why my daughter couldn't become the next ruler of Hsipaw. I believe that girls are as capable as boys. So does our neighbor, the Prince of Mongyai. He has already proclaimed that the eldest of his eight daughters shall succeed him."

"That's true. Our Shan society has come a long way since your uncle Sir Sao Hke's time." Thusandi thanked her lucky stars for having such an open-minded husband.

"Frankly though, I hope that our feudal system will be history by the time our child is old enough to take over."

Thusandi did not reply. She understood how Sao longed for a change to a democratic form of government. However, she had learned quickly that time was measured differently here, and that decades could pass before Sao's dream became a reality.

One day, Sao announced, "I've told the secretary to start looking for a suitable nanny for our baby."

"Aren't you rushing things a bit?" Thusandi asked. "The baby isn't due for another six months."

Although Sao had always been calm and collected in their relationship, Thusandi saw him change into an overprotective and worried father-to-be. His advice touched and amused her. "You must take more vitamins." "Have you finished your Ovaltine?" "I don't think you should play tennis any more." "Have you taken your nap today?" "I'm afraid you're doing too much for a woman in your condition."

Contrary to this, Thusandi was feeling relaxed, confident, and filled with boundless energy. She did not see why she should behave like a semi-invalid. After all, pregnancy and childbirth were routines that she regularly observed at the maternity home. She planned to spend extra time there and learn, firsthand, all she could about childbirth and infant care, to augment her book knowledge gathered from Dr. Spock.

IT WAS THE NIGHT OF THE FULL moon of *leun shee,* the fourth month, when the princely baby announced its arrival. Sao and Thusandi's mother, who had come from Austria for the occasion, were feverishly loading two cars to take Thusandi to Namtu and the Danish doctor. The trip to the private hospital of Bawdwin Mines had been carefully planned and was to take only one-and-a-half hours. Two miles out of Hsipaw, Thusandi exclaimed, "Turn back immediately, I can't make it to Namtu."

They returned to the East Haw, where their first daughter was born, less than two hours later, with the help of Nang Noom. The baby was beautiful and perfect, with a crop of jet-black hair framing her smooth pink face. Sao raised concern among his subjects by carrying the tightly wrapped little bundle back and forth through the upstairs corridor. They could not remember any Shan prince ever holding a newborn baby, or being so close to the process of birth. The old man in charge of the private chapel warned that Sao could lose his protected status and become vulnerable to evil spirits. Sao shrugged off these warnings.

Astrologer Saya Ba Han and Chief Minister U Htan arrived within minutes of the birth. The astrological chart of the newest Hsipaw princess was scratched onto palm-leaf, to serve both as a birth certificate and a reference for future readings. Although Shan parents, as a rule, waited to name their children, Thusandi was unwilling to follow this tradition. She had no objections to the manner in which the name of her daughter was to be selected; she was born on a Thursday, therefore her name had to begin with the letter B, M, or P. Each day of the week had certain letters of the alphabet assigned to it, which determined the initials of the child's name. While Thusandi held her daughter, examining her little toes and fingers, she overheard relatives and advisers suggest suitable names.

"I like the Sanskrit name Papawaddee", a cousin suggested.

"Out of the question," Sao responded.

"What about a Shan name like Mawk Kham?"

"I don't like that either." Sao realized what was happening. In true Shan fashion, his relatives were intruding into his life, and he did not appreciate it.

"Thusandi and I will make this decision," he said as he turned his back to the crowd and went back into the bedroom to be with his wife and daughter.

They decided on a Sanskrit name—Mayari—which sounded sweet and had its origin in Buddhist history; and the astrologer approved. The prefix "Sao" was automatically added to show that she was a member of the ruling family. According to Shan customs, Mayari would retain this name all her life, not even changing it in matrimony.

For a while, the baby princess became the most important person in the East Haw. Nai Nai, the nanny, was a close second. She had been selected from a number of suitable applicants even though she was in her middle sixties. A trained nurse and midwife, she had outlived her husband and children and dedicated much of her life to those in need of her skills. She spoke Shan and Burmese but no English. She had been converted by

Baptist missionaries while attending nursing school. Although the Buddhist household staff respected her for her age and profession, they eyed her religious affiliation with suspicion. Moei worriedly inquired of her mistress whether Nai Nai would try to make a Baptist out of their little princess.

Thusandi was not concerned about such matters. In view of the health hazards to which so many small children of the area succumbed, she wanted a nurse by her side to help raise her daughter. Terrified that malaria-carrying mosquitoes, deadly scorpions, and poisonous centipedes could find their way inside the mosquito net of the crib, Thusandi sneaked into the nursery several times each night. During the day, she suspiciously eyed every visitor, wondering if he was a carrier of smallpox, tuberculosis, leprosy, typhoid, or any other disease endemic to the area. Sometimes she lay awake half the night wondering what it would have been like to raise her child in Austria, away from all these hazards, within reach of a pediatrician. Nai Nai's competence and reassurances slowly eased Thusandi's fears and helped her to enjoy the normal development of her beautiful baby.

At eight months, Mayari joined her parents in her first official function. The invitation to the event, issued by the chief minister, read: "The Saophalong and Mahadevi of Hsipaw invite you to the Name Giving Ceremony of their daughter, the princess, on the eleventh day after the full moon in the month of Hnadaw in the year 1318. The Ceremony will take place in the East Haw at 10:00 A.M. You are requested to attend. Presents will not be accepted."

Dignitaries, the state's three most senior Buddhist monks, and hundreds of invited guests filled the rooms and terraces on the first floor, which had been emptied of furniture and covered with thick carpets. Auntie Gyipaya, the oldest close relative, was chosen to perform the ceremony. A huge silver bowl in front of her held special ingredients for the auspicious ritual: water scented with tree bark, flower petals, and perfume; a variety of nine gemstones including diamonds, rubies, emeralds, sapphires, and pearls; and a bundle of special leaves for which an attendant had searched the jungle for an entire week. Thusandi carried her daughter, who was dressed in the pink lace gown Thusandi had worn for her own baptism in Austria, past the guests to a platform sofa set up for the occasion. Seated below the monks, Auntie Gyipaya pronounced that the princess should henceforth be known as Sao Mayari. She used the special leaves to sprinkle scented water on her niece, bestowing special blessings over her. It proved to be too much for the little princess, who was taken to her nursery. She was not present to acknowledge the gifts from her father: jewelry, a horse, and a large orange plantation; nor did she participate in prayers and the festive meal that kept the guests busy for hours.

ONE DAY THE PEOPLE OF TAPOK, the village to the north, brought Thusandi what they thought to be a very special present: a beautiful live parrot. The bird's head was purple, and so were the top feathers of his graceful, long tail. His beak was bright red, and the feathers of his body and wings were a range of greenish yellow colors, becoming vivid gold on the bottom of his tail. Thusandi noticed immediately that his wings had been clipped.

"I appreciate your gift," she said, "but I'm only accepting this beautiful bird so that I can set him free. Please don't ever again take a creature from the wild and bring it to me."

Thusandi thought she had made it clear previously that she would never hold captive any animal that had been born free. Her predecessor, the Mahadevi of Sao Ohn Kya, had been known to keep bears in a small pen near the moat, even though each one of them had ultimately killed its handler. Once before, villagers from a remote area of the state had brought Thusandi a baby leopard. She had been unsuccessful in making the leopard eat, and it had been unable to grow strong enough to be released into the wild. It had been a horrible experience to watch helplessly as the beautiful leopard kitten grow weak and listless. Without the assistance of a veterinarian—none was within eight hundred miles—the little leopard had died in her care, probably of starvation. She had been terribly upset, and word had gone out that creatures of the wild were not acceptable as presents. Unfortunately, the villagers of Tapok had not put birds in that category.

Bukong examined the parrot and assured Thusandi that the clipped feathers would grow back within weeks, after which the bird could be returned to the wild. He took responsibility for the parrot's care and hurried to the bazaar in search of a large birdcage and a selection of fresh fruit.

The guava trees near the kitchen were selected as the perfect place for the parrot's cage; somebody was always nearby to keep an eye on the bird and chase cats away, and the foliage of the trees provided the right combination of shade and sunlight.

The bird was not a fussy eater and enjoyed ripe bananas and melons from the first day of his captivity. On the second morning of his life under the guava tree, he had visitors. A flock of approximately sixty parrots, all identical to him, descended upon the trees. Their deafening chatter drowned out all other noises and made everybody in the Haw hurry to see what was happening. The chattering flock stayed for a few minutes, then left as abruptly as it had appeared. "I've never ever seen parrots this close to a house before," Bukong said, shaking his head in wonderment.

The parrots returned every morning at the same time. There was no doubt in anybody's mind why they came. After a few weeks of loving tender care by Bukong and visits by his feathered family, the parrot appeared ready to fly again. One morning, a little while before the daily visit, Bukong opened the cage while Sao and Thusandi posted themselves nearby. They watched apprehensively as the bird approached the opening of his cage. He did not leave, but remained perched on the open door of his prison. He and everybody else waited until the noisy flock landed once more on the branches of the guava trees. This visit proceeded like all the previous ones, with one exception; when the birds flew away, their friend left with them, while his caretakers cheered.

And the parrots never again returned to the guava trees by the kitchen entrance of the East Haw.

Nine

THE SECOND DAY IN HIS BAMBOO
prison was coming to an end, and Sao saw that he was no closer to regaining his freedom than the day before. On the contrary. He had learned from his interrogators that General Ne Win and his army had staged a coup d'état and put thousands of people, including the entire elected government, in prison. Sao could no longer hope for Prime Minister U Nu to intervene on his behalf. At best, the United Nations and world opinion would put pressure on the Burmese Army's so-called Revolutionary Council, but it would take time, and Sao wondered if he had enough of that precious commodity left. He looked at the palm of his right hand, examining his lifeline in the dimly lit hut. The palm reader at Rangoon's Sule Pagoda had warned him repeatedly that his lifeline showed a break in his thirties; and he was beginning to think that he had reached that point.

Sao stretched out on his mat and closed his eyes. He was so tired, and the news of the coup had shattered the hope that his horrible situation would soon end. Even if his secret letters reached his wife and Jimmy Yang, he could not see what they could possibly do to get him out of this bamboo cage. He sat up abruptly as he heard footsteps approaching; he would never give his captors the satisfaction of seeing him sad and discouraged. The sound of boots became fainter. Sao let down his guard, feeling relieved that he did not have to face another uniformed interrogator. He took his wallet from the inside pocket of his jacket and, for the first time since his imprisonment, looked at the snapshots of his daughters. Thusandi always made sure that he had the newest photos of the children with him when he went away. Seeing the smiling, happy faces of the girls hurt so much that Sao quickly put the pictures away. He could not bear to think what would happen to his wife and children if he did not live. He groaned and covered his face with his hands. Terrible guilt feelings swept over him. He should not have ignored the warning signs that had pointed toward this catastrophe and could not believe that he had been so stupid.

Sao had ample time to dwell on these recriminations. He was not going anywhere, and his tormentors had tired of his refusal to cooperate. He knew why he had been blind to the internal threat by Ne Win and his army. It was because the people had rejected them during the elections two years ago. Their political party, the Stable AFPFL (Anti-Fascist People's Freedom League) had lost dismally, in spite of the army's ruthless intervention at the polls. The voting public of the Union of Burma, who had endured Ne Win's military caretaker government for two years, wanted no part of it. The people's mandate had gone to U Nu, of the Clean AFPFL, who had then been sidetracked by his ambitious general for a two-year period. Instead of winning the confidence of the people during its two-year rule, the army abused its power and earned the hatred of the voters.

Sao remembered how convincingly he had argued that Ne Win had been put in his place by the mandate of the people, that he could not rule the country without their approval and cooperation; and that Ne Win, still licking his wounds, would not attempt another takeover for years to come. How utterly wrong he had been. He and many political leaders—U Nu, Sao Hkun Hkio, U Ba Swe—had failed to foresee the army's power play. Sao bent his head and started to hit it with both fists.

His good judgment had not only failed him two years ago, his lack of it went back much further. Sao reproached himself for capitulating when sixty-seven buhengs had besieged him to accept the leadership of Hsipaw State after the British had regained Burma from the Japanese. They had refused to accept his father and older brother because of their blatant collaboration with the Japanese occupation forces. Although Sao had planned to continue the formal education he had received in Taunggyi and Darjeeling, he had acquiesced to the will of his people. Without doubt, it had all started in January 1947 when he was proclaimed ruling Prince of Hsipaw.

After this fundamental mistake, there were others he gradually admitted to himself. Sao became more and more confused and upset as he tried to search his memory for all his errors in judgment.

"Enough of that," he said firmly to himself. Sao saw clearly that he would destroy himself if he allowed self-doubts and self-accusation to sap his strength. He could not permit that to happen; he had to prepare for tomorrow's war of nerves with the Military Intelligence men.

Sao wished he had something to read, anything to occupy his mind. But his attaché case filled with books and papers had disappeared when he was taken to Ba Htoo Myo. He had spent his free moments in Rangoon and on the plane reading technical material about the salt project in Bawgyo. The equipment was on its way to Hsipaw, and he was ready to start operations as soon as he returned home. The salt wells of Bawgyo had been worked for hundreds of years and provided salt for Hsipaw State whenever the regular supplies from Burma proper were disrupted. But the salt was very bitter due to high levels of magnesium chloride, and eliminating this required a special refining process that he was finally able to install. The northern Shan states would subsequently become self-sufficient in a very important staple—salt.

Many projects needed his attention, and here he was, cut off from all of them because of the political ambitions of one man. Sao had been told repeatedly that Ne Win feared him, even though he did not see himself as posing a threat. Deep down he sensed that he was in great danger, that something irreversible could happen to him. He remembered having had that feeling before, several years ago, on the road from Lashio to Hsipaw.

Sao had been in the process of boarding the Friday Union of Burma Airways (UBA) plane in Lashio to fly to Rangoon for another session of Parliament. A jeep had sped toward the DC-3, stopping short of the stairs used by the passengers to board. A breathless aide to the special commissioner had waved a letter at Sao. "Sir, this is urgent—from the commissioner."

Sao had read the note with concern and disbelief. It was an official request that he postpone his trip to Rangoon in the interest of national security—the commissioner promised to explain in person. Sao rushed to the special commissioner's office once the pilots had agreed to delay the plane's departure. The plane crew welcomed this opportunity to make a beef-run to Lashio bazaar, since the sale of beef, for religious reasons, was prohibited in Burma proper.

Hom Hpa, the commissioner, was waiting at the door. "Come in, my royal brother. We have to talk. One of my wives will keep Thusandi company."

"She'll stay. We both want to hear why I shouldn't go to Rangoon today." Sao took Thusandi's hand, leading her into Hom Hpa's office. The jovial tone of the commissioner did not indicate a national emergency, yet Sao felt very suspicious.

"So what's going on?" Sao said impatiently. "The pilots are holding the plane for me."

"I can't let you go on this flight," the commissioner said, as if this were a routine request.

Sao looked at him in disbelief. "And why not?"

"Because Colonel Chit Myaing, in charge of the Northern Command, has to go to Rangoon on this flight. He says he fears for his personal safety if he goes on the same plane with you. His presence at a staff meeting is more important than your attendance of Parliament. That's why I'm ordering you to take next Tuesday's plane to Rangoon."

"You can't be serious," Sao said angrily. "I carry no arms, I've never threatened anyone, and I'm going on this plane. If the colonel is afraid of an unarmed member of Parliament, that's his problem, not mine." Sao gave the commissioner a contemptuous look and started toward the door, pulling Thusandi with him.

"You must obey me. We've got to please the Burmese Army," the commissioner said, rushing to the door and trying to prevent Sao from leaving.

Sao had reached the door when he stopped, turned around, and made a surprise request. "I will stay behind on one condition: You put in writing what you have just told me."

"Sure. I'll dictate the letter in your presence and you can correct me," he replied, obviously relieved.

Sao was satisfied and sent word to the plane that they could take off without him. He wanted the commissioner's letter to document his charges of harassment by the Burmese Army.

On the road back to Hsipaw, Sao and Thusandi were traveling behind their police escort through a densely wooded area when they suddenly heard rifle shots. Sao pushed his wife down to the floor and yelled at the driver to speed up. As the car wheels squealed, more shots rang out, hitting the trunk of the car. When their car caught up with the jeep, Sao turned to look back; nobody was following them and the jungle had pulled its veil of secrecy over those who had fired the shots at them.

Sao remembered every moment of the rest of their return to Hsipaw, every noise aside from the humming of the motor. He sensed then and there that danger loomed ahead, that something unspeakable could happen. But he did nothing about it, and after a few years, concerns about this event faded away. An obviously false sense of security had overtaken him again.

If only he were given the opportunity to make some decisions all over again. Sao thought of the secret meeting he had held with the founders of the first Shan insurgent group, the Noom Seuk Harn. They had pleaded for his leadership, but he had sent them away, lecturing that the only way to resolve legitimate grievances was through parliamentary channels. How utterly wrong he had been.

Sao stood up and began pacing the squeaky floor, four steps in each direction before the matted wall made him turn back. He looked down at the wrinkled pants of his suit; he had had no bath, no change of clothes for two days. How he craved for a hot jetlike shower to wash away this forty-eight-hour nightmare. The only water available to him was in the tea that his prison guards brought regularly.

"I must have another chance at life," Sao kept saying over and over again.

THAT NIGHT, WHEN SAO FINALLY dozed off on his grass mat, he had a happy dream. He was crossing the Namtu River in a dugout canoe, with the children on the canoe floor in front of him. Their black hair was shining in the sunlight, and their little suntanned hands clutched the rim of the boat.

"Take us across the river to the orange plantation," he said to the oarsman, who stood in the bow, guiding the dugout with one oar. The water was calm and cool, allowing their canoe to glide over it with hardly a ripple. Halfway across the river, the children began to sing nursery rhymes in their clear, young voices: "Twinkle, twinkle, little star," "Baa baa black sheep, have you any wool?" "Kookaburra sat on a tall gum tree." Sao joined them and their carefree song echoed from one bank to the other. Then he heard the sweet sound of strings and flutes rise from the depth of the river and lift their simple melodies toward the sky. With every new song, the sound of another instrument joined in until a full, invisible orchestra supported the vocal trio. Sao did not want this happy journey to end, and the river seemed to grant his wish; the canoe kept gliding toward the other bank, which seemed to move farther and farther away.

"Papa." One word broke the spell and silenced the music. "Papa, I want to go home," Mayari said to him as she turned her frightened face toward him. "I'm afraid when the river sings."

His daughter's worried face awakened Sao and ended his dream. He opened his eyes and, seeing nothing, closed them again to cling to the happiness he had just experienced.

He loved his two beautiful daughters beyond words, and he felt their presence within him. That gave him peace, at least for a while. He imagined how they would run toward him, arms outstretched, expecting to be scooped up by him when he returned home. Kennari, now aged three, had started to reproach him for going away so often, making it very clear that she wanted her father to be home where he belonged. He smiled when he remembered how she used to wait for him by the front door early in the morning, how he would take her by the hand and walk to the chapel for meditation. And when they returned from that ritual, they usually delighted in waking up Thusandi and Mayari, now aged six, so they could all have breakfast together.

Sao felt a great sense of satisfaction that his children had the happy and secure childhood he had never experienced. Thusandi was a wonderful mother to them, and he was trying to be the caring father he himself had never had. Sao could not remember his own mother, who had died of cholera when he was two years old. He had fond memories of his stepmother, but she had fallen victim to pneumonia when he was twelve. After that, he had no place he could call home. His father continued to take and discard one wife after another, abandoning his children to the care of cousins and kindly aunties.

No wonder he now found himself reliving his childhood through his own children. Sao chuckled when he thought of the complex electric train set he had bought for Mayari when she was only two years old. He had never admitted to himself that this toy wasn't solely meant for his beloved

Family portrait of the Prince and Princess of Hsipaw with their daughters, Mayari (left) and Kennari (right).

toddler. When he set the trains in motion, she had watched them race around the track, her dark brown eyes sparkling and her delighted laughter filling the room. Children, wife, electric train, bed, tiled bathroom, verandah—all these symbols of home kept tugging at Sao's heart. He was homesick and without hope.

Ten

THE WICKER CHAIR NEXT TO
Thusandi on the terrace was empty, not unusual with Sao's busy schedule
of meetings in Taunggyi and Rangoon. But this time the empty chair had
a different meaning; there was a frightening possibility of it remaining so.
Thusandi closed her eyes and hoped for a vision, a spiritual experience,
something supernatural to connect her with Sao, wherever he was. She had
heard of, even seen, such occurrences after she had arrived in Hsipaw and
accepted them as part of Shan life. That took some time though; while
growing up in Austria, she had been taught to regard anything supernatural, including astrology, as suspect and unbelievable.

Earlier that morning, Thusandi had attempted to consult Saya Ba
Han, their astrologer, to get a reading of Sao's horoscope. She had waited
impatiently for him until her messenger brought disappointing news: Her
trusted old astrologer sent his apologies—he was afraid to pass the military
guards at the gate. Thusandi acknowledged with a sad smile how alle-
giances could change within twenty-four hours. She was not angry, merely
disappointed in a man whom she had considered to be loyal and apolitical.
He had always rushed to the East Haw at a moment's notice whenever a
foreign visitor wanted to have a horoscope done to take home as a souvenir,
a conversation piece at diplomatic cocktail parties. Since Saya Ba Han
spoke no English and visiting diplomats no Shan or Burmese, Thusandi
was often asked to interpret—at times a rather sensitive task. She smiled
when she thought of one of the most memorable episodes.

The ambassador from a southern European country, with his attractive young wife and their poodle, had called on Sao and Thusandi for lunch.
The ambassador had seen Saya Ba Han's elaborate astrological charts on

palm-leaf in Rangoon and wanted to order one for himself. He also asked for a reading of his horoscope. Sao excused himself while Thusandi took their guests and Saya Ba Han into the study. No sooner had they sat down than the astrologer said, "The young lady here is not this man's wife."

"What did he say?" the ambassador asked impatiently.

Thusandi was not about to reveal what she had just heard. "He said that you travel a great deal," she replied, thinking quickly. Then she turned to the astrologer. "You're wrong. They have been in Rangoon for three years—everybody knows they're married."

"No, his wife is on another continent. I'm sure of that."

The ambassador looked at Thusandi expectantly. She had done enough translating to come up with other noncommittal statements until Saya Ba Han changed the subject.

Thusandi never shared with anybody what the astrologer had revealed about the status of this ambassador's wife. A year later, the Rangoon diplomatic community was shocked by a scandalous discovery: The woman whom this very ambassador had officially introduced as his spouse was, in fact, his mistress. His wife was in Europe attending to the children and their Catholic education.

Now Thusandi turned her attention to the thick, yellow piece of palm-leaf with its elaborate inscriptions. She was able to decipher the record of Sao's birth but could find no predictions about his life. The symbols and numbers referring to planets were meant to be interpreted by trained astrologers, not by her. She gave up with a sigh.

She really wanted some form of insight into the future but did not know how to achieve this. Before that day, she had not considered such things, although she had once been present when an extraordinary incident occurred. The event had in turn led to an amazing disclosure by Sao. Thusandi remembered every detail of that day several years ago as vividly as if it had taken place yesterday.

ONE AFTERNOON WHEN SAO returned from his office, Thusandi was waiting for him outside, under the portico. She rushed to open his car door before the attendant could get there. "I'm so glad you are home—you won't believe what happened," she said anxiously.

Sao recognized by the uneasy way in which she greeted him that something extraordinary must have occurred. Her usual calm and composure had vanished. Instead, she grabbed his arm with both hands, trying to lead him into the cool drawing room. Noticing her sweaty palms and the pasty color of her face, Sao knew that she was frightened. He led her through the drawing room to her favorite corner on the east terrace.

"Tell me, what happened?" he asked after he eased her into a comfortable wicker settee. "I want to know."

"You won't believe me. It doesn't sound real," she sighed, staring past him into space.

Sao started to suspect that she had run into one of those paranormal experiences that seem to happen often in the Shan states but seldom in the Western world. He had always believed in reincarnation and in life on different planes, but after four years in an American engineering school, he had not felt comfortable discussing these topics with Thusandi.

"I'm listening, Liebling," he said, stroking her shoulder.

Thusandi began in a tense voice. "It all started an hour or so ago. Ai Tseng, the sweeper, came and begged me to hurry to his house. He said that his wife was very ill and that she kept asking to see me."

"And then?" Sao asked when Thusandi hesitated.

"I hurried to their little house with my medical kit and an ampule of penicillin. But it wasn't the usual infection—it was something else." She stopped again and shook her head. "You won't believe what she did." Sao held her hand and waited till Thusandi had calmed down enough to continue.

"Ae Kham, the Shan woman, has never been to school and has never been known to speak a word of English, Yet, she sat up on her mat, looked at me, and said in perfect King's English, 'Madam, please don't worry about me, I shall be just fine. But I do thank you so much for coming.' Her husband, their children, and several neighbors listened and seemed to be amused rather than shocked. I guess I was the only one who panicked and felt like running away. But, of course, I couldn't."

"So, what did you do then?" Sao prompted her.

"Well, I acted as if we had always spoken English to one another and told Ae Kham to lie back and tell me how I could help her. She said, 'You

have helped me simply by coming to my side when I needed you.' I
touched her forehead and realized that she was running a very high fever.
When I offered to call the doctor, she said, 'No, thank you, that won't be
necessary. I shall be perfectly fine.' She sounded determined, and I sat by
her side for a while, wondering what I should do. I was just about to step
outside and ask Ai Tseng a little more about the history of his wife's illness
when she started speaking again. But this time it was not English, neither
was it Shan or Burmese. One of her neighbors understood and responded—
in Chinese."

"And then? What happened next?"

"Nothing, really. Ae Kham went to sleep and I left. A few minutes
ago, Ai Tseng came to tell me that his wife woke up and her fever was
gone. She couldn't remember anything and wanted to know why there
were so many people at her house."

"That means she is well again, and you have no reason to worry any
more," Sao said, looking at her with his caring smile.

"But don't you understand? This whole thing was simply not normal. That woman was possessed!"

"And what if she was?"

"It frightens me—I am confused. What if you or I become possessed
by some spirit? I just can't believe these things are happening." Thusandi
nervously fidgeted with her rings, pulling them off her left ring finger and
slipping them back on again.

"Please believe me—you have nothing to worry about."

"How do you know?" she asked Sao with disbelief in her voice.

"From experience, my dear. I never told you that I too have seen
things like that. And I learned that we have nothing to be afraid of. There
is a lot more to life than we humans can understand."

Sao would have continued, but Thusandi interrupted him, something she usually did not do. "I want to hear what you yourself have experienced—tell me!"

"Okay, but I want you to know that I have not told this to anybody
else; neither has Hkun Oo, who was with me when this happened. This
isn't easy for me, you know." Sao looked very serious, and his calm voice
had a soothing effect on Thusandi. She made herself comfortable on the
settee by pulling her feet underneath some cushions and leaning her head
on Sao's shoulder. Slowly and deliberately, he started talking.

"A few months before I left for America, Hkun Oo and I took a trip to the China border. Since there are no hotels anywhere upcountry, we had to stay at the inspection bungalows that the Public Works Department of the government maintains in most towns along the roads of the Shan states and Burma. We had to take everything with us—our bedding, our valets, our guards, and a cook. The cook's name was Mahmoot, and he had worked for me off and on for years. After five days on the road and every night in a different PWD bungalow, we spent the last night in Lashio, which as you know is not far from here.

"Mahmoot cooked and served our dinner in the sparsely furnished dining room of the wooden bungalow. That evening he made the best *biriani* and *purees* I have ever had—I can still taste them. After the meal, Hkun Oo and I read for a couple of hours. There was no electricity, and my eyes got tired from the flickering light of the gas lamp. The other half of the large bedroom that Khun Oo occupied was already dark, and I was about to turn out my little bedside lamp when I heard a knock at the door. It was Sang Aye, the valet. He came to tell me that Mahmoot was very ill with another one of his malaria attacks. I decided that Mahmoot should be taken to the hospital immediately and told Sang Aye that I would personally go along. A few minutes later, four of us, including the driver and Hkun Oo, took Mahmoot to the hospital by jeep and entrusted him to the doctor and nurse on duty. Although Mahmoot looked very ill, we expected that he would recover in a day or two, as he always had from his previous malaria attacks." Sao stopped, took a sip of tea, and continued.

"We returned to the bungalow and went to bed. Hours later, I was awakened by an insistent knock at the door. I asked who it was, but nobody answered. The knocking continued. I finally lit my gas lamp, put on my slippers, and went to peer out the door. The very Mahmoot whom we had taken to the hospital a few hours ago was standing outside the bedroom door. I asked him what in the world he was doing there in the middle of the night when he was supposed to be in the hospital. He told me that he had come to assure me that he was all right. By that time, Khun Oo had awakened and come to the door as well. We both told Mahmoot to wait right there for us while we'd throw on some clothes. We insisted on taking him back to the hospital. 'Very well,' he said—that was always his favorite expression. I suggested to Hkun Oo that we didn't need the driver, with the hospital only about ten blocks away. We got dressed and hurried to the door, but Mahmoot was gone. He wasn't anywhere in the bungalow or in the servants' quarters; none of our people there had seen him. I checked my watch. It was two-thirty in the morning." Sao paused. He noticed that Thusandi was listening intently.

"I assumed that Mahmoot had started walking back to the hospital. Hkun Oo and I wanted to catch up with him and make sure he got back to his hospital bed. So we got in the jeep and drove the most direct route to the hospital. No sign of Mahmoot. We tried another route, to no avail. Then we stopped at the hospital to check if Mahmoot had somehow gotten back within such a short time. As we entered the building, a concerned nurse ran toward us and said how very sorry she was. I said she should be sorry to let a sick patient like Mahmoot run out on her like that in the middle of the night. She looked at me in disbelief.

'What do you mean, I let Mahmoot out?'

'You must have, otherwise he could not have come and gotten us out of bed.'

'You are wrong, sir! Mahmoot never left his bed after you brought him in. He died at two-thirty right here, in my presence. Follow me and see for yourself.'

"When we saw Mahmoot, peaceful in his bed, we had to believe that, physically, he had never left it that night. But both of us were roused from sleep by an apparition of this man, at the very moment he died. We not only saw him, we talked with him. Strange as it may seem, I found nothing abnormal about it all. That's when I lost my fear of spirits. I had met one, and he was kind and gentle, with concern for me.

"We are surrounded by spirits, but we usually lack awareness of their presence. And when they allowed me a glimpse into their world, I was grateful."

Sao and Thusandi sat on the wicker settee for a long time, holding hands without speaking. She closed her eyes and allowed the events of the afternoon to pass through her mind again. What she herself had experienced and what Sao had shared with her contradicted everything she had been taught as a child in Europe. Ghosts and witches had their place in the literature of the romantic era and in fairy tales, not in real life. In school she had been discouraged from pursuing thoughts and questions that ventured beyond the culturally accepted. Now she felt as if some of those barriers within her had fallen, and her thoughts were unencumbered and had become her very own. The feeling of fear was no longer there; Thusandi was at peace with herself and her surroundings. She squeezed Sao's hand gently, hoping that he would understand how much his own story had helped her.

THUSANDI PUT SAO'S PALM-LEAF horoscope back in the safe and walked through the flower garden to the chapel, a small two-story wooden building at the east end of the compound. A large room on the ground floor served as storage for the throne, white umbrellas, and other ceremonial equipment. It was also a favorite refuge for scorpions and deadly centipedes, as doors and windows remained closed for years on end. Thusandi climbed the stairs to the second floor. She liked the wide verandah with its carved, wooden balustrade that extended the whole way around the building. From there she could look down on hundreds of terraced paddy fields to the east. They looked dry and idle, since it was too early for rice cultivation and too late for the winter crops of onions and garlic. A few rotund water buffaloes, each with a resident paddy bird on its back, were grazing along the irrigation ditches.

Thusandi's heart filled with pride when she recalled how Sao had given these and all other paddy fields in Hsipaw State to the tenant farmers who actually tilled them. These fields—tens of thousands of acres—had been the property of the ruling prince since their creation hundreds of years ago. Sao had been troubled by this hereditary system of land ownership from the day he had been enthroned. He had often told Thusandi that it was an unfair and exploitative medieval practice, and that he was going to change it. He did. One day, several years ago, he decreed that all paddy land in Hsipaw State was the property of those who worked it. The jubilant response by his subjects was very gratifying. But the Burmese Army was less pleased: It was suspicious that a feudal lord cared for his people and deprived himself of a substantial source of income.

Their household expenses increased sharply as a result of Sao's generous deed. For the first time ever, they had to buy bags of rice for the East

Haw as well as for the households of their twenty-six servants. Rice for the family was a traditional part of a servant's salary.

Thusandi turned her back to the fields and opened the double doors to the chapel itself. Sunlight flooded the large room and focused on the golden Buddha statue surrounded by fresh, fragrant flowers from her garden. She sat on a grass mat on the floor and looked more closely than ever before at the large Buddha above her. The face of the finely crafted statue radiated peace, strength, and harmony. She longed for some of these qualities herself; her mind was restless and scattered. She closed her eyes and tried to meditate, hoping to be infused by peace of mind. But nothing happened. Thusandi wished she had joined Sao when he had practiced meditation; she intuitively felt that she would seriously pursue it one day soon.

On the way back from the chapel, she stopped under the enormous banyan tree that shaded a little shrine for the guardian spirit of the East Haw. His miniature house stood on four high stilts and served as a resting and feeding place for the spirit. Offerings of fresh water, cut-up fruit, and cooked rice were made to him once a week by the household staff. Sao had consistently tried to discourage the tradition of spirit worship as incompatible with Theravada Buddhism. But his opinion fell on deaf ears; his people saw nothing wrong with believing in the teachings of the Buddha and, at the same time, looking after the spirit who protected them.

Thusandi had looked at the spirit house before, out of curiosity. On this day, though, she stopped for a different reason: She wanted to enlist the guardian spirit's help in contacting Sao, wherever he was. She went down on her knees, in the way she had asked various saints for favors as a child, and begged for Sao's protection. Eyes closed, hardly daring to breathe, she knelt on the bare ground under the shade of the banyan tree. She waited. Thusandi did not hear voices, she did not have visions, nor did she sense anything unusual, until a sudden breeze caught the leaves of the tree and coaxed them into making their own music. The wind chimes on the chapel's verandah blended with their tender melody.

"Is this a message?" she asked. There was no answer except the one in her heart, confirming what she wanted to believe—that Sao was all right and would return home one day soon.

WHEN THUSANDI STEPPED INTO the cool foyer of the East Haw, she heard the happy laughter of Kennari, her younger daughter, who had opted not to accompany her sister Mayari to school for the day. She was beating her nanny at Schwarzpeter, a card game her grandmother had sent from Austria. Thusandi was not ready to join in this carefree activity and tiptoed past the playroom to her bedroom suite to be alone.

She thought of Kennari's third birthday, which was one week away. Sao had taken an extra suitcase to Rangoon to bring back presents for her, which were unavailable in Hsipaw. He would undoubtedly find a way to be home by then, Thusandi thought; he never missed being with his family on birthdays.

Then her mind turned to the full-moon night of *leun hsam*, the third month, three years ago. The Bawgyo Pwe was, once again, in full swing, but Thusandi stayed away, since their second baby was due any day. This time she had planned to stay home for the delivery and call Sayama Nang Noom, the maternity home's nurse-midwife, to assist. It was nine o'clock in the evening, and Sao and Thusandi sat on the terrace and watched the man in the moon.

"Let's walk a bit," she said to Sao, "I'm getting a backache." After a round on the moonlit front lawn, Thusandi realized what the backache signified. "The baby—it's coming—hurry and send for the midwife."

Sao panicked again, as he had three years earlier when Mayari was born. This time, though, his mother-in-law was not at the East Haw to join in the joy and the responsibility. He immediately dispatched the driver to fetch the midwife, and then he and Thusandi waited together. They didn't know that Nang Noom, the midwife, had gone to the Bawgyo Pwe and, lost among the tens of thousands of festival-goers, was nowhere to be found. When the nurse finally arrived at the East Haw two hours later, the second-born princess was already bathed, bundled up, and nestled in the arms of her happy mother. Sao had been at Thusandi's side, giving her support and encouragement, and their daughter was born with the help of Nai Nai and Moei.

"Another beautiful girl," Sao announced proudly, "healthy, with black hair and light skin, and born on a Monday just like me."

"We must find the right name for her," Thusandi said.

"It'll have to start with the letter K, G, or Ng," Sao responded.

With the help of the astrologer and relatives, they chose the Sanskrit name Kennari, referring to one of four perfect women around Gautama Buddha, as well as to a mythical bird of Shan and Thai legend.

That was three immeasurably happy years ago, Thusandi thought as she followed the sound of laughter to join her daughter Kennari in the playroom.

Eleven

SAO AND THUSANDI HAD LONG
ago made plans to keep the family together and provide for the children's
primary education at home instead of sending them off to boarding school.
Since the local government school was unable to provide a good education, Thusandi opened the trilingual Foundation School in a building just
outside the East Haw compound. The Hsipaw Sawbwa Foundation, Sao's
charitable trust, took financial responsibility, and Thusandi assumed the
administrative duties.

Shan, Burmese, Chinese, and Indian boys and girls flocked to the
private school in larger numbers than expected. Their parents understood
the value of a good education and wanted their children to be proficient in
Burmese, Shan, and English from kindergarten age. A respected Anglo-
Burmese teacher was appointed as headmistress, and she, in turn, chose her
Shan assistants.

Every morning Mayari and Nang Sein, Moei's daughter, led a group
of eight children, the sons and daughters of household staff, from the East
Haw to school. They marched off in brightly colored clothes, carrying
their books in woven Shan bags and their lunch in lacquer food carriers.
Whenever it pleased her, Kennari tagged along.

On the days of upheaval in March of 1962, Thusandi was comforted
to know that her children would enjoy routine school days. The Burmese
military had not yet made any attempt to interfere with the operation of
the school. Final exams were only days away, after which the three-month
summer vacation would begin. When Sao returned, they would probably

Students and teachers of the trilingual Foundation School, located just outside the East Haw compound.

go away for the hottest months, April and May. Thusandi liked the idea of going to Taunggyi, the cool capital of the Federated Shan States. But Sao would not care for it, she thought. He had been spending so much time there, attending never-ending meetings and sessions of the Shan State Council, especially since the ruling princes had finally handed over their powers to an elected central Shan government. Contrary to his hope that he would be freed of his political obligations, Sao had been elected to represent his people in the Shan State Council and in Parliament. Consequently, his responsibilities had not decreased, especially with rising tensions between the dissatisfied Shans and the Union government. Sao would not want to go to Taunggyi.

The perfect place for a summer vacation would be Namhsan, six thousand feet above sea level and the capital of Tawngpeng State to the north. They were always welcome guests at the Grand Haw of their neighbor, the Prince of Tawngpeng. Thusandi thought back to their visit to Namhsan the previous year, when the temperatures in Hsipaw had felt like the burning heat of a potter's kiln.

EVEN THOUGH IT WAS EARLY morning when they loaded their cars with children, nannies, and body-guards, the summer sun was already exacting its toll.

"I don't want to go," Mayari said. "I want to go in the pool."

"How about a swim in the Namtu River instead?" Sao asked. He received an enthusiastic reply from both children and from his wife. It was a rare occasion when Sao agreed to take them for a swim anywhere except in their blue-tiled pool.

They reached Thatay, the only crossing point of the Namtu River on the road to Namhsan and the Namtu-Bawdwin Mines. One car at a time had to cross the river on a rope-guided ferry. An ageless Shan woman held the concession and ferried all motorized and pedestrian traffic across the river. She lived on the other side with her family. When she saw a car approaching, she hurriedly set her ferry in motion, guiding it with a large oar. She recognized the prince, and a big smile spread over her brown wrin-kled face, exposing a row of teeth blackened by decades of chewing betel nuts. "Sahtoo, Sahtoo, Sahtoo," the old ferry-woman exclaimed respect-fully, bowing and folding her hands in front of her face as she knelt on the moist ground. Then she adjusted the planks so that the Mercedes could drive onto the wooden deck. Sao and his family were standing on the ferry, watching the swift current push them to the other bank, when they saw a peculiar sight. Fifty feet downstream, a large water buffalo waded into the river and started swimming across, ignoring the calls of his young keeper to turn back.

"Oh no," Thusandi shouted in dismay, "he's being swept away." In spite of the strong current, the buffalo continued on his course, and the boy gave up recalling his charge. When the old woman noticed Thusandi's concern, she explained, "He does it every day, Royal Mother. He swims to the other bank to feed in the jungle. But at night he always comes back to his master, my grandson. I wish I knew why he doesn't like the jungle on our side of the river."

While the other cars waited their turn at the ferry, Sao drove ahead to the bathing spot that he remembered from his childhood. It was perfect.

Crossing the Namtu River on a one-car ferry.

The meandering river had carved a cove that was filled with clear, calm water. Large-leaf teak trees provided shade along the gravelly bank. Sao held his younger daughter, Kennari, as she splashed and played. Thusandi had to prevent Mayari from following the water buffalo's example and venturing out of the cove into the swiftly flowing river.

The winding, one-lane road to Namhsan proved to be less enjoyable. "Are we there yet?" was the question asked by one or the other child after each of the hundreds of hairpin curves the driver had to negotiate. During the four-hour-long ascent, they encountered a few trucks and two mule trains carrying tea from the Palaung Hills to brokerages in the valleys. When they reached the altitude where tea bushes thrived, the scenery changed. Well-groomed tea plantations in place of jungle covered the hillsides, and white pagodas reached toward the blue sky from every mountaintop in sight. They saw many Palaung villages from a distance but only passed through one, which reflected the relative wealth of the tea-growing hill tribe. The houses appeared more permanent than in the valleys, constructed of wood instead of bamboo. The Buddhist monastery was the largest and best building in the village, indicating the religious devotion of its inhabitants. Thusandi had seen Palaung women before, and she marveled once again at their colorful costumes and heavy silver jewelry adornments. Their caps, dark blouses, and heavy skirts were well suited for the cool temperatures; Thusandi reached for the children's cardigans.

The town of Namhsan itself kept company with the clouds. Situated on a mountain plateau, it was peaceful and cool, away from the steaming valley and from the politics of the lowlands. The Prince of Tawngpeng and his Anglo-Burmese Mahadevi had not lost their rambling palace in World War II. It was built on the highest point in the town and was comfortable and large enough to accommodate their many children and occasional guests. Every room had a fireplace, and even during the hot season they were all in use.

The biggest attractions of Namhsan were the numerous gable-roofed Buddhist monasteries and a modern tea factory. It was run by a solitary Englishman who, with a small staff, dried and roasted tea leaves for sale in the Shan states and in Burma. The area did not produce enough tea for export, though the quality was excellent. Mr. Brown, the English manager, was primarily a trained forester and timber expert; tea was his hobby. He

The Prince of Tawngpeng in Namhsan, surrounded by his Palaung people.

was also a passionate hunter and felt that Namhsan was a perfect location for him. The Palaungs were even stronger believers than the Shans in not taking life, so there were no hunters to compete with him. Plenty of wildlife roamed these hills: big cats, wild pigs, rhinoceros, bears. He showed Sao and Thusandi huge tiger tracks outside his bedroom window. They were fresh; the tiger must have been there the previous night without rousing the avid hunter or his dog. Sao and Thusandi disappointed the Englishman when they showed more interest in the tea factory than in his hunting stories.

Back at the Grand Haw, the Prince of Tawngpeng presented Thusandi with a large tiger skin, pierced in many places by spears and pellets from a muzzle-loading gun.

"Thank you very much," she said looking somewhat puzzled.

"You know we don't kill," he said, "but my villagers had no choice. This tiger ate three of them, not far from here."

Surprised and shocked, Thusandi asked, "How could that happen?"

"The tiger stalked them when they were picking tea. He first killed a child, then he came back for an old man. My people knew that he would return again when he was hungry. So they armed themselves and went after him. But they didn't get him until he took one more victim, a young girl."

"How terrible!" Thusandi said. "Tell me, why didn't Mr. Brown go after the tiger?"

"He would have if he'd been here. But he was on home leave when it happened. He was actually quite disappointed that he missed the man-eating tiger."

"They are very rare," Sao said. "I've only heard of one in Hsipaw State, when I was a young boy."

"Why do they become man-eaters?" Thusandi wanted to know.

"I'm not an authority on this," Sao said, "but people say that tigers who are too old to hunt sometimes stumble onto easy prey—people. And once they feast on humans, they'll come back for more."

Thusandi wasn't sure that she wanted the tiger skin, but she could not offend her host by refusing to accept his gift.

After a few days of relaxation and long walks through the Mahadevi's extensive flower gardens, Sao invited Thusandi for a jeep ride. He wanted to see if they could reach the Palaung village of Punglong, which was actually located in Hsipaw State, from the Tawngpeng side. His host had discouraged him, saying that after a certain point only mules could manage the terrain. However, Sao decided to see for himself. A few years ago, he had approached Punglong from the Hsipaw side, with Thusandi, to open the new road to Punglong. He had helped his Palaung villagers build it by themselves so they could transport their tea to the markets down below by truck rather than by mule and horse.

After about ten miles, the gravel road narrowed and assumed a steep downhill course. Soon it turned into a winding path, hugging the side of the mountain. Sao ignored Thusandi's pleas to stop, turn around, or do anything other than continue. "It's got to get better," he said as he inched ahead, clutching the steering wheel. He was wrong. A forbidding cliff around the next curve put an abrupt stop to forward progress. Sao carefully examined what was ahead and admitted, "I give up. This is only suitable for goats—and fools. But look—that's Punglong over there." He pointed at a large village that was nestled on the side of the next mountain.

Thusandi, shaken up from the rough ride and annoyed with her husband's stubbornness, recognized the village and searched for binoculars in her overstuffed Shan bag. She did not say a word to Sao; that was her way of expressing displeasure. Instead, she dwelled on their official visit to Punglong a few years before.

Three Palaung villages in Hsipaw State had requested that their royal couple open the nine-mile stretch of road that they had carved out of the mountain to connect them with the state's road network. After a five-hour drive, Sao and Thusandi had finally reached their destination—the beginning of the new road. Palaung children from the villages had lined the road, and a welcoming committee of Palaung village elders—all of them men—had jumped from a truck to greet their honored guests. Sao had cut the first ribbon, invoking blessings for road and people and had given a short speech. That scene had been repeated three times along the road, at each of the three Palaung villages that had worked together on the project. Finally, they had arrived in Punglong, where a big festival had been staged for them, consisting of music, dances, songs, flowers, beautiful girls, excited children, and mountains of food. The district headman himself had prepared a special meal for his prince and had served it in a bamboo tent erected for the occasion. Sao and Thusandi had eaten their meal in public, the inhabitants of the 150 Palaung households watching their every move. Thusandi remembered some mouth-watering dishes she had never tasted before: salads of deliciously sour ants' eggs and crunchy pigs' ears, fragrant and delicate fried blossoms of some kind, and a deep-fried fatty worm that lived in bamboo shoots. The latter had not inspired her, but she had tasted it anyway, without regrets.

The villagers had waited patiently until each of them had had a chance to speak to Sao and Thusandi. They had expressed their pride and gratitude over the new road, which would take the yearly 650,000 kilograms (more than 700 tons) of tea they produced to market. The buheng had also announced that the next communal work project had already begun: a pipeline to provide the villages with water. For as long as the inhabitants of Punglong could remember, they had carried every drop of water one-and-a-half miles from a stream to their village.

As Thusandi focused her binoculars on the village once more, she wondered if the water pipeline had been completed yet. The happy memories of their visit to Punglong also made her feel more forgiving toward her husband.

"Can we go back now?" she said to Sao, smiling for the first time since they had left Namhsan.

"I'm sorry, dear. That was a stupid thing to do," Sao said, shaking his head.

"I agree. Let's try to get out of here."

Sao had to back up for several miles until he found a spot where he could turn the jeep around.

They stayed in Namhsan for three more days without attempting another excursion. Sao realized that the only passable road led down the mountain, to Hsipaw and beyond.

After several cool days and cold nights in the mountains of Tawng-peng State, they looked forward to returning home. The children missed their toys and familiar surroundings. Sao wanted to return to draft plans for the salt project, and Thusandi had to oversee preparations for the coming Water Festival.

Hsipaw's temperatures had climbed well above the one-hundred-degree mark, and the air-conditioning units in the East Haw were over-taxed. Sao and Thusandi spent the evening on the lawn, letting their bare feet rest on the cool grass. Although they were tired from the drive home, they stayed up until midnight, enjoying the night air and talking about their short holiday in Namhsan. Thusandi planned to sleep late the next morning before assuming her normal routine.

"WHAT TIME IS IT?" THUSANDI asked Sao as she stretched and tried to wake up in response to a gentle yet determined knock at their bedroom door.

"Five-thirty—and I haven't any idea what this is all about," Sao answered as he reluctantly got out of bed and searched for his slippers. He went to the door, and Thusandi heard the excited voice of Bukong, the head of the guards, muttering something about a snake. Why would Bukong wake them at dawn on the morning after their return because of a snake, she wondered, rubbing her eyes and sitting up in bed.

"There is a python in the chicken house," Sao said as he hurriedly threw on his khakis and a sport shirt on his way out.

"I want to come too," Thusandi shouted after him, but he did not wait. Even though she had planned to sleep late, she stumbled out of bed and got ready to follow Sao to the area behind the moat where they kept their experimental livestock.

She had always hoped to see a python when they trekked in the jungle, but had never done so. Now there was one in the teak chicken house that Ah Wah, the Chinese carpenter, had built according to Sao's hand-drawn plans. This edifice had not been constructed for ordinary chickens, but for two dozen Rhode Island Reds that Sao had imported from halfway around the world. He wanted to improve the stock of the local jungle hens, which were shy, small, and laid a small number of tiny eggs. When the giant imports arrived, they were lodged in the custom-made chicken house together with a selection of the local breed. Thusandi often went to look at this artistic structure, which was complete with balconies and an enclosed, covered patio to ensure that the prize chickens would not be inconvenienced by the monsoon. She expected to see a docile python curled up among the fowl.

As she turned the corner by the moat, Thusandi heard the commotion. Chickens were cackling wildly, something was making a slashing sound, and men were shouting. Over it all, Sao's commanding voice shouted, "Don't shoot! Do not shoot yet!" Several women and children stood at a respectable distance from the chicken house, which was the source of all these noises. Thusandi, driven on by curiosity, was stopped ten yards short of its entrance by Bukong, who rushed out of the enclosure as she approached. "Sao Mae, you must go back to the Haw. Please take these women and children with you—away from here. We may have to shoot the python."

"But why in the world would you want to shoot the python?" she asked, pressing forward a little more slowly.

"Because it has eaten most of our Rhode Island Reds. It couldn't get the local hens." Bukong shouted to be heard over all the cackling and slashing noises.

Thusandi realized very quickly that her naïve notions of an encounter with a friendly python were merely a figment of her imagination. "Can't you do something other than shoot?" she shouted at the top of her voice.

"Zinna and Sang Aye are trying to catch it, but the python is beating at them with its strong tail," Bukong said before he ran back into the scene of the action.

She was determined to catch a glimpse of the marauding python and hurried toward the entrance. An inner voice stopped her from opening the door. Thusandi noticed a crack by the hinges and pressed her right eye over it. Her mouth fell open as she saw chicken feathers flying and the long tail of the giant snake slashing back and forth ferociously. "Oh no," she mumbled to herself, realizing that Sao was somewhere inside. Thusandi was pressing down the door handle when Moei caught up and started to pull her away. "You are not safe here—you must go back," she shouted with such authority that Thusandi turned to look around. Moei's face was dark red, her eyes were wide with horror, and she was out of breath. She continued to implore her mistress. "Please come back, Sao Mae—to the guardhouse. Nobody is safe here till the python is dead."

Thusandi paid heed and followed her maid, ordering everybody else to back off to a respectable distance. "What do we have to worry about if the snake survives?" she asked Moei.

"If it gets away, it'll return to feast again when it gets hungry. And if the python can't find any chickens, who knows what it will eat," Moei said, as if she spoke from experience.

"Have you ever seen a python here before?" Thusandi asked Moei.

"No, not this close to town and to people," Moei answered. "But we've seen giant lizards come and steal eggs and chicks." She paused for a minute before she continued, "My mother told me about a python carrying away a baby from her village when I was little."

That information alarmed Thusandi, and she wished Sao would leave it up to the guards to deal with the grand robbery. Instead, he was inside, amid cackling chickens, an angry python, and three guards intent on restoring order in the chicken house. She knew how much these agricultural experiments meant to Sao and how determined he was to make his Rhode Island Reds project succeed. Only a few months ago, the secretary was dispatched to Rangoon to meet the fowl shipment and to fly the birds up to Hsipaw without delay. At this moment the chickens were experiencing a severe case of culture shock.

Thusandi didn't know how long she had been standing in the ever-growing crowd of women and children when she heard shots, several popping sounds in succession.

The thought of killing, even a rogue python, upset her. Neither she nor Sao believed in any type of hunting; they respected life in all forms. Despite this, Sao must have given the orders for the shots she just heard.

The racket in the chicken house died down, and there was no more slashing—only a few cackles. Sao and Bukong emerged from the chicken house. Behind them, Zinna and Sang Aye dragged out the dead python. Sixteen feet long, its slick body resembled a knotty walking stick, with clearly defined bulges distributed along its shiny expanse. It was a magnificent reptile in spite of the bulges caused by the many chickens it had swallowed whole. The python was beautiful, with a golden-brown skin and a pattern of symmetrical dark brown diamonds, large in the center and small on both sides. Its pointed, inconspicuous head looked disproportionately small, and Thusandi was mystified how the snake could swallow the plump hens in one piece. Even when Sao explained to her that pythons unhinged their jaws for large-sized snacks, she remained incredulous.

Thusandi mourned the death of the python, and Sao mourned twenty Rhode Island Reds; only four of them had survived. All the local hens had managed to evade the hungry intruder.

A FEW DAYS LATER, WHILE THE python was still on everybody's mind, the incident with the king cobras occurred. It heightened Thusandi's concern for the children's safety around the East Haw.

Two bricklayers from Mandalay were doing repairs around the Haw while keeping a fearful eye on Ballah, one of the watchdogs who had settled down under an old tamarind tree, sixty feet from them. Ballah made a sudden move and came running toward them and they jumped. Then they saw the reason. An angry king cobra, six feet long, was chasing the dog away from the foot of the tree. Maung Win, one of the men, swung into action. He had been tattooed with antisnake venom and never missed an opportunity to show off his invulnerability and his courage in the presence of poisonous snakes. And a king cobra, the deadliest of the species and the only one known to chase after people, provided a special challenge. He ran toward the snake, caught it by its tail, and smashed its head with full force against the ground, killing it instantly. Maung Win examined the foot of the huge tree and pointed at a hole. "This must lead to the snake's den. And the partner will soon come out and look for its mate."

He settled down near the hole, waiting quietly, until about twenty minutes later when the second king cobra emerged. Maung Win acted with lightning speed, dispatching the reptile the same way as the first. The guards who had assembled to help if necessary heaved a sigh of relief, expecting that the cobra nest was now empty. They were wrong. Over the next two days, four more king cobras emerged from the hole under the tamarind tree. Maung Win killed all but the last one. One of the body- guards took care of it the Shan way—with a jungle knife. He hacked the snake in half and swung at its head. But before he could finish, the upper half of the cobra crawled back into its hole. The Burmese bricklayers and the Shan guards assured an almost hysterical Thusandi that the cobra would die there and not resurface again.

Thusandi could not put this incident behind her and did not let her daughters out of her sight. Lying awake at night, she imagined what would have happened if the king cobra had chased one of her girls rather than Ballah, the watchdog. She could not believe that she had allowed the children to play under that or any tree. She also wondered why the cobras had never emerged from their nest when Mayari and Kennari had played their hide-and-seek games there. If the snakes had avoided the children, she was not sure if she was justified in ordering any snakes found in their compound to be killed. She thought with envy of her childhood friends who were raising their children in safe surroundings, far away from venom- ous reptiles.

THE WATER FESTIVAL, everybody's favorite event and the most enjoyable part of the New Year celebrations, provided a welcome diversion to the shaken residents of the East Haw. The festivities started on the night of April 13, when according to the Burmese calendar, the year 1322 ended. They lasted for three days. It was never clear to Thusandi on which of these days in April the New Year really began. To add to the confusion, the Buddhist calendar proclaimed the new year to be 2505, not 1323. The Burmese kings had rearranged the calendar according to non-Buddhist beliefs, acknowledging that the king of the *dewa* (Hindu gods) descended to earth for the commencement of the new year. He remained on earth for three or four days, and everybody celebrated until he returned to his realm.

On the evening of April 13, Sao and Thusandi joined local dignitaries in the chapel to await the dewa's arrival. Outside, three orchestras played simultaneously, creating a disharmonious medley. Precisely at 9:40 P.M. a deafening racket began. The sound of guns, horns, and bells reverberated from all parts of the town, making certain that nobody would miss the significant moment. As soon as year 1322 had ended, the minister of ceremonies poured water on the ground and led a sequence of prayers. Two hours of music and dance followed to welcome the visitor from the other world: first Burmese court music, then Shan music and dance. Tattooed members of the Hsipaw police force performed Shan sword dances to the beat of their drums and gongs.

Bukong, the head of the bodyguards, playing a drum with a traditional Shan band of percussion instruments.

Hsipaw townspeople performing songs and dances during the Water Festival, in front of the East Haw.

The next three days were dedicated to the Water Festival, an event unlike any other. Thusandi had been initiated to this the year she had arrived, but she never tired of throwing buckets of water anywhere, anytime, at anybody whom she encountered. Only Buddhist monks were spared. On the first morning, Sao packed the Mercedes with wife, daughters, Moei, and a dozen large containers filled with water. Then he drove to the houses of relatives to surprise them with an involuntary shower, regardless of their age, dress, or place. They, in turn, reciprocated and drenched the well-wishers. Soaking wet, Sao and his accomplices got into the car to raid another household. Much laughter, shrieking, and splashing accompanied the unorthodox housecalls. The streets of Hsipaw were lined with countless children using large water pistols, made out of bamboo, on passersby. Neighborhood groups had set up toll booths where everyone was stopped and treated to dance performances and more buckets of water.

When they returned to the East Haw, they had barely enough time to put on dry clothes before hundreds of groups of well-wishers arrived. First came three floats loaded with uniformly dressed university students home on vacation. They asked for permission to perform some songs and dances—their own creations—on the front lawn. They sang of a good New Year and of blessings for their prince, families, country. Then the water throwing started with good cheer and humor. When a few daring nieces tried to follow the fleeing Thusandi into the Haw, Sao was ready on the balcony above the entrance. He unleashed a true waterfall onto the would-be intruders and stopped their advance. Soaked household staff served refreshments to the departing revelers.

The wet celebration lasted for three days. Households, neighborhoods, villages, and towns paid each other visits and strengthened good relations by wishing each other well. A spirit of joy and caring prevailed, and nobody seemed to mind when their house got flooded and their hair soaked. The children were so involved in the dousing activities that it was an additional week before they discontinued what they had enjoyed so much.

Thusandi never received a satisfactory reply when she asked for rhyme or reason behind this madness. "We're trying to make the monsoons big and early," some said. Others explained to her that it was a cleansing ritual. "We've got to wash away all evil and bad deeds so we can start the new year fresh and clean." It made most sense to Thusandi when people said, "It's so hot—we can't go on without this cool-down."

When the car, the furniture, the floors, and the clothes had dried out, Thusandi sat down to write a letter to her family in Austria. She wanted to describe this, her all-time favorite festival, to them. After several attempts, she realized they would not understand. She smiled when she imagined how they might react if someone were to pour a bucket of water over them.

Twelve

FROM THE BEDROOM VERANDAH, Thusandi could see the road leading up to the East Haw. She was anxiously hoping for a car to deliver Sao or some news of him. But all she saw was an occasional bicycle or a stray dog and, in the background, a few pillars of the old Grand Haw. She smiled when she remembered what Sao had said to her about the old Haw: The only good thing resulting from World War II was its total destruction. He had not liked a single thing about it and dreaded the thought of ever having to live there. Thusandi often put her imagination to work and envisioned what it must have looked like. The picture albums had all disappeared, but she knew from the remaining foundation that it had been a rambling one-story building. Auntie Gyipaya filled in a few details about the interior of the old Haw—large, dark halls, no privacy, no indoor plumbing. Sao's grandfather had built it when he returned to Hsipaw after his remarkable experience in Burma proper.

His name was Sao Hkun Hseng, and he had been brought up in the Burmese royal palace in Mandalay. In 1882, he incurred the displeasure of King Thibaw and fled to Rangoon, which was already in British hands. There he suspected two of his followers of plotting against him and had them shot, as was his right under Shan law. To his surprise, the British tried him for murder and sentenced him to death. Later on, Sao Hkun Hseng was released on condition that he leave British-held territory. He returned to Hsipaw, rebuilt the town—which had been ravaged by warring Shans—and helped establish the boundary between Burma and the northern Shan states when the British took Mandalay in 1886. A year later, he was the first Shan prince to acknowledge the supremacy of Queen Victoria. In return, he was granted an exemption from tribute for ten years and received support for his claim to three smaller neighboring states. Sao Hkun Hseng traveled to England twice, was received by the queen, and was made a Companion of the Order of the British Empire. And before he died, he married one of the wives of Thibaw, the last king of Burma. Thusandi wondered what he would have thought of his grandson's Austrian-born Mahadevi living in the English-style East Haw. From the day of their arrival, she had felt grateful for this comfortable and modern home that Sao Ohn Kya had designed for himself after his years in England. He too chose not to live in the old palace of his grandfather.

Thusandi had accompanied Sao on many visits to other Shan princes and had seen their Haws, old and new, big and small. Some of them charmed her, but none came close to the East Haw in stateliness and comfort, with one possible exception. The Government House in Taunggyi was built for the British chief commissioner of the Federated Shan States, which was then a protectorate administered separately from Burma proper.

Taunggyi as seen from the balconies of Government House was a lovely garden town surrounded by deep-green forests and rocky hilltops. Trees that Thusandi had already seen in Sakandar, but which were uncommon in most parts of the Shan states, stood everywhere in the park surrounding the stately mansion and in the gardens of the attractive stone houses. But aside from the blue jacarandas, the pink cassias, the white acacias, and the graceful silver oaks, people also grew pears, cherries, and apples. The cool temperatures of this hill station, almost five thousand feet above sea level, always restored color to Thusandi's cheeks, which had a way of paling in Hsipaw.

She enjoyed the European flavor of Taunggyi and its colorful gardens, but Thusandi never missed a chance to visit Inle Lake, thirty miles to the East, downhill in a low-lying basin of Yawnghwe State; it held a strange fascination for her. The Prince of Yawnghwe was usually in Rangoon, attending to his duties as the speaker of the House of Nationalities. His relatives took care of the Haw and the many guests who came to see the lake and the Intha lake dwellers. Once, while Sao attended meetings in Taunggyi, Thusandi toured the lake in a motorboat, which first had to struggle through a three-mile canal choked with water hyacinths, a scourge imported by Europeans. The shallow lake, twenty miles long and twelve miles wide, was smooth as a mirror and reflected the surrounding

Sao Kya Seng (second from right) with the Saophas of Hsamonghkam (front) and Mong Nai (second from left) after a directors' meeting of Kambawza School, Taunggyi. The British headmaster (left) was in charge of this private high school, financed by the Shan Saophas.

mountains that jutted into the cloudless blue sky. Inle Lake was the home of the Inthas, who lived by and on its water.

Thusandi's motorboat headed first for the guesthouse, which stood on stilts in the center of the lake. It was used for visiting dignitaries, and wilting garlands on the verandah were reminders of the most recent visitor, Marshal Tito of Yugoslavia. As the noisy motor churned the still waters, they passed men of all ages standing in peculiar shell-like boats and rowing with one leg wrapped around a long oar. One hand was always free for activities like fishing, gardening, or moving real estate to another location. Thusandi watched two of the leg rowers take a chunk of land to their village and secure it to the lake bottom with four long bamboo poles. Some of these floating islands were turned into fertile vegetable gardens with mud scooped from the lake bottom; others served as a land base for houses. Thusandi's imagination worked overtime when she thought of the possibilities that this movable real estate offered: People could pull their bamboo poles and move if they didn't get along with their neighbors, or they could just turn the house toward another direction. There was no reason why entire villages could not change location.

Thusandi and her hosts visited a few of the seventeen Intha villages situated around the fringes of Inle Lake, which were accessible only by boat. They stopped to see silk weavers working at their looms, creating glamorous longyis with intricate zigzag designs and brilliant colors. The boat became weighed down with dozens of silk longyis that Thusandi purchased; she knew how much they would be treasured by family and friends. There was continuous traffic on the waterways between houses and villages. Around every turn, they encountered lake dwellers going about their daily activities; small children rowed themselves to school, women took products to floating markets, and men set bamboo traps for their daily catch. Every Intha they questioned assured them that life away from their lake was unthinkable. Surrounded by hill people who tilled the land, the Intha's destiny depended on the shallow waters on which they lived.

THUSANDI PANICKED. SHE COULD not imagine that there would be no more travels with Sao in the future. She thought about their plans for a voyage to Japan and the United States in a year's time. They had already looked into shipping lines. No, she thought, nothing could possibly happen to interfere with these plans. Sao had been to Japan several times as a member of Burma's delegation to negotiate Japan's war reparations. But Thusandi had stayed home to look after the children and to represent Sao during his absence. She had never been east of Burma except for one unforgettable visit to China.

It took place when Burma and China were negotiating an agreement about the disputed boundary between the two countries. As a member of the Border Commission, Sao had already been on several inspection tours along the Shan State segment of the boundary with China. When he was getting ready for another trip, Thusandi pleaded, "Please take me along—I want to set foot on Chinese soil."

"The border is closed. The Chinese won't let anybody go across who isn't on the commission," Sao said.

"You could at least try to take me," Thusandi persisted. She suggested that the Chinese authorities probably would not turn her away if she joined their small group. Sao raised more objections and pointed out that, being white, she was probably not welcome on the other side of the border. But he finally gave in.

On a crisp morning in December, their convoy headed northeast following the Burma Road, the route of the Allied supply line to Chiang Kai-shek's troops in World War II. Leaving the sleepy town of Hsenwi behind, they started climbing toward Kutkai, a hill station. Tawng, one of Thusandi's new nannies, came from there. Like the majority of Kutkai inhabitants, she belonged to the fiercely independent Kachin ethnic group. The women wove their own bright red wool skirts and leggings, outdoing each other in intricate designs. Heavy silver jewelry, handcrafted by the men, adorned their black blouses and black-and-red woven shoulder bags. Women were not only conspicuous by their striking dress but also by their presence everywhere; they worked in fields, tended to shops, carried water, and did all other chores. Kachin men appeared to be passive bystanders while their women worked.

After leaving Kutkai, the scenery provided a stark contrast to the lush jungle they had passed through earlier that day. The high plains were barren save for occasional clusters of blooming wild cherries, plums, and peaches. Jet-black rocks jutted out of the smooth, red surface of the earth. The beauty of this infertile stretch of land was disturbing. Sao pointed out how erosion had taken its toll after trees had been felled and grasslands torched. Thusandi saw people on the roadside mix cow dung with straw and set the "cakes" out to dry. This was the prevalent fuel of India and China, which she had only read about before.

Eight hours later they reached the border town of Muse, 170 miles farther on the Shweli River, just in time to see a sunset they would remember forever. The rays of the setting sun transformed the Shweli River into a wide, winding band of pure gold, glistening and gleaming as if the world's treasures had found their way into its fold. Hundreds of wild geese played on the golden river, and their mysterious calls beckoned people on both banks to listen. They frolicked back and forth, undecided whether to stay in Burma or fly toward the burgundy red mountains of China.

Sao had decided to show Thusandi the sights of this northernmost part of the Shan states before crossing the border into China. The next day, they drove twenty-five miles farther north through the Shweli valley toward Namkham. The fertile valley, densely populated, appeared prosperous; houses were large and of permanent material, stone water fountains dotted the roadside, and well-fed children with rosy cheeks played at the side of the busy road.

Ox carts, people on foot, and bicycles were headed toward the village of Se-Lan for the bazaar, which took place every five days. To see this well-known event was an opportunity not to be missed. Thusandi asked Sao to stop there for a while, and he reluctantly agreed to this unplanned detour. The scene at the market reminded Thusandi of the Bawgyo Pwe: hill tribes in colorful dress, merchandise of every description, and food stalls advertising their menus with tantalizing smells. Against Sao's wishes, Thusandi bought some fried, dried milk-dough, a delicacy available only in the Namkham area. The tradition of making milk into thin dough, wrapping it around bamboo sticks, and letting it dry was introduced to the area by the Mongols, who were the only people in the area who made use of milk. The fried chips of milk dough had a peculiar sweet-sour taste, and its scent permeated the entire market.

"While we're in Se-Lan, I'd like to see the site of Vieng Nang Mon. That was the capital of the Shan Empire in the thirteenth century," Sao said.

The terraced layers of the ancient town were still clearly visible, even though thick clusters of bamboo and a large array of vines and bushes had covered the site. No archaeological excavations had been attempted, but local enthusiasts had cleared away the jungle from a few defensive walls and a bathing area. One of the village elders was at work with his jungle knife when Sao's party arrived. With great pride he showed them elaborate stonework, almost one thousand years old, which he and his villagers had uncovered. What an idyllic place for a capital this must have been, Thusandi thought, as she stood on one of the ancient terraces. Below them the river glistened as it meandered west, giving life to the valley's earth and people.

On reaching Namkham, the town marking the border between the Kachin and Shan states, they went to see the two-hundred-bed teaching hospital set up by Gordon Seagrave. Thusandi had read his book *Burma*

Surgeon while she was in America, and she had envied Sao for knowing this remarkable man, whom she thought of as Burma's Albert Schweitzer. She had long looked forward to making his acquaintance and telling him how well his nurse-midwives were performing at the maternity home in Hsipaw.

The one- and two-story hospital buildings were unlike any structures around them. They were built with countless round river stones bound together by mortar. Roofs, windows, and doors looked as though they were borrowed from English cottages and did not really belong in this part of the world. Dr. Seagrave proudly showed them the inside of his hospital: the basic though spotless operating room where he had performed thousands of goiter and stomach operations—his specialties—as well as much other surgery; the wards, filled with patients who had come from near and far to seek help from the famous doctor; and the nursing school, where young Karen, Kachin, and Shan women received the best training in the country. The white-haired surgeon described how he had started building his hospital almost forty years earlier and how he never wanted to leave his "hospital in the hills" (the title of his third book). When funds permitted, he planned to add another building, so that he would never have to turn a patient away for lack of space. Sao and Thusandi drove away worrying who would carry on this dedicated surgeon's work when he could no longer guide the scalpel. They had noticed that his hands shook from time to time for no apparent reason.

In the evening, they rested at the Public Works Department bungalow in Muse—hotels were nonexistent. The four drivers approached Sao in a state of alarm: There was not a drop of gasoline available in the entire Muse-Namkham area, and the tanks were nearly empty. Zinna, the senior driver, had checked every single petrol pump, to no avail. However, he had received one valuable hint: Dr. Seagrave was known always to have an extra supply of gasoline. In order to keep his appointment with the Chinese general the next day, Sao had no choice but to head a convoy of four cars back to the hospital. Dr. Seagrave was pleased to help, and Sao gladly made a generous donation toward the new building.

Finally, early next morning, Sao's convoy approached Pangsai, the border post on the Burma side, where three other members of the Border Commission were to join him. Pangsai consisted of a few ramshackle buildings remaining after the destruction of the core of the town. Nothing suggested the importance this border post had had fourteen years ago, when countless trucks had passed through on the Burma Road carrying supplies into China. Since the border had been closed for over a decade, there had been no incentive to rebuild. Sao found his three colleagues in a coffee shop, where two men in Chinese uniform were devouring bowls of noodles as if they had never eaten before.

"They're always so hungry when they come over here," the shop-keeper said in Shan. "They haven't got any money, but I can't see them starve," she continued, shrugging her shoulders as she placed another dish on their table.

The Burmese border patrol met Sao and his group at the coffee shop. From there a young officer escorted their car down the gorge to the small stream that separated the two countries. It was only when they were close to the bridge that the new and substantial buildings of Wanting, the Chinese border town, came into view. The officer, the four men, and Thusandi stepped onto the bridge and walked about thirty feet to the center. That was where Burma's jurisdiction ended. They waited until two Chinese soldiers met them, their rifles at the ready. After the Burmese officer

Wanting, China, from the Burma side. In the 1950s the bridge to Wanting was closed, as regular border crossings were not permitted.

addressed them in Chinese, one soldier marched back to his guard post while the other blocked the way. Thusandi had expected a slightly warmer welcome and wondered whether her presence made the difference. She was not sure that she was right to have insisted on coming along. It was almost ten minutes until a dozen men in uniform poured out of the main building and marched onto the bridge. They carried no arms. Their leader saluted Sao and said in Burmese, "Please follow us. The general is expecting you." He cast a suspicious look at Thusandi, the white woman in Burmese dress, especially when she did not turn around to go back to the other side with the Burmese officer.

General Li greeted them in his austere office, which was furnished with a plain table, six chairs, and a large portrait of Chairman Mao. An orderly served jasmine tea while the general, through an interpreter, tried to establish Thusandi's nationality. He seemed greatly relieved when he heard that she came from neutral Austria, and he invited her to join in a tour of the area.

And it was a memorable tour—through very clean and tidy streets, past buildings devoid of people.

"Over here are the dormitories for our men." General Li proudly pointed at a long row of low buildings made of corrugated iron.

Still, there wasn't a soul in sight.

A few hundred yards down the road, the general showed them the women's dormitories. They stopped to take a look inside: clean cement floors and two long rows of cots, one like the other, each covered with a blanket.

This looked like a camp and was probably not in use at the moment, Thusandi thought. She decided it was best if she did not ask any questions. But she was curious about where the families lived and when these dormitories would fill up.

Then they saw the children. They were of all ages up to twelve or thirteen, and of both sexes. It was not easy to tell girls from boys, however, because they wore identical uniforms of blue cotton overalls with long sleeves. Dozens of them surrounded the jeeplike military vehicle and giggled shyly as General Li talked to a few of them. "They are taking a break right now," he explained, "but they'll return to the classroom in a few minutes." Several women wearing blue pants and Mao jackets came out of the building to herd their charges back inside. As the children turned their back on the visitors, it became obvious that their overalls were split from the waist down through the crotch, now and then exposing a partially bare bottom.

Thusandi could not contain her curiosity any longer.

"General, why the split in these children's overalls?"

"Because it's so much more efficient. The children are directed to relieve themselves in the fields behind their dormitories. That way nothing is wasted—neither resources nor extra energy."

Thusandi and Sao exchanged looks before Sao asked a question.

"When do the children return to their parents?"

"They don't. The Party looks after them, educates them."

"You mean there is no family life?"

"No. I already showed you the separate quarters for men and women. Of course, we have places where couples can get together when the time is right," he said with a smirk.

After a pause, the general continued, "This is a model commune, you know. We've brought people from the eastern provinces to populate the area. Our comrades work in the fields and in the iron industry nearby."

"What about the local people?" Sao asked.

"They didn't want to cooperate," the general replied wistfully. "Some of them crossed the river into your country. Others . . . well, we had to eliminate them. It was well worth it. We are very proud of this worker's paradise, you know."

Sao did not say a word; neither did the other three men. Thusandi could tell from Sao's frown that he was very upset. She had shuddered when she heard the word "eliminate." It reminded her of the terrible crimes against humanity that had been committed in and around the country of her birth while she was growing up.

As their tour continued, they came across troops of workers marching from one field to another, guided by leaders who blew shrill whistles. All their faces looked young and enthusiastic, reminiscent of the marching Hitler Youth that Thusandi had seen as a little girl in Austria; the uniforms and race were different, but the zealous expressions were the same.

The general made a final stop at the commune's general store and mentioned that Burmese currency would be accepted for any purchases. Very few items were available for sale—a few silk scarfs, some embossed leather purses, and two or three bales of brocade. Thusandi was trying to make a selection when Sao whispered to her in English, "Don't you buy anything! I don't want to support this miserable system with so much as a penny."

But Thusandi did not listen. She felt compelled to take back a few souvenirs to convince herself that she had been to China.

As Thusandi later recalled the trip to China and this particular incident, she felt deep remorse at her insensitivity to Sao's request. She had upset him terribly when she had bought those useless souvenirs, which she had never even looked at in the years since. Her regret at not having supported Sao by a simple economic statement against the repressive Chinese system lingered on.

MOEI CAME LOOKING FOR HER mistress, sighing with relief when she found her on the verandah.

"What is it, Moei?" Thusandi turned to her maid in anticipation of some good news, any news.

"It's time to plan for Kennari's birthday party," Moei said, knowing that this was one of the few subjects Thusandi might be willing to discuss on a day of such horrendous events.

But Thusandi shook her head. "That can wait till later," she said dejectedly.

"Not really," Moei countered. "Our little princess is so excited about her third birthday. She should not be disappointed."

"I guess you're right, Moei." Thusandi straightened up and folded her arms. "The children must not suffer because of all this. We'll have a grand celebration."

Then the two women put their heads together and made elaborate plans for a combined Shan-Austrian birthday party. They talked about the children's birthdays of years past and discussed how the traditional festivities could be improved.

Mayari and Kennari had always enjoyed a Western birthday party with lots of beautifully wrapped gifts, a big cake, and candles. It had taken a while for them to yield to the Shan custom of giving rather than receiving on their birthdays. Thusandi had insisted on including that tradition in their family celebrations.

On her daughters' birthdays, all children of the East Haw staff were invited. Dozens of little boys and girls filed into the drawing room, barefoot, wearing their finest. They sat down on the carpet without saying a word, intimidated by the building that they entered only on special occasions like these. Quiet as church mice, they waited until the birthday child—or her mother—handed each of them a gift package containing an item of clothing, a toy, and sweets. Little hands clutched the precious parcels until it was time to eat cake and drink fresh lime juice. Then they relaxed and behaved like children anywhere in the world at a birthday party.

The year before, when Kennari was only two, she had shed lots of tears about all the packages she had to give away. Older and wiser, she was looking forward to this year's party.

"Moei, I'm so afraid. What if the prince doesn't come home for the birthday." Thusandi fought back her tears and looked at her trusted maid for reassurances.

"The prince will return, and maybe the prime minister will come along again, too." Moei's loud voice sounded so convincing that Thusandi paid attention.

"Could be," Thusandi said. She became more hopeful when she recalled the surprise of Mayari's first birthday five years before.

IT WAS A HOT DAY DURING THE hottest month of the year, and the birthday activities at the East Haw had started early. The driver and Bukong were busy taking meals to fifteen monasteries, the staff children were already leaving the drawing room, and Mayari was shrieking with delight as her father whirled her round and round. Sao had to stop playing with his daughter because he had to go to Lashio to meet U Nu, the prime minister, who was visiting there.

It was two o'clock when Sao phoned from Lashio and announced to his wife that he was bringing the prime minister and forty other guests for tea at the East Haw. "We'll be there in two hours," he said.

That announcement set everyone at the East Haw in motion. Mehta, the cook, baked a hundred cupcakes within an hour; Kawlin and the kitchen boy produced a supply of cucumber sandwiches; and other servants set up tables for sixty people in the drawing room. Thusandi hurriedly sent cars to fetch the state ministers, a few town elders, and relatives. By the time Sao arrived with his guests, everything and everybody was ready, looking as if such large surprise tea parties were a daily affair.

U Nu greeted Thusandi by saying, "I've been wanting to meet you. That's why I asked the prince if he'd invite me to tea."

"I'm so pleased that you came," she replied, "especially since it's Mayari's first birthday."

"Yes, I know. That is why I propose we all go to Bawgyo Pagoda and say our prayers on your daughter's behalf."

That was precisely what they did, after they had had tea and small talk with fifty-five sets of ears straining to hear every word that was said. In the car on the way to Bawgyo, there was no audience. U Nu sat between Sao and Thusandi, listening intently to their views and concerns about the political situation in the Shan states. U Nu not only listened, he came to realize how disenchanted Sao's people had become with Burmese domination of the federation.

"We must preserve the Union of Burma," U Nu said. "Otherwise we're doomed."

"In that case, you'd better control the military," Sao replied quietly.

"I will, believe me, I will," U Nu said with great emphasis before getting out of the car to offer his prayers at the white pagoda of Bawgyo.

Thirteen

ON HIS THIRD DAY IN PRISON,
Sao received a change of clothing and permission to take a bath outside his
hut. It was not the type of bath to which he was accustomed; however, he
relished each drop of the cold water that his guards had brought him in
two large buckets. Pouring it over his head and shoulders with deliberate
care, he made certain that every inch of his tired body came in contact with
the cleansing liquid. Though humiliated by the presence of four heavily
armed military guards, Sao felt physically refreshed for the first time since
his arrest. He decided that he had to establish a routine of physical and
mental exercise in order to maintain his strength.

Back on the squeaky wooden floor of his hut, Sao tried to do all the
yoga exercises he could recall. As he stretched his tired limbs and coordi-
nated his breathing, he wondered if Thusandi was continuing with yoga by
herself; they had exercised together whenever they could. Lately, he had
been away from home often, a fact he now regretted very much. His efforts
and sacrifices of fifteen years had been nullified in the early morning hours
of March 2.

Sao remembered that he had recognized serious problems in the
Union of Burma as soon as he had returned from the United States with his
degree and his firsthand knowledge of a working democracy. It had been
obvious to him that the federated states of the Union had not been treated
equally with Burma proper. The latter had begun to prosper, with new fac-
tories, large construction projects, and social programs, but the states had
not even received their due share of budget allocations. Sao had been con-

vinced all along that redress for these inequities should be sought in Parliament; the federated states could certainly count on their constitutional guarantees. What a fool he had been! Having been locked up for three days without cause indicated clearly what General Ne Win and his revolutionary council thought of the country's Constitution—that it was a superfluous piece of paper to be discarded. Ne Win had considered the states worthy recipients of one thing only, his army, which had spread like a cancer into all corners of the Union.

Things would have turned out differently if General Aung San, the founder of the Union of Burma and its army, had lived instead of falling victim to an assassin's bullet. Sao had trusted him, and so had many other Shan, Kachin, and Kayah leaders. It was the main reason they had agreed to join Burma proper to form the Union, with the right to secede after ten years.

Soon after Ne Win, a power-hungry upstart, assumed leadership of the army, its unscrupulous treatment of the hill people had started. Sao and his fellow rulers had been powerless to protect their people from the atrocities committed by the Burmese Army, who behaved like ruthless occupation forces rather than protectors of the land. Sao had been outraged when the buhengs of Namlan, Mongku, and Kalagwe reported looting, rapes, and murders committed by the military. Once when he had been prospecting near Namlan, Sao had arrived at the site of a torched village where burned-out homes were still smoldering. He had abandoned his search for minerals in order to help the victims. Families had lost their possessions and feared for their men, who had been abducted as forced laborers. Sao felt horrified and frustrated to witness the aftermath of this unprovoked rampage by the military, knowing that he was unable to promise that such an outrage would never happen again. He remembered how he had demanded an investigation and the punishment of those responsible. But the commanders, from Ne Win on down, responded with arrogance and mockery. After all, they had the guns and the power. Nevertheless, Sao had firmly believed that the Constitution and the will of the people would eventually prevail.

Even now, looking down on his prisoner's clothing, Sao still held onto that conviction. He thought of Mahatma Gandhi and refused to abandon hope.

Having learned that most of his colleagues had also been imprisoned, he hoped to catch a glimpse of some familiar face when he was allowed outside his hut. But he did not see anyone who looked like a fellow prisoner. It was strange that not even his brother seemed to be in Ba Htoo Myo. They had seen each other at the Taunggyi military outpost shortly after Sao's arrest, but had been prevented from talking.

Sao was suspicious of his isolation and wished he had stayed in Rangoon, as originally planned, instead of going to Taunggyi; he would have been among all the others who had been taken prisoner. He wondered what the Burmese had in mind for him. He suspected that there was a reason for the lack of attention he had received from his jailers since their first attempt at questioning him. Sao knew he was powerless, at the mercy of a ruthless general and his men. He had never been in this position before, and he was surprised at how calm and fearless he had remained in the face of such adversity. There was little else he could do except wait for the next move by the men in uniform.

Sao had always thought and planned for the future. Now, however, it was too painful for him to anticipate the next day, the next week, the next month. He did not know if those days, weeks, and months would ever come. Sao turned his thoughts to the past, seeking strength and hope from memories. When he did not think of his wife and daughters, Sao thought back to his favorite projects.

Mining and farming were of equal importance to Sao. When he was in the United States, he had often wondered why he had decided to study mining engineering rather than attend an agricultural college. But since his return, he had been satisfied that he could pursue both interests, that he did not have to choose one or the other. Thusandi had frequently pointed out that he could only afford to be a farmer because he was not dependent on crops for their livelihood. Sao had to admit that so far his agricultural experiments had been financial disasters. However, he was convinced that the orange plantation would, one day, make up for all previous losses.

Sao thought of the pineapple plantation in Loikaw, which had been his favorite project three years ago. He had employed hundreds of people to clear away the jungle that covered two rolling hills near the village of Loikaw, three thousand feet above sea level. His workers had become quite skilled in removing huge tree stumps with tractors, and in preparing the red soil for plants, which had arrived in huge trucks from Maymyo. When the fields finally abounded with endless rows of pineapple seedlings, Sao was immensely pleased with his creation. He remembered the time when four hundred rice farmers had come to pay their respects to him. After a short ceremony in the East Haw, he had invited them to see his pineapple plantation, although it had been nearly impossible to arrange for the ten buses at such short notice. The rice farmers had stood amid the never-ending rows of pineapple plants, awestruck by the transformation of a formerly jungle-covered hillside.

"I must bring my children here," said one of the farmers to Sao. "They have to see this, so they can have a dream for the future."

Sao wanted to show his people what could be done. The problems that arose at the time of the harvest did not diminish his success in their eyes; nor did they discourage his agricultural experiments.

By the time the delicately sweet and juicy pineapples were ready for the markets of Mandalay and Rangoon, prices had dropped sharply, barely covering the cost of picking and transporting the delicious fruit. Sao had not foreseen such developments and immediately started planning a cannery for his pineapples, an obvious solution to the marketing problem. After closer scrutiny, he had to abandon this plan. His harvest produced enough fruit to keep a cannery busy for only three weeks of the year, and it was anybody's guess if and when local farmers would decide to grow pineapples and justify such an endeavor.

Sao had also experimented with other crops on the same piece of land, especially ginger and coffee. Both looked promising, and he was anxious to return to his plantations.

His main focus however, continued to be mining. Sao was pleased that years of preparation had brought his Tai Mining Company to the point where operations could begin. The Australian geologist whom he had hired had walked to the remotest corners of the state to examine the sites of promising ore deposits. Together they had decided that a vein of rich lead and silver ore in the Kalagwe area should be the first site for mining operations. The site was ready, so was the crew, and the equipment was on its way. Sao was desperate to be free again—free to mine, free to farm, and free to proceed with the salt plant that was almost operational when he had left Hsipaw two weeks ago.

SAO SMELLED SMOKE. AT FIRST
he wondered if his senses were playing tricks on him, taking him back to
the campfires that had burned all night when he had visited the mining
sites. But the smell of smoke became more intense, and he realized that
there was a major fire in the area. Sao had always rushed to the scene of
fires around Hsipaw to take command of fire-fighting activities. He recognized the smell of burning houses and pressed against the four walls in
turn, trying to catch a glimpse of the outside through the bamboo matting. He could not see any signs of the fire; his nose provided the only
information. It crossed his mind that the army camp might be burning.
He dared not hope for such good luck. Hearing no sirens and no excited
human voices, Sao assumed that another Shan village closeby must have
been torched by the Burmese military, perhaps as punishment for one civil
disobedience or another.

A wave of rage welled up in Sao as he remembered how Burmese soldiers had burned down several villages, two hundred homes in all, not far
from Hsipaw. They had surrounded the area and captured the villagers
fleeing the inferno, torturing all of them and killing many. Some of the
men who had lived had come to Sao to tell their story. The Burmese interrogators had suspected them of harboring an imaginary Shan rebel army
that, they claimed, Sao had been training and hiding in their district.
Finding nothing—no secret arms cache, no private army—the Burmese
still made the innocent civilian population pay with their lives and their
belongings. And then Ne Win's Tatmadaw (Burmese Army) denied that
this outrage ever happened. News of this and similar crimes did not spread
beyond the Shan states because the Burmese press was unwilling to arouse
the displeasure of its army, the rising power in the Union of Burma.

At approximately the same time, another incident brought about the
literal occupation of the area around the town of Hsipaw. Army units had
pitched camp and taken up positions at all strategic points: on both sides
of the Namtu bridge, at the train station, along the three roads leading
into town, and on Lookout Mountain. The Burmese Air Force arrived in
Hsipaw with a helicopter and six fighter planes. News about their mission
soon leaked out. They were searching for a small, unauthorized plane that

had supposedly landed north of the town, at the foot of the Palaung Hills. A Palaung villager had been returning home from picking tea and reported seeing the plane. He said he spent half a day trying to get into the locked cabin. The military, already nervous because of frequent flyovers of unidentified high-altitude aircraft, went on a high-powered airplane hunt. Their aircraft and ground forces searched for two days, using the Palaung tea leaf picker as a guide. When no plane and no clues materialized, the Palaung villager confessed that he had made up the story because he had been lazy and was returning home with an empty basket. To explain why he had not picked more tea leaves, he had fabricated the story about the mysterious airplane. An embarrassed military command put a seal of secrecy on the whole affair and on the fate of the hapless Palaung villager. He was never seen or heard from again.

A few weeks after that incident, the troops occupying strategic points around Hsipaw withdrew to their permanent outposts and garrisons. Sao presented every case of the army's brutality and aggression to the Shan State Council, which was the official government, since the ruling princes had surrendered their individual powers. And he was only one of sixty-six delegates, all of whom had similar stories to tell.

Sao cursed himself that he had been so blind to the steady progression toward military dictatorship. Had he been more realistic, a better judge of Ne Win's ambition, he would not be in prison. And his mind would not be tormented by fears for his wife and children. He was not afraid for himself—thoughts of torture and death no longer disturbed him. But when he allowed his mind to dwell on the possible fate of Thusandi and his daughters, Sao had to hold back his feelings of anguish and despair.

Fourteen

THUSANDI PACED THE FLOOR,
stopping whenever unusual sounds broke the silence. The scheduled plane
to Lashio had flown over Hsipaw on time, and she nurtured the dim hope
that somehow Sao would come home, even though she had not gone to the
airfield to see if he got off the plane. She realized it was unwise to entertain
hopes for Sao that could deliver him into the arms of enemies, who still
seemed to be searching for him.

A jeep drove up and stopped under the portico. Thusandi heard a
familiar voice call out to Kawlin, "Please tell the Mahadevi that we are
here to see her."

The local doctor, accompanied by his wife, had come on an unsolic-
ited house call. "Go and sterilize the syringes; boil them for at least ten
minutes," he ordered Kawlin in such a loud voice that it must have carried
to the guardhouse.

Then Dr. Khin Aung and his wife followed Thusandi to her bedroom
suite. "Can we talk here?" he asked.

"Yes, we can." Thusandi assured him. "Please tell me that you have
news of my husband," she pleaded as she motioned her unexpected guests
to sit down.

"I've come to tell you all I know, Mahadevi. I'm the only person outside of your household whom the military guards at your gate did not turn
away. We can't stay long and you must listen carefully. I don't know when I
can come back." Dr. Khin Aung sat at the edge of the chair, his hands
folded under his chin, his eyes fixed on her face with unmistakable concern.

"What is happening? Tell me what is going on," Thusandi pleaded. "Why is the Burmese Army looking for the prince? Why am I under house arrest?"

"You see, I was right," Dr. Khin Aung said, turning to his wife. "She really doesn't know what's going on."

Then he turned to Thusandi and said, "The army under General Ne Win overthrew the government of the Union of Burma early this morning. The entire leadership of the country has been arrested, and martial law has been declared."

"No, this can't be!" Thusandi jumped to her feet. "Are you sure, doctor?"

"Yes, Mahadevi, I'm absolutely sure. And I am very worried about you, us, and our country."

"What about my husband? What do you know about him?" She was still standing in front of the doctor, until his wife put her arms around Thusandi's shoulders and eased her back onto the sofa.

"He was not found in Rangoon when the military searched Jimmy Yang's house. We assume that he got away. You must be extremely careful now. The military is capable of anything, especially in these times of turmoil. Think of your children and all the people who depend on you. We'll try to come and see you whenever we can."

Moei waited outside with the syringes. She did not seem surprised that Dr. Khin Aung put them back in his bag, unused. She started to carry the doctor's bag to the jeep, but he urged Moei to stay with Thusandi and not leave her alone.

Thusandi was still sitting on the sofa, with her eyes fixed on a gecko on the ceiling; he was lying in wait for insects that managed to make it through the screens. Her thoughts were far away, trying somehow to connect with Sao, wherever he was at the moment. She instinctively knew that he was alive. She hoped he was free, and that maybe he was on his way to join the Shan rebels, the Noom Seuk Harn, whose leaders had tried to convince him to lead them. Sao had sent them away, more than once, refusing to accept that the only recourse the Shans had was secession from the Union of Burma and armed struggle to achieve it.

Thusandi knew she had to stay calm. She wished she had been a better student of the various meditation masters who had been their guests.

"Sao Mae, Sao Mae," she heard her daughters call for her as they returned from the little schoolhouse on the other side of the moat. The children—her best reason to stay calm—ran toward her and clutched her outstretched hands.

"Sao Mae, I want to go swimming," Mayari told her mother in Shan. Thusandi was relieved to hear her daughter insist. She was not capable of decisions herself. Splashing in the pool, designed by Sao for his family, was exactly what she needed to rid herself of the tension and to pass time. The children were unconcerned by the day's events. Mayari took no notice of the fact that the guards at the gate wore different uniforms. And both girls were used to their father being away for weeks on end, attending meeting after meeting in Rangoon and Taunggyi.

When her daughters were asleep on their father's side of the bed, Thusandi thought about the warnings that had been given by the country's astrologers for February, the previous month. They had predicted the worst possible conjunction of planets, a dangerous phenomenon and one that had not been seen since 3000 B.C. To avert disasters of major proportions, people everywhere in the country had banded together to pray. When February ended peacefully, everyone heaved a sigh of relief, their faith in the power of prayers affirmed.

Only two weeks earlier, the Yunnanese community of Kyaukme, which represented the commercial center of Hsipaw State, had brought their New Year's parade to the East Haw, for the first time ever. They too had been worried about the disastrous predictions for the year ahead. The Chinese dragon (brought to life by fourteen boys) and many aquatic creatures (danced by little girls) had performed on the front lawn, determined to change the course of the planets and frighten away the evil spirits. Spellbound, they had watched the dance of the fierce dragon as he followed a winding pattern around his own red body, continuously chasing a globe that swirled before his angry face. The children had not been able to take their eyes off a magical shell; when it opened, a beautiful girl with lights in her hair emerged, only to be attacked by a stork. She withdrew to safety in her shell just in time to avert harm from the stork's evil beak. Thusandi herself wished for a shell to protect her and her family from danger. For the first time since her arrival in Hsipaw, she began to long for the personal safety of her life in the West. Exhaustion and the rhythmic breathing of her children finally brought sleep.

THE NEXT MORNING, THUSANDI awoke hoping that the events of the previous day had been a bad dream. But the nightmare continued. She was still upstairs when Kawlin came and said, "Sao Mae, the lieutenant and his orderly have come to disconnect the telephone and take it away."

"Don't even try to argue with him. I'll take this matter up with the colonel," Thusandi said calmly, although she was becoming increasingly alarmed. Yes, they were turning the East Haw into a prison.

A little later, Mehta, the cook, returned from the bazaar on his bicycle. Burmese soldiers at the gate searched him, his basket, even his little daughter who had gone along for the ride. Then he had to sign a roster, as did everybody who left or entered the East Haw.

The postman had to surrender all mail—and there was always plenty—to the military gatekeepers, who passed it on to their superiors. When Thusandi tested the system by sending Kawlin to the post office with a letter, it was taken from him at the gate. The letter from Sao that she so desperately hoped for would not get through. She kept telling herself he would find a way, a messenger.

Thusandi called together the servants and the wives whose husbands had been arrested. "As you know," she said to them, "things changed yesterday. The Burmese Army has taken over, the prince is not here, and I am under house arrest. If you stay with me, you may be harassed by soldiers, and your friends may be afraid to come and see you. You have served us well, but you are free to go. I release any and all of you who wish to leave and find other employment. Those of you whose husbands have been arrested will receive their salaries regardless of where you live."

After her statement, there was silence. Then Kawlin spoke up. "I am staying with you, Sao Mae."

"Have you considered that you also may be arrested if you stay?" Thusandi asked him.

"I am not afraid of them," was his terse response. Then Moei spoke up, then Nai Nai, then Mehta, then Ai Tseng, the gardeners, Pa Saw, and all the others, saying they wished to stay. Bukong's wife told Thusandi they wished to pay their respects to her and were prepared to place their well-being into her hands.

Thusandi was touched and encouraged by this loyalty, but she also felt the added weight of responsibility that was now all her own. She was glad she had decided to keep enough cash in the East Haw to run the household for a year if need be.

After they filed out, she was left alone to wait—to wait for visitors, for mail, for news from Sao. The clock seemed to stand still, and nothing came.

Next day, there were visitors again, but they were not welcome ones. Another contingent of Burmese soldiers embarked on a frantic search of the chapel, the pump house, the cement walkways, and the swimming pool. All they found was one bullet from World War II, which was dislodged from the chapel roof.

After four never-ending days of uncertainty and worry, Thusandi decided that she could wait no longer. With both children in school for a few hours, she could drive away and not alarm them by her absence. When they were at home, the girls did not leave their mother out of sight for any length of time without getting panicky. For the first time since the driver was arrested, Thusandi went and got the Mercedes out of the garage. Then she asked Moei to accompany her to see the commanding colonel in Kyaukme, twenty-four miles away.

"But, Sao Mae, you are not allowed to leave the Haw," Moei pointed out.

"I don't care! I must go and find out where the prince is," she said to her maid. "And how are they going to stop me at the gate?"

"They might shoot," Moei replied.

"We'll just have to see, won't we. You don't have to come with me, Moei. I can go alone."

"I am not afraid for myself—I fear for you," Moei said.

"Then, let's go!" Thusandi said before Kawlin and Nai Nai had a chance to come up with serious objections.

Thusandi drove the heavy black car and insisted that Moei sit in the back seat, at a distance from her. She drove toward the open gate, guarded by six armed soldiers, and stopped there.

The sergeant in charge rushed to the car window and said, "I have orders not to let you leave the East Haw compound."

"And I am going to see Colonel Tun Oung in Kyaukme and talk to him about that," Thusandi answered.

"I have my orders. If you continue, I will have to shoot," the sergeant shouted.

"Okay, go ahead and shoot!" Thusandi shouted back as she stepped on the gas pedal and drove past the dumbfounded soldiers.

They did not shoot.

The twenty-four miles to Kyaukme seemed endless. On the first leg of the trip, Thusandi and Moei did not say a word to each other. As they drove through the jungle, they were on the lookout for dacoits, for Burmese soldiers, for Shan rebels, for anything. But they saw only an occasional bullock cart, a few buses, some jungle fowl, and a big swarm of vultures devouring something that had been run over. Thusandi's mind was on the meeting with the colonel, to whom she had given a piece of her mind when he led the first search of the East Haw. Her mind raced as she worried about whether she would succeed in seeing him, about the risk she was taking.

Moei broke the silence. "Sao Mae, please turn back, I beg you."

"Why? Are you sick?" Thusandi, startled, slowed down and turned her head to look at Moei.

"No, but I am so afraid."

"Afraid of what, Moei?"

"They might shoot us, Sao Mae."

"I doubt that. The guards at the gate had a good reason, and they decided not to fire." Thusandi tried hard to sound convincing. As they came closer to Kyaukme, she herself became increasingly concerned and doubtful that she was doing the right thing. The fearful plea from Moei added to her own nagging doubts. But she could not turn around now. She simply had to carry out her plan—if necessary, alone.

"I am going to see the colonel," Thusandi said, "but you can wait for me at the teashop in the next village."

"No, Sao Mae, I want to stay with you. But I wish you would turn around. I am so afraid for you." Moei took her prayer beads from around her neck and settled down to recite her prayers.

They approached the garrison, which was located at the junction of the main road to Mandalay and the turnoff to Kyaukme. When Thusandi pulled up to its gate, the guards seemed to be expecting her. They explained politely how to proceed to the colonel's headquarters. While she concentrated on finding the right building, Moei had a chance to look around.

"Sao Mae," she shouted, "look to your right!"

"What is it?" Thusandi asked as she slowed down even more.

"It's our men—Zinna, Bukong, Sang Aye."

"Where?"

"There—along the side of the building. They're working."

Thusandi saw them. They were clearing the ground around the wooden barracks while armed guards watched them closely. Thusandi was tempted to speak to her employees, but she decided against it. They did not need any further complications. However, she did not reckon with Moei, who rolled down the window and shouted her brother's name— "Zinna!" The two armed guards swung around and pointed their guns at Moei and the car; the Shan prisoners kept working as if they had not heard or seen anything.

"Quiet, Moei!" Thusandi said sternly as she continued the slow drive. "One more word out of you and we could all get shot, including your brother and the other men." It occurred to her that these guards looked more threatening than the ones posted outside the East Haw.

Colonel Tun Oung, a tall and slender dark-complexioned Burmese, did not seem surprised to see his visitors. An adjutant showed Thusandi and Moei into his office, where the colonel got up from his desk, stretched out his hand, and greeted Thusandi. After motioning to the adjutant to leave, he addressed her, almost jovially. "What can I do for you, Mahadevi?"

She did not answer immediately, and the colonel continued speaking in Burmese. "Please have a seat, and then tell me what brings you here."

Thusandi sat down and made sure that Moei was next to her, even though sitting on a chair beside her mistress made Moei very uncomfortable.

"Why are your officers in Hsipaw treating me so badly?" Thusandi was direct. She did not make the slightest attempt to skirt the issue, which would have been the Burmese way of handling such matters.

"They are not treating you badly," the colonel said with emphasis. "We are only trying to protect you, on the orders of our superiors."

"I see," she said. "You and your superiors put us under house arrest, take away our phone, confiscate our mail, arrest some servants and intimidate the others. And that you call protection?"

The colonel looked uncomfortable but said nothing.

"What exactly is it that you are protecting us from, Colonel?" Thusandi continued.

The colonel was not prepared for such directness. It was simply not the way women in Burma were supposed to interact with the authorities. They were expected to be meek, helpless, and tearful, not confrontational and defying.

"You are a foreigner," he finally said, "and foreigners are not good for our country."

"I see," Thusandi said. "If that is the problem, then I insist on making immediate contact with the Austrian ambassador."

That suggestion did not seem to please the colonel.

"Look," he said, "our troops exchanged gunfire with one hundred fifty Shan rebels ten miles from the East Haw yesterday. And I am responsible for your safety."

"Frankly, I think I'd be a lot safer if your soldiers would keep away from us. Don't you?"

Thusandi sensed that the colonel was somewhat sympathetic to her. He did not play the role of the Burmese Army's tough advocate very convincingly.

An uncomfortable silence settled in until Thusandi spoke again, in a softer, more conciliatory tone. "Bohmugyi, I have two small children to consider before I do anything foolish."

She waited to let him reflect on this statement and on her change of attitude. Then she practically pleaded with him. "Please, Bohmugyi, let me move around town freely, give me the phone back, and let me have my mail. I promise I won't cause any trouble."

The colonel seemed to think about her suggestion—a good sign, Thusandi thought. He scratched his head and looked out the window. Then, he said what she hoped to hear. "Your phone will be returned to you tomorrow. And you can leave the East Haw for short errands around town. But you must inform the soldiers at the gate where you are going. I can't make any promises about your mail. We'll have to wait and see."

"Thank you, Bohmugyi, thank you very much." Thusandi said, smiling for the first time since she had entered the office.

"I do have one more question though."

"All right, go ahead."

"Where is my husband?"

The colonel didn't hesitate to answer. "I assume he is where all the others are, in protective custody. I've heard nothing to the contrary."

Thusandi was careful not to show her surprise and disappointment at his answer. "I would like to know more, Colonel. Where and how is he and when can I see him? I am worried about my husband—he needs medication and special diet." Thusandi no longer sounded cool and collected. She stopped and took a deep breath.

"I can assure you, Mahadevi, that our army will treat all who are in protective custody very well. We'll let you know when and where you can visit your husband and when you can send supplies to him." The colonel got up and indicated that their meeting was over.

Thusandi thanked him as he walked her to the car. When she drove away, she saw him in the rearview mirror as he stood in front of his office, watching the black Mercedes speed away.

THE NEXT DAY BROUGHT results. The lieutenant and his orderly returned the phone, mumbling something about having checked the license for it. Of course, there was no such thing as a phone license. A few hours later, he returned with two letters that must have arrived a few days previously. One was from Thusandi's mother in Austria, the other from a friend in Colorado. Since they were in German and English, the lieutenant requested that Thusandi translate them into Burmese for him. She did so orally as the little lieutenant stood listening intently to what a mother had to say to her daughter, and what one college friend said to another. Thusandi kept a straight face; she was grateful for little favors and handed the letters back to the diligent officer when she had finished. Maybe she would gradually get to see more of her mail, which was now her only link to the outside world.

Thusandi finally received newspapers, the English-language *Nation* and the Burmese *Myanmar Alin.* There she saw long lists of the country's leaders who had been taken into protective custody: Prime Minister U

Nu and his entire cabinet, the Supreme Court justices, the president of the Union of Burma, who was a Karen, members of Parliament, most Shan princes, and many other Shan and Kayah leaders. But Sao's name was not on any of the lists, at least not yet.

In the evening, her sister-in-law, the wife of Sao Khun Long, arrived unexpectedly from Taunggyi. Nang Lao passed the gatekeepers without problems. She had come to see her mother, who lived in Hsipaw town and had fallen gravely ill. For Thusandi, the moment had finally come when she could find out firsthand what had happened to Sao.

Nang Lao whispered to Thusandi that Sao had been arrested by the Eastern Command in Taunggyi, but the two women had to wait for the children to be in bed until they could talk freely. On the terrace, at last, Nang Lao recounted the events of March 2 in Taunggyi. After listening to the detailed account of Sao's arrest by Burmese Army officers at Taunggyi Gate, Thusandi could no longer cling to her hopes that somehow he had gotten away. She found little consolation in knowing that he was being held in Ba Htoo Myo in the southern Shan state of Lawksawk, at the site of the Burmese military academy.

"Do you know if the brothers saw each other after they were arrested?" she asked Nang Lao.

"Yes they did, at the military outpost by the gate. Several people who were questioned and later released saw them there."

"At least they're together now." Thusandi tried to find something encouraging about this horrible news.

"No, they aren't. My husband was taken to Aungban, not to Ba Htoo Myo," Nang Lao responded.

Thusandi's heart began to pound when she imagined Sao alone, without his luggage, in an army prison. What an outrage, a terrible injustice.

Nang Lao showed Thusandi a newspaper report about Sao Khun Long's arrest. "It is strange that Sao Kya Seng's arrest wasn't reported anywhere," she said wistfully. Thusandi did not comment. She felt alarmed, as if something was terribly wrong.

Thusandi did not sleep much that night; she had to regroup her thoughts, curtail her imagination, and look at her situation realistically. Sao was not free; he had not escaped to Thailand through the jungle. And he was not going to send her instructions as to what to do and where to go. Her sister-in-law had suggested that Thusandi take the children to Taunggyi and stay with her until they both would be permitted to see their husbands in the nearby army prisons.

Nang Lao left the next morning to spend a few days with her mother. Thusandi had a very strong feeling that she should wait at home for something or someone.

That someone materialized a few days later. Kawlin announced that the new captain in charge of the Hsipaw army outpost had come to see her. Thusandi did not expect this to be a pleasant encounter; most likely another house search, she thought to herself. But when she saw the captain waiting for her in the private study, she immediately noticed some things of significance. First, the captain was alone, without an orderly at his side. Second, he was not Burmese—his features were Kachin: long nose, large eyes, and pronounced cheekbones.

"You want to see me," she said cautiously.

"Yes, madam," he answered. "I am the new commander here, and I want to introduce myself." He spoke Burmese with an accent, she noticed.

"Thank you, I appreciate that," she said, wondering what his motives were.

"I am sorry for what's been happening to you," he said awkwardly.

Thusandi was surprised but decided not to respond. She sensed a certain compassion and sincerity from this unexpected source. The Kachins were known to be the best soldiers in the Burmese army, and they had been originally trained by the British. But they were hill people with closer ties to the Shans than to the Burmese. Their allegiance had not yet been tested.

"I would like to help you, madam," he said, handing her two letters that had been opened and stamped as censored. "I came across these letters among your mail and decided to bring them to you before anybody else saw them."

Thusandi felt shivers going down her spine when she took the two envelopes, which had Burmese stamps on them. She did not recognize the handwriting on the envelopes, but she knew they were from her husband. She pulled out the first letter—it wasn't really a letter, just a small piece of paper from a pocket calendar—and read Sao's words: "Liebling, I am . . . in the army lockup at Ba Htoo Myo. . . . I am still OK." The note bore the date of the military takeover. Nervously, she pulled out a larger piece of paper from the second envelope and read Sao's letter, which gave her more details about his arrest and some suggestions as to whom she should contact to get him out. He obviously did not know that there had been a coup d'état.

Her hands were shaking when she asked, "Why are you giving me these letters, Captain?"

"They are meant for you, and they may become very important. Don't tell anyone right now. And I suggest you keep them in a safe place."

"How can I ever thank you, Captain?" Thusandi was close to tears, but she owed it to this valiant officer not to let anyone suspect their secret.

"You need not thank me," he said modestly. "I had to do it. I am so sorry for you, for the prince, and for the country."

Then the captain quietly left the study and drove away in his jeep. He returned a few days later, again alone, and told Thusandi that Sao was still all right, still at Ba Htoo Myo. She never saw the captain again. He was reassigned to another area a week later.

Fifteen

❖ ❖ ❖ ❖ ❖ ❖ ❖ ❖ ❖ ❖ ❖

AFTER LEARNING FROM HER
sister-in-law of Sao's arrest, Thusandi phoned Colonel Tun Oung and
requested permission to send clothing and correspondence to her husband;
the colonel offered to forward them for her. Thusandi wanted the Burmese
Army publicly to accept responsibility for holding her husband captive, so
she considered the colonel's offer to be a good sign. She carefully packed a
box, not too big, not too small, with clothing, toilet articles, medication,
and writing paper, and wrote an open letter to Sao with family news and
words of encouragement. Then she drove again to Kyaukme, with Moei,
and delivered these items by hand to the colonel. After an almost cordial
reception and reassurances from the colonel, Thusandi felt confident that
she would soon receive mail from Sao through official channels.

Instead, complications of another nature arose. Agricultural machinery, mining equipment, and supplies for the salt project arrived in
Kyaukme and needed to be processed. Thusandi asked the equipment
manager of the Tai Mining Company to handle the arrangements. When
he arrived in Kyaukme, however, he was arrested and the shipments were
confiscated.

On the same day, two American friends on their honeymoon called
from Mandalay, saying that they were on their way to Hsipaw for a prear-
ranged visit. No sooner had they completed their call than the Military
Intelligence Service (MIS) lieutenant arrived on the doorstep, denouncing
Thusandi's contact with foreigners. He made it clear that the visitors
would not be allowed to proceed to Hsipaw. Two days later, the army-con-
trolled newspapers printed an article claiming that two NATO agents had
been stopped from meeting with the Mahadevi of Hsipaw.

Thusandi often lay awake, listening to the chimes of the clocks at night and the temple bells of the nearby monastery in the early mornings. Sometimes bursts of machinegun fire intruded on the soothing sounds of chimes and bells. Her imagination played tricks on her when she focused her eyes on the long shadows cast by the chilly light of the moon. She thought she saw spirits dancing toward her bed as messengers from another realm. During those seemingly endless nights, she was starting to lose hope that their family would ever be whole again.

But the morning sun would restore her confidence that a positive turn was just around the corner. She was desperate to establish contact with Sao—receive his mail, send him messages, and, above all, insist that the Burmese Army acknowledge responsibility for his arrest.

One Sunday morning, Nai Nai, one of the few Shans who had become a Baptist, returned from her church service with good news. "Sao Mae," she said to Thusandi, "my friend Grace told me that her husband has seen the prince in Ba Htoo Myo several times."

Thusandi dropped the newspaper she was reading and stared at her old nanny, who continued, "My friend Grace and her husband belong to the Karen people. He is an army captain, but his heart is not with the Burmese. I stayed with them in Rangoon years ago."

Thusandi motioned to Nai Nai to come closer. She glanced around the drawing room, assuring herself that nobody was nearby to overhear their conversation.

"Nai Nai, is your friend going back to her husband in Ba Htoo Myo soon?"

As Thusandi whispered this question, Nai Nai nodded with a knowing smile. She understood her mistress so well that she was ready for her request.

"She is taking the bus back tomorrow morning," Nai Nai said.

"Would you consider . . . ?" Thusandi did not have a chance to finish her eager question.

"I'll go with her," Nai Nai said assuredly, as if her decision had already been made.

"Oh, Nai Nai, will you really do that for me?" Thusandi sat down on the floor, took the arthritic hands of her trusted, seventy-two-year-old nurse, and held onto them as if she would never let them go.

"Sao Mae, I have already talked to my friend. She says that nobody will question the visit of an old woman like me."

Thusandi jumped up as if she were going on the trip herself. But within moments, she sat next to Nai Nai on the floor again. "You will take a letter from me and see to it that he gets it."

"I promise. And I'll stay there until I can bring back firsthand information." Nai Nai sounded sure of herself.

"But are you strong enough, Nai Nai? This is going to be strenuous and not without danger," Thusandi said with concern. She thought of Nai Nai's fainting spell, which had alarmed them several months ago.

"Jesus will help me," was the answer of her devout nurse.

Early the next morning, Nai Nai left the East Haw, officially to visit some of her relatives in Lashio.

After a week, Thusandi began to anticipate Nai Nai's return with ever-increasing anxiety. Every time some army officers came to the East Haw, she feared that Nai Nai's secret mission had been uncovered. She was relieved when they only wanted to get her signature on another statement, do another search, or question her about something she had said or done to their displeasure.

When Sao heard the clicking of heels outside his bamboo prison, he knew that somebody important had finally come to see him. He half expected Colonel Maung Shwe, in charge of the army's Eastern Command, because he had refused to answer to the lower-ranking officers in their attempts to speak to him. Sao got up from his mat, determined to meet his interrogator eye-to-eye. When the door was flung open, Sao recognized the pudgy, mustachioed face of Colonel Lwin, the despised head of Military Intelligence. No doubt he had been sent by Ne Win, his master, to whom he was known to be absolutely devoted. Despite being a prisoner, Sao did not act like one; he stood regally, measuring the stocky man in uniform from head to toe without saying a word. The colonel looking uncomfortable, dismissed his armed followers, and closed the door. It seemed that he did not want witnesses to the impending conversation.

Trying to sound cordial, the colonel began by addressing Sao with his Burmese title. "Sawbwagyi, I've come to offer you your freedom as part of a deal. The supreme commander and I have a proposal that'll benefit us all. Should we sit down?"

"I'll stand," Sao said icily, folding his arms and looking squarely at the man who was reputed to be ruthless, cruel, and dishonest.

"Sawbwagyi, it'll be in your interest to cooperate with us." The colonel's tone became noticeably cooler. He paused long enough to give Sao a chance to reply.

Sao said nothing.

"Well, I'll just come directly to the point. I expect that'll make you more responsive." The man whom the Shans referred to as "Ai Noot," or "mustachioed adolescent," became sarcastic. "The Revolutionary Council can try you for treason . . . or you can join our cause."

This statement sounded so absurd to Sao that he looked at the colonel in utter amazement. He did not even feel angry, nor was he the least bit afraid.

"You can't possibly be serious," Sao said.

"Yes, I am very serious."

"Your Revolutionary Council can charge me with anything they want. But no court is going to convict an innocent man."

"They're our courts now. They do what we say," the colonel snapped back. "And we know a lot about you."

"Like what?"

"You've been financing the Shan insurgents, you have secret dealings with SEATO, and you've been plotting the secession of the Shan states from the Union. You are a traitor."

"You know, Colonel," Sao said calmly, "I do wish I had done all of those things. Then I wouldn't have to stand here and listen to you now."

The colonel's face turned red, and he looked like he was ready to stomp out of the hut. He was obviously not used to prisoners talking back.

"Don't tempt us," he said to Sao in a controlled but threatening voice. "We can make life difficult for your wife and children, too."

This statement had a calculated effect on Sao, who had been dreading such a possibility from the moment he was arrested.

"So what's your deal?" he asked.

With a smirk on his face, the colonel pulled a sheet of paper from a folder and handed it to Sao. "All you need to do right now is sign this."

Sao took it and stepped toward the lightest corner of his hut. Adjusting his wire-frame glasses, he began to read what he was expected to sign.

"No," Sao said, returning the paper to Colonel Lwin, "I can never agree to that—never in a million years."

"In that case, I'll give you some time to think about the consequences. And I'll be back." Without warning, the colonel lunged toward
Sao, grabbed his glasses, and pulled them abruptly from his face. "You
won't need these until I return."

THUSANDI SAW THE FRIGHTENING
headlines in many Burmese-language newspapers: "Prince of Hsipaw was
never arrested by the Burmese Armed Forces—his whereabouts are
unknown." As she read and reread the malicious articles, her hands were
shaking and her teeth began to chatter. It was what she had feared the
most—that General Ne Win and his MIS chief, Colonel Lwin, would
play another dishonest game. If they did not admit to having arrested
Sao, they would not have to account for him. Thusandi swept up all
newspaper articles and headed straight for Colonel Tun Oung's office
once more. She almost forgot to take along Moei, her constant companion.

"What is the meaning of these lies about my husband, Colonel?" she
said as she shoved the newspaper articles under his nose.

As he looked at the headlines, the colonel acted surprised. "You
know, newspapers print all sorts of things," he said cautiously.

"We both know, Colonel, that the newspapers print only what this
military government permits." Thusandi became more agitated and continued without sitting down. "You know as well as I that Sao Kya Seng
was arrested in Taunggyi on the day of the military takeover. These lies
must be repudiated immediately."

The colonel's response was unexpected. "I agree with you," he said. "I
suggest that you write a letter stating the true events. Send it to me, by
messenger, and I'll see to it that the newspapers get your letter."

Thusandi scrutinized his face for overt signs of insincerity but could
not detect any. She slowly folded the newspapers and put them under
her arm.

"Okay, I'll try that. But if I see no results within two weeks, I'll find
another way to inform the public." With that she turned around and
walked out of the colonel's office.

FOURTEEN DAYS AFTER SHE LEFT, Nai Nai returned to the East Haw in a pedicab.

Thusandi rushed Nai Nai into her bedroom suite, where they could talk freely. Her heart was pounding, and the palms of her hands were wet with perspiration.

"Did you see him?" she asked tersely.

"I'm sorry, no. But he is still there, in Ba Htoo Myo. At least, he was when I left." Nai Nai pulled a letter out from the bodice underneath her aingyi.

Thusandi's face lit up in anticipation until she recognized the hand-writing on the letter—it was hers.

"Why did you bring the letter back?" she asked dejectedly.

"The captain did not dare keep it. He saw no way of getting it past the MIS guards."

"Nai Nai, please tell me anything, anything at all about him," Thusandi pleaded.

"I don't know, Sao Mae." She paused, folding her hands, her eyes downcast.

"What don't you know?" Thusandi was growing increasingly alarmed.

"I don't know if our lord will ever come back."

"Why are you saying a thing like that to me, Nai Nai?" Thusandi said, raising her voice in fear and desperation.

"The first week I was there, the Karen captain kept saying that he would find a way to get me close to the bamboo hut where the prince was confined. Every day he promised that I would soon get to see the prince when he was outside for his daily exercise. So I waited. Then, suddenly, on the ninth day, the captain came to his quarters during the day and told me, 'Nai Nai, please pack your bags and leave immediately. Something terrible has happened. Forget what I told you, and don't ask any more questions about the Prince of Hsipaw.' I couldn't get another word out of him, but I knew that I had to respect his wishes."

Thusandi did not look at Nai Nai. She stretched her head backward and stared at the ceiling.

"What do you think he tried to tell you, Nai Nai?"

"Oh God, I wish I knew, but I don't. The night after I left Ba Htoo Myo, I had a strange dream about the prince. I saw him riding on a cloud up into the sky, waving sadly at the children and me as we watched him rise toward heaven."

Neither one of the two women said any more. They sat quietly, each deep in her own thoughts, until the children came storming up the stairs to demand their time with Nai Nai.

SAO WAS ALONE AGAIN AFTER Colonel Lwin left with his glasses and the paper he refused to sign. Sao missed his glasses, even though he had nothing to look at or read. He could not remember ever being without them except when he was asleep. He felt incomplete, disoriented; but wasn't that exactly what the colonel had hoped to achieve? Sao expected it to be only the beginning of more serious harassment, especially since he would never acquiesce to their demands. He had had hours to think without interruptions. The evening meal had not been delivered to him; it was the first time that his jailers withheld food.

But Sao was not hungry. After refusing food on the first day in captivity, he had forced a few bites of rice down his throat at each of the two meals that had been brought to him daily. He still felt physically strong, but he was losing weight rapidly. Possibly this was due to dehydration, he thought. Sao avoided drinking the unboiled, unfiltered water that was left for him in an earthenware jug, and the small kettle of tea he was given once a day did not last long.

He wondered how long it would be before Colonel Lwin returned for another confrontation and what would happen when Ne Win and his clique realized that he would never cooperate with them. Sao wished fervently that he could somehow protect his wife and children, yet to compromise his principles was not an option. His enemies could not really expect him to become their stooge, to act as the Burmese Army's spokesman and bring his Shan people into their camp. Ne Win was surely not so desperate or stupid as to believe that Sao would ever consider such a betrayal. No matter what the consequences, he could not sacrifice his principles. Sao found comfort in his Buddhist belief that each individual's life was shaped by its own karma; that his wife and children's future would be determined by their previous deeds, not by the decision he made. Even if he went against his principles, he could not help them; he would only accumulate negative karma for himself.

Sao dozed off when the cool, moonless night descended upon his hut. He was exhausted from his ordeal and from the heat of the day, which was compounded by the tin roof and the lack of moving air around him. He had learned to welcome the nights, when, though alone, he felt a strong spiritual connection with those he loved, with the caring world beyond his bamboo bars.

The sound of numerous boots approaching and the beams of powerful flashlights woke Sao abruptly. Colonel Lwin had decided to return under the cloak of darkness. Ne Win's henchman swept into the hut. A captain and four heavily armed soldiers pointed their automatic weapons at Sao. This time the colonel ordered them to stay. Sao backed up against the wall as two soldiers pointed their powerful flashlights directly at his face. Blinded by the strong light, Sao closed his eyes and leaned against the flimsy wall for balance. "So, what's your decision?" Colonel Lwin asked tersely.

"I haven't changed my mind. I won't be used by you."

"How unfortunate. Aren't you concerned about your fate? And that of your wife and daughters?" The colonel came so close to Sao that he had to turn to the side to avoid inhaling his adversary's hot, agitated breath.

Sao did not respond, and that made Colonel Lwin furious.

"I demand that you speak to me, you hear?" he shouted.

When Sao remained silent, the colonel whispered something to the lieutenant next to him. Then he turned around and left abruptly.

Sao was powerless to resist the next move by Colonel Lwin's men. With lightning speed they pushed Sao away from the wall, pulled his arms back, and handcuffed him.

"We have orders to take you to the colonel's office." The lieutenant led Sao outside, making sure that the other armed men stayed very close.

Sao saw no point in resisting, even though he was greatly alarmed. He expected the worst. Why else would they take him out at night, in handcuffs? He breathed deeply, appreciating the night air as it soothed the tightness in his chest. He put one foot in front of the other until they came to a wooden building, dark and seemingly abandoned for the night. When they reached the other side of the long building, Sao saw lights and heard voices. "Bring him in. Hurry."

The soldiers pushed Sao into an office where Colonel Lwin was awaiting him, seated behind a heavy teak desk.

"Sorry about the restraints—regulations, you know." As the colonel made these remarks, the lieutenant removed the handcuffs from Sao. "Please sit down, Sawbwagyi, I have to ask you lots of questions."

Sao was somewhat relieved, yet tired, and accepted the offer. He took a seat across from the colonel and began rubbing his wrists.

"You were the secretary of the Association of Shan Princes, weren't you?"

"Yes, I still am."

"Did you negotiate with any foreign powers?"

"No."

"But you favored secession of the Shan states from the Union, didn't you?"

"I personally didn't, but the right of secession is guaranteed under the Constitution."

"Rubbish." The colonel's face turned red. "The Constitution isn't worth the paper it's written on. That's why our commander in chief has torn it to pieces. Spare me any mention of it."

"The people will fight for it, whether you like it or not."

"No they won't, if we eliminate troublemakers like you." Leaning forward in his chair, the colonel stared angrily at Sao.

"You can't scare me, Colonel. My conscience is clear and my cause is just."

"Wrong. You're to blame for the Shan rebellion and for the threat to the Union."

Sao got angry. "You know very well why our people are up in arms. It's because of you—your oppression, your lies."

"Thank you, you've just given me proof of your treason. But I'll give you one last chance. Join our side, help us defeat the insurgents, and you'll prosper with us."

"I'd rather die," Sao said defiantly.

Colonel Lwin jumped to his feet, and leaning across the table, he said in a low voice, "You just decided your fate." Then he turned to the lieutenant. "Take this prisoner to his new quarters. And take extra measures."

Sao was not only bound with handcuffs but also with leg-chains, before he was taken to a bare, tiny cell made of corrugated steel. The dirt floor stank of human excrement, and there was no way to get fresh air. Sao was overcome by nausea. He wondered how long he would have to endure these conditions. He suspected then that his situation would only deteriorate, that his fate was already sealed.

Sixteen

AFTER NAI NAI'S RETURN, IT DID
not take Thusandi long to decide that she wanted to move to Taunggyi
with the children. She would be able to stay with her sister-in-law, Nang
Lao, and contact Colonel Maung Shwe, in charge of the Eastern Command
headquarters. Moreover, Sao's sister was close to death and wanted to see
her and the children one more time. Thusandi wrote a letter to the Eastern
Command, with copies to Colonel Tun Oung and the captain in Hsipaw,
informing them that she was moving to Taunggyi within two weeks. Two
days later, the captain appeared in person with the army's response; she was
prohibited from leaving Hsipaw.

The Water Festival came and went, but the entire community lacked
the enthusiasm that had always characterized this occasion. For the children, though, it remained a joyous event. Mayari and Kennari surprised
their mother with bucketsful of water several times a day for the duration
of the festival. Groups of villagers came to pay their respects to their
Mahadevi, but the townspeople stayed away, save for some close friends
and relatives. The simple Shans from the villages were not afraid to record
their names at the gate and be questioned by military guards. They
expressed their sorrow and anger over the political situation. Their absolute faith in the safe return of their prince gave Thusandi renewed
strength.

She realized that the responsibility to make plans for the future
rested upon her shoulders. The burden of making decisions was a lonely
one; even the close relationship she had shared with her husband had not

prepared her for this. Thusandi spent hour upon hour on the balcony, looking at the green waters of the Namtu River flowing past the East Haw, unaware of what had happened to its residents. She missed Sao terribly, but she also longed for contact with people who considered themselves her equal and who would express their thoughts and opinions freely. Everybody around looked to her for decisions, moral support, financial help, and strength, and she did not think she could continue to provide all that without some support for herself.

People soon started to take advantage of that need. Men and women she had never seen before came to tell Thusandi that Sao had been sighted in various places: near Rangoon, in the Insein jail and at the army camp near Mingaladon airport, and in Mandalay. They could provide proof of these sightings, but that would, of course, require money. Thusandi grasped at every flicker of hope and sent well-funded messengers in all directions. Most of them never reappeared, sending ambiguous messages instead. Others came back reporting a near success and requesting more money.

When word spread of Thusandi's gullibility, astrologers and messengers of spirits joined in beating a path to Thusandi's receptive ear and open purse. She chose to believe what she wanted to hear: that Sao was alive, well looked after, and that he would be released soon.

But she also wrote to General Ne Win, to Colonel Lwin of the MIS, and to Colonel Maung Shwe of the Eastern Command, requesting permission to see her husband and to correspond with him. She also carefully checked the newspapers for the correct story about Sao's arrest, for which Colonel Tun Oung had assumed responsibility. When the story did not appear within a few weeks, Thusandi wrote a letter explaining the true circumstances of the arrest and, through messengers, sent copies to all major Burmese newspapers. Then she waited and hoped that at least one paper would have the courage to print the true story.

A week later, Kawlin came into the study, triumphantly holding up the newspaper *Myanmar Alin*.

"Sao Mae, they printed what you had sent them," he said, still out of breath after hurrying back on his bicycle.

"Let me see," she said, almost knocking over the chair as she jumped up.

Thusandi beamed as she read the front-page article, which gave the correct version of Sao's arrest in Taunggyi and quoted her as the source for the information. She was so happy and relieved that she wished she could have embraced Kawlin.

As Kawlin turned around to leave, he said, "Sao Mae, you should expect visitors in uniform any minute now."

He was absolutely right. Within ten minutes, a jeep drove up and came to a screeching halt under the portico. Kawlin, ready for this visit, rushed out to show the local army captain and the MIS lieutenant into the study. The latter held a newspaper in his hand. He had opened his mouth to address Thusandi when he caught sight of the *Myanmar Alin* on Thusandi's desk.

"Did you write that article?" the lieutenant shouted.

"Yes, I most certainly did."

"You were not allowed to do that." He became more agitated.

"Well, you left me no choice. You and your superiors didn't give the newspapers the correct version, so I had to." Thusandi stood calmly, with her arms folded, looking down on the lieutenant who was eight inches shorter than she was.

He came one step closer to her, and his face turned red. "You will pay for this," he yelled. "You are making things very difficult for us."

"What am I making difficult for you?" Thusandi challenged him, hiding her alarm.

The lieutenant did not reply. Instead, he glanced at the captain, who had not uttered a word. But the latter remained silent, obviously uncomfortable.

Finally, the officious lieutenant spoke again. "Yes, you have made things very difficult for us, and you will be punished."

But this threat did not have the desired impact on Thusandi. Instead of showing fear and remorse, she defied the little lieutenant.

"If you and your heroic commanding officers want to punish me for speaking the truth, so be it. I am not afraid of you." With that, she walked away from the two uniformed men, out of her study, and up the stairs to her private quarters.

Although Thusandi had not lost her composure in front of the officers, she was deeply concerned. She paced the floor of her bedroom suite at ever-increasing speed. She felt like running—running away from this nightmare, back to Austria or to Colorado, where she remembered feeling safe and protected. How much more could she bear? She thought that she would break under the mounting pressures.

Then Thusandi thought of what Sao had to endure, cut off from his loved ones, deprived of his freedom and of basic necessities. She simply could not do his tormentors the favor of breaking down. It occurred to her that she had not listened to music during all these days of misery. She stopped at the record player to select one of her favorite records, a gift from Sao. When the first notes of Mozart's Piano Concerto in F-major filled the air, she sat down, closed her eyes, and thought of the many times she had enjoyed this music with Sao at her side.

THE RAINS STARTED EARLY THAT year, and everything that was rooted in nature began to grow. Even dry fence posts awakened and established new roots, surprising villagers with an unintended hedge around their homes and gardens. Whenever the sun prevailed over the subtropical downpours, Thusandi took the children to the orange plantation across the Namtu River. The trees were laden with tangerines and oranges that grew bigger after every rain shower. Many branches could only bear their burden of fruit by bending to the ground; others broke before workers could put up support posts. If only Sao could see this bumper crop from his favorite agricultural project, Thusandi thought during each visit. She assured herself that he would most certainly be back to oversee the harvest in December.

Although Thusandi had sent letters and packages to Sao through all available channels, she had never received confirmation that any had reached him. As long as none of these mailings were returned to her, she wanted to believe that some of them must have found their way to him. That is, until the day when she was given a devastating letter from the office of Colonel Maung Shwe's Eastern Command. Thusandi was informed that the Burmese Army had never arrested Sao Kya Seng and that his whereabouts were unknown to the government of General Ne Win. Within days, many of her packages for Sao were returned to her as undeliverable by the local army captain. Thusandi sensed that great suffering lay ahead.

3/2/62

Liebling

I am writing this *secretly*.
I am being locked up in the army lockup at Lon Htoo myo at Taunggyi. Please ask Khin my Clerk to request Tommy Clift to use his influence to get me out. There is also Ko Hla Moe. Millie can help here. Miss y[ou] all. Conditions here are not clean. Hope to see you all again soon. Cheer up yourself!
I am still ok.

love

[signature]

A letter sent on March 2, 1962, by Sao Kya Seng, the Prince of Hsipaw, to Thusandi shortly after his arrest near Taunggyi, during a countrywide military coup.

To,

      Mrs Sao Kya Seng
      The East Haw
      Hsipaw N.S.S

Subject;-   Appeal to send Clothings and Letters.

Reference-   Your Letter dated the 1st August 1962.

        Sao Kya Seng, Sawbwa of Hsipaw have never been taken into custody by the Defence Service. Only Sao Kya Zone, brother of the Sawbwa was found in Taunggyi and detained by this Command. It is learnt that when the house of Sao Kya Zone was searched, Sawbwa of Hsipaw was absent.

                           Commander.

Rel. 25/8/62

Letter from the Burma Army's Eastern Command denying that Sao Kya Seng was ever arrested. It was in response to repeated letters and parcels of clothing sent by Thusandi to her husband through local military authorities.

When Dr. Khin Aung and his wife made one of their regular visits to Thusandi, they found her clutching one of the boxes that had been destined for her husband. Her eyes were red, swollen, and blank. Moei, who was by her side, got up and whispered into Dr. Khin Aung's ear, "We've tried everything to cheer her up, but nothing works. Please help."

The doctor nodded to Moei and walked to Thusandi's side, gently removing the box from her grasp. Bending over her, he spoke in a low and compelling voice. "Mahadevi, we must talk. Can we have a cup of tea on the verandah?"

She did not answer. However, she got up from her desk and followed the doctor as if she were in a trance. She did not even realize that she had not said a single word of welcome to her guests.

Only when they were seated on the verandah did she begin to speak. "What do I do now, doctor? They deny ever having arrested the prince. I fear the worst." Thusandi broke down in tears again, almost convulsing.

"We don't know why they are doing this, and we don't know what it means," Dr. Khin Aung said. "But I feel that you should try something different. Your present approach to General Ne Win and his men isn't working."

"What can you suggest?" she asked, between sobs that had become gradually lighter.

"You must have spent some time thinking about other options," Dr. Khin Aung said. "What do you feel you should do next?"

"I've been thinking about moving to Rangoon with the children. That way, I could approach the leaders of this military government personally."

"Excellent idea!" Dr. Khin Aung shouted. "I really think that is the best possible next step. It'll be good for you and the children to live in the city. You'll be less isolated there."

"Do you think they'll give us permission to move?" Thusandi sounded in control of her emotions again, weighing her options, willing to continue her struggle.

"I don't see how they could object," Dr. Khin Aung answered.

"I wasn't allowed to go to Taunggyi, remember," Thusandi said pensively.

"Perhaps because the prince is held nearby. But they won't stop you from going to Rangoon." Dr. Khin Aung sounded so convinced that Thusandi became a bit more hopeful.

"What if they do?" she asked him.

"Then we'll just have to insist that you need medical treatment only available there. And believe me, I do carry some clout when it comes to matters like that."

For the first time in days, Thusandi felt slight stirrings of hope again, hope that the door to freedom, shut for months, was finally inching open again, letting in a faint shimmer of light.

SAO COULDN'T SEE HIS WATCH, but the horrible night appeared endless. His mouth and throat were parched, and he longed for the unboiled, unfiltered water he had rejected in his bamboo hut. He sat on the dirt floor in a corner, thinking that his experimental livestock in Hsipaw was enjoying much better accommodations than he was. However, it didn't matter to him any more. Through meditation Sao had overcome his nausea, and he was concentrating on the dryness in his mouth. He had learned how his mind could control physical discomfort and mental anguish. Now he had to make that happen. And he did, until he found a few hours of merciful rest.

At the first crack of dawn, the MIS captain present at last night's interrogation came with a question. "The colonel wants to know if you have changed your mind."

Sao shook his head. He saw no reason to speak to him.

"Isn't there anything you wish to convey to the colonel?"

Again, Sao slowly shook his head.

It did not take the captain long to return. He came with a jeep, overloaded with five armed soldiers.

"I have instructions to transfer you to another place of detention," he said as he carefully pulled Sao up from the dirt floor. "I'm taking you in this jeep."

Sao shuffled out of his cell and lifted his head toward the eastern morning sky. Was this the last time he would see the sun rise over the Shan hills, he wondered? Then Sao turned toward the waiting jeep.

Seventeen

AFTER ELEVEN MONTHS OF
isolation in the East Haw, Thusandi was at last permitted to move to Rangoon with her children. It was a crisp January morning when she boarded the train at the Hsipaw station. Hundreds of well-wishers had assembled to bid her farewell and were invoking every guardian spirit's blessing for her journey. As Thusandi stepped into the railway carriage that was to take them away, she knew a chapter in her life had ended; she sensed that they were leaving their home in Hsipaw that morning, never to return. The premonition that had overcome her on Lookout Mountain some eight years ago had fulfilled itself: Peace was gone from the valley, and her happiness lay in the past. The engine's whistle cut into Thusandi's heart like a dagger, as it spelled out its shrill message for all to hear.

The rocking motion of the train had a soothing effect. It reminded Thusandi of the daily rides to high school in Austria, when her only concerns had been good grades and the weekend skiing. A couple of decades and many thousands of miles lay between those memories and the present reality. She closed her eyes, wondering if Sao could somehow sense that his family was leaving Hsipaw. Thusandi tried to suppress the recurring doubts that Sao was still alive. They had lately tormented her at night, when time stood still and shadows danced on the bedroom wall. She refused to let them torment her by daylight; Sao had to return to their lives.

The train ride to Mandalay, less than two hundred miles away, would take most of the day because of the many scheduled stops, the hilly terrain, and the Gokteik viaduct. Thusandi had seen the silvery marvel of engineering from the road, and today she would cross it for the first time. Sao had told her how his men protected the bridge, so important to the economy of the northern Shan states, from the Communist insurgents in 1947. He had planned to take Thusandi on a special train, one day, over the steel trestle railway bridge built by an American company for the British in 1899. After Naung Peng station, she started looking out for the gorge of Gokteik and the shiny steel structure connecting two rugged hills. As the train descended toward the gorge, there was no sign of the bridge. They passed through a chain of tunnels, short and dark. The children squealed with delight each time the compartment was enveloped by darkness. Although this was the dry season, the tunnels smelled musty, and an unexpected chill struck the passengers. When the train finally crossed the magnificent bridge, Thusandi stretched to see the river at the bottom of the gorge through the leaves of the dense jungle. Somehow the bridge, an engineering wonder, did not fit into this wild, undeveloped part of the world.

On the other side of the gorge, they stopped at Gokteik station, a heavily armed military outpost; then the train started climbing again. Thusandi savored every remaining moment in Hsipaw State. Twelve miles outside Maymyo, they reached the border of Burma proper.

The Railway Hotel in Mandalay provided a welcome stopping place for a bath and a change of clothing before Thusandi and her party boarded a night train to Rangoon.

"How long till we get to Rangoon?" Mayari asked as soon as they settled down in their first-class compartment.

"When you wake up in the morning, we'll almost be there."

"I'm not going to sleep," she said. "How many hours till we get there, Sao Mae?"

"I think sixteen," Thusandi said as she pulled her daughters close to her. "Imagine, one entire night on this train. And then, we'll be in Rangoon."

Thusandi turned her attention to the receding lights of Mandalay as the night express rumbled southward. No moonlight illuminated the dark night that had settled over central Burma. Now and then a flicker of light signaled that they were passing a village or a small town. She closed her eyes and thought of Sao, wondering about his physical and emotional condition. A faint smile spread over her face when she imagined how pleased he would be with her; she had left everything under her control in Hsipaw in best order. Household, staff, and dependent relatives were provided for, the school had enough funds to continue operations, and the citrus harvest was completed. By establishing the new orange plantation, Sao had, unknowingly, provided Thusandi with a source of income much needed at this time of upheaval. The unexpected bumper crop of several hundred tons of oranges and tangerines had helped Thusandi financially, since most of their assets had become inaccessible to her under the military government. She glanced at their suitcases on the luggage rack, amused that a few were stuffed full with cash and jewelry. For a while, at least, she would have no financial worries in Rangoon, where one of their two houses was ready for her arrival.

Thusandi was confident that she would adjust to life in the Burmese city, even though her Rangoon household would be modest by Hsipaw standards. What concerned her was the state of mind in which she found herself more and more frequently. Double vision made her see chairs with eight legs rather than four. She was unable to concentrate, and her memory was unreliable.

The children were sound asleep when the train made a lengthy stop in Pyinmana. Pa Saw, one of the nannies, returned with disconcerting news from the platform: During the past week, Karen insurgents had attacked several trains on the stretch ahead of them, causing heavy casualties.

After speeding through the night for another hour, the train stopped in the middle of nowhere. The station ahead of them was burning, and Thusandi nervously watched through the window as fires illuminated the sky. The northbound train had been attacked, and she feared they might be next; the lights of their railway carriages were an easy target for an ambush.

After two hours of uncertainty, the train started moving again and slowly passed the burned-out station and the damaged northbound train. Some people with emergency medical kits were attending to the injured passengers. Others waited for a relief train to take them north again, away from the scene of horror and bloodshed. Thusandi was powerless to help, as her train did not stop but picked up speed on its way south.

The dawn broke soon after they left the scene of civil war behind. As daylight flooded the compartment, Thusandi and Pa Saw looked at each other with relief and renewed confidence. The children and Tawng, the other nanny, had slept through the hours of uncertainty and fear, and woke up excitedly for the remainder of their first train journey from Hsipaw to Rangoon.

"WHY ISN'T PAPA HERE TO MEET us?" Kennari asked her mother when a group of friends greeted them at Rangoon's railway station.

Thusandi, bending down to her little daughter, said calmly, "Papa had to go on a trip again. But he'll join us at the new house when he gets back."

The house, off Ady Road, was a few miles away from the inner city, not far from Inya Lake, in a residential area popular with foreigners. The U.S. Embassy housing section was close-by, and so was General Ne Win's private residence. Thusandi and Sao's one-storied house was devoid of luxuries, but Thusandi knew that it would be adequate for the simple life she would lead until Sao returned.

The cars with several trusted Shan servants and the truck with household necessities arrived from Hsipaw late the same evening. Hla Tin, Sao's personal secretary and driver, who had been stuck in Rangoon since the coup, had done his best to prepare house and garden for them. Thusandi was grateful to find that Hla Tin was eager to continue working for her, and hoped that he would provide the secrets of how to survive in Rangoon. Hla Tin had had no choice but to stay in Rangoon; he was informed that he would be arrested as soon as he returned to Hsipaw for having been in the service of the prince. Thusandi wondered why the army did not arrest him in Rangoon. The MIS knew where to find him. They were probably too busy with thousands of important detainees and could not concern themselves with such little people.

In her new surroundings, Thusandi enjoyed the feeling of being inconspicuous, a luxury she had not known for a year. She hoped that this was an indication of more personal freedom for her, of the end of the de facto house arrest she had endured since the military takeover. The following day made her change her mind.

Early in the morning, Pa Saw knocked at the bedroom door to

inform Thusandi of two visitors in a jeep. She did not recognize the two young men in longyis and Burmese shirts who stood on her porch.

"What is it that you want?" she asked them in Burmese, looking them over rather suspiciously.

"We've been sent by the War Ministry to discuss your visit to Rangoon," the taller of the two men answered.

"First of all, I would like to see some identification," Thusandi said assertively, "and second, I am not visiting Rangoon. I've come to live here."

"That'll depend on your compliance with our restrictions for you," the man responded as he handed her his ID card. She inspected it carefully and decided that he was, indeed, an MIS officer by the name of Lieutenant Pe Win. She saw no reason to invite him into the house. Thusandi handed the ID card back, folded her arms, and said to him in a frosty tone, "I'm ready to hear what you have to say, but please understand that I am very busy."

Lieutenant Pe Win did not seem pleased with the chilly reception and responded in an equally cold manner. "You are here on probation, and if you don't comply with our rules, you'll be sent back to Hsipaw."

So much for the hope of being lost in a crowd, Thusandi thought to herself. She said, "What are your rules for me, Lieutenant?"

"You may not interact with any foreigners, and you must stay away from any large gatherings. And most of all, don't cause any trouble. We'll be watching you very closely." He abruptly turned and got into the jeep, next to the driver, who had already started the engine.

Thusandi shook her head and returned to her bedroom. She had not expected that they would catch up with her so soon. On the other hand, the lieutenant had said nothing about being confined to the house, nor had he mentioned the mail. Maybe his threats should not be taken too seriously.

Thusandi was surrounded by five of her trusted Shan servants and a local Indian gardener, but she felt safer on this hidden cul-de-sac than she had during the past eleven months in the East Haw. Their house looked like everybody else's in the neighborhood. She was not the only person with a Mercedes, and she and the children blended in with the crowds in the city streets and markets. People still turned their heads to look at the tall Caucasian woman who wore longyi and aingyi and a traditional Burmese hairstyle, but generally they did not recognize her as the Mahadevi of Hsipaw. She shopped for all the items necessary to make the house a temporary home. Every time they left the house and turned from their side street onto Ady Road, Hla Tin, the driver, pointed out to Thusandi that the same jeep began to follow them. There was no doubt that she was being watched closely.

Before the unpacking was done, a stream of visitors began to arrive, most of them Shan relatives, students, and Burmese friends who were not afraid to associate with Thusandi. A young man, conveniently positioned in the driveway, took careful notes on who came at what time and how long each visit lasted. Occasionally, he would go to the back door and ask one of the servants if he had the correct spelling of a specific visitor's name.

One evening, Mehta, the cook, tired from producing gallons of lime juice for the never-ending stream of visitors, announced to Thusandi that two "palefaces" were at the door, and he could not understand what they wanted. (People did not put her in the paleface category; she had long ago been adopted as one of their kind.)

"Okay, I'll go and see if I can help them," Thusandi said. She had only been in Rangoon for three days and did not expect that any foreigners would be looking for her. She was wrong. The couple, deposited at her doorstep by a taxi, turned out to be the Austrian ambassador to Burma and Mrs. Kolb. Thusandi had corresponded with him at the embassy in Karachi, which was also accredited to the Union of Burma.

"How did you ever find me?" asked an excited and dumbfounded Thusandi. She ushered her guests into the living room.

"We have our sources," he responded, "and we came directly from the airport."

"I simply can't believe that you are here."

"You are the main reason for our visit to Rangoon. We have been very worried about you."

"I am so glad to see you," Thusandi said. "I have so many questions."

"So do I," the ambassador responded.

They talked and talked, in German. The ambassador wanted to hear about everything that had happened since March 2, 1962—to Thusandi, to Sao, and to the country. He listened carefully and expressed relief that she had come through the ordeal intact, both physically and emotionally. After hours of listening to Thusandi's story, the ambassador shocked her when he said, "I urge you to leave for Austria, immediately, with the children, of course."

"I can't do that. I must try to obtain the release of my husband," she said emphatically.

The ambassador and Mrs. Kolb exchanged glances before he said, "I must tell you that your husband is not in the hands of the Burmese military government."

"That's ridiculous," Thusandi said heatedly. "You are buying this regime's big lie. He was arrested in Taunggyi and I have proof of it, in black and white."

The ambassador remained quiet for a while. Finally, mincing every word, he said, "Whatever happened, we don't know, but your husband is not in their custody anymore."

Thusandi immediately tried to convince the ambassador otherwise. She refused to consider the implications of his statement. Instead, she gave him many convincing reasons why Sao was alive and well, in the hands of his captors.

Ambassador and Mrs. Kolb finally left for the Strand Hotel, promising to return. They also assured her that their suite in the hotel would be a safe haven for her and the children should they require one.

As soon as the guests had left, the man from the driveway came pounding on the door.

"Who were those two foreigners who stayed for hours?" he demanded.

"It so happens that was His Excellency, the Ambassador of Austria, checking up on his citizens, who are virtual prisoners in this country," Thusandi shouted at him before she slammed the door shut.

Lying awake most of that night, Thusandi tried to convince herself why the ambassador's information about Sao was wrong. She had received convincing testimony from two informants that Sao had been seen recently: in solitary confinement in Insein Jail, separated from most other Shan princes who were kept there, and then in the army camp near Mingaladon airport. However, nobody had furnished any proof of these sightings. She desperately clung to the hope that he was alive, but she was tormented by doubts and a feeling of near panic.

Tomorrow, she would attempt to see General Ne Win himself to ask him for the same privilege that the wives of all other detainees had been granted: to correspond with her husband. According to reliable sources, the general had informed MIS chief Colonel Lwin that he would personally handle the case of the Prince and Mahadevi of Hsipaw.

SHE WAS ABOUT TO LEAVE WHEN U Khant, her trusted friend and brother of UN Secretary General U Thant, drove up in a jeep. With him was Bo Setkya, one of the historic Thirty Comrades of World War II, who at one time had been General Ne Win's military commander. He had left the armed forces years ago and established himself as a successful businessman. Thusandi was genuinely pleased to see him again; he and his wife, the actress Win Min Than, had been welcome visitors to the East Haw several years earlier. When Bo Setkya handed Thusandi a big bouquet of flowers, she was touched and surprised. Such a gesture was totally uncharacteristic for a Burmese man.

"How nice of you to visit," she said with a smile. "I wish I had more time to chat with you."

"Are you on your way out?" U Khant asked when she hesitated to invite them in.

"As a matter of fact, I am going to see General Ne Win," Thusandi said as if she did so every day.

"What for?" Bo Setkya asked. The tone of his voice left no doubt that he strongly disapproved of that idea.

"Because he is the one person in the country who holds my husband's fate in his hands. I must get to him."

"Wait, Mahadevi! Please hear me out before you do that," Bo Setkya said. He spoke with such authority that Thusandi decided to listen.

As soon as they were seated in the living room, Bo Setkya spoke. "I know Ne Win very well. Believe me, you must not confront him." He paused as if to make sure that his words were heard. "He is absolutely unpredictable, and I doubt very much that he will respond favorably to any request from you. When he gets irritated, Ne Win is capable of anything."

"What could he do to me?" Thusandi challenged Bo Setkya.

"Lots of terrible things, Mahadevi."

"I am not afraid of him or anybody," she said contemptuously.

"Who would look after your daughters if you were deported?" Bo Setkya didn't wait for her reply to this rhetorical question and continued, "And what would happen to your children if you had some kind of 'accident'? Those can be arranged easily, you know." He paused again.

"Then there are the children themselves." Bo Setkya left no doubt that he knew from experience what an angered Ne Win was capable of doing.

Thusandi had heard enough. Last July's massacre of hundreds, maybe thousands, of university students flashed through her mind. Ne Win had ordered his troops to shoot unarmed protesters and to take the dead and wounded to Rangoon University's Student Union. Then he had the building blown up with the dead and wounded inside. She knew several grieving mothers whose children vanished forever.

She shook her head, looked at Bo Setkya, and, supporting her chin with her clenched fists, said to him, "Say no more, please. I'll listen to you and wait."

"Good," Bo Setkya exclaimed, obviously relieved. "Promise me you'll only think of yourself and your children," he pleaded.

"Why, no! I must think of Sao first. He is suffering more than we are."

Bo Setkya had a deep voice and quite a presence. He leaned forward in his chair and looked at Thusandi with almost hypnotic power.

"I know that you are brave. That is why I have come to tell you what I know about the prince."

Thusandi lowered her eyes, fearing what he would say next. She remained silent and waited till Bo Setkya continued.

"I am sorry to tell you that the prince is no longer alive. He was killed near Ba Htoo Myo several weeks after he was arrested."

He paused, expecting some kind of reaction from Thusandi. But she looked as if she had gone within, unaware that he and U Khant were still there. They sat in silence for minutes until she calmly said, "No, this is simply not true. I know he is still alive. He was seen right here in Rangoon a few weeks ago."

"Whoever is telling you that is lying," Bo Setkya said forcefully. "I have many loyal followers in the army, and this information comes from one of them. Believe me, Mahadevi, I would not give you this news if I were not absolutely certain that it's true."

Thusandi turned to U Khant and asked him, "Do you believe that my husband is alive?"

"I'm sorry, I don't," was all he said.

Thusandi just sat there, calmly, and smiled as if they had talked about matters of no importance. Then she turned her head and looked out the window, at the velvety white gardenias blooming on her hedge.

"We should take our leave from you." Both men slowly got up and reluctantly left Thusandi.

Eighteen

❖ ❖ ❖ ❖ ❖ ❖ ❖ ❖ ❖ ❖ ❖

AFTER THE TALK WITH BO SETKYA,
Thusandi postponed her plans to visit General Ne Win. Instead, she wrote
him a letter in Burmese, requesting again the same privileges granted to
the wives of other detainees. She wrote six copies of the letter by hand and
sent them by various routes, hoping that at least one would reach its destination. Then she waited for a reply, a messenger, a phone call telling her
that she could see Sao or, at least, write to him. But her wait was in vain.

The time in Rangoon passed more quickly than it had in Hsipaw,
and life was more normal. Thusandi became friends with Elsebet, a Danish
neighbor, whose husband was in the country on a World Health Organiza-
tion assignment. The ever-present Burmese man in the driveway did not
pay any attention to these neighborly visits. He only wrote down names of
visitors arriving by car. Elsebet cheered up Thusandi and made her long for
the carefree friendships she had known before coming to Burma. The Scandinavian neighbor introduced her to other foreigners, who unequivocally
urged Thusandi to leave the country.

Her phone calls were monitored more carefully. Conversations in
Burmese and English met the approval of the censors, while those in Shan
and German were crudely interrupted with the statement "You must speak
a language we can understand."

Thusandi saw many Shan women living in Rangoon to be near their
imprisoned husbands, hoping for their release or for permission to visit
them. She also met with wives of Burmese leaders who were in the same
position.

Mabel was the English-born Mahadevi of Mongmit, wife of Sao

Hkun Hkio, the Prince of Mongmit, who was also head of the Shan State and foreign minister of the Union of Burma. Mabel had been living in England with their children until several months before the military take-over. Now she was stuck in a large house in Rangoon and was unable to leave, since the Burmese had confiscated her British passport. She was very outspoken and very angry, and most Shans and Burmese avoided her, fearful of the army. But Thusandi sought Mabel's company. At a time when everybody counseled her to lie low and not make waves, she wanted to be near this defiant and fearless Englishwoman. However, she decided against protesting with Mabel in front of the Ministry of Defense, carrying a poster demanding the release of all political prisoners. It was the only protest seen in Burma after the July student demonstrations had been put down so brutally. Thusandi wanted to have the army's acknowledgment that Sao was in their hands before joining any public demonstration.

THE AUSTRIAN AMBASSADOR AND Mrs. Kolb paid Thusandi another visit before returning to Karachi. Ambassador Kolb's first question was, "Have you decided to go back to Austria?"

"One day, maybe, but not now," Thusandi said determinedly.

"I can understand your hesitation, especially after what you told me. But I wish you would start making arrangements, even if you're not going back for some time."

"I suppose you have a point. But I must try to help Sao first."

The ambassador did not respond, but he and his wife exchanged worried glances.

Thusandi wasn't seriously considering such a step. She shuddered at the thought of returning to a cold climate and to the grayness of life in Austria. But once Sao was released, they might want to retreat to her former home for a time to recuperate.

"Do you know that General Ne Win visited Austria a few months ago?" the ambassador asked Thusandi.

"Yes, he went for medical treatment, didn't he?"

"More precisely, he came to see our top psychiatrist."

Hearing this, Thusandi sat up straight in her chair and leaned forward. "Don't tell me he saw Professor Hoff."

"Why, yes. Do you know him?" The ambassador seemed surprised.

"Of course I do. One summer when we visited Austria, Sao also got to know him fairly well. Professor Hoff was even planning to visit us in Hsipaw before all this happened." Thusandi's face lit up with hope and excitement. She saw a new opportunity to approach Ne Win, and the ambassador did not discourage her.

"Let me also tell you that arrangements are being made for Professor Hoff and his assistant to come to Rangoon. He was invited to continue the general's treatment here."

Thusandi didn't know whether to be glad or furious about this information. She saw an opportunity for some high-powered intervention on her behalf, but she also felt strong resentment against the professor for accepting a ruthless dictator as his patient.

"I think I owe Professor Hoff a long-overdue letter," she said to the ambassador. "He may know about the changes in this country, but he has not heard what happened to us."

"I'd be happy to have your letter delivered through diplomatic channels."

"Thank you, I'll take you up on that." Thusandi felt a surge of energy and optimism. Who could have better access to Ne Win than his psychiatrist? And she strongly believed that Professor Hans Hoff, chairman of the Psychiatric and Neurological University Hospital of Vienna, would use his good offices to help her as much as he could.

Before the Austrian ambassador left for Karachi, he made arrangements for another embassy in Rangoon to maintain contact with Thusandi and forward her mail to him by diplomatic pouch. He also indicated that the Austrian foreign minister, Dr. Bruno Kreisky, would appeal to U Thi Han, the Burmese foreign minister, to send the Prince of Hsipaw and his family into exile in Austria.

Thusandi wasted no time in writing to Professor Hoff, informing him that Sao had been imprisoned by the Burmese Army a year ago and that she had neither seen him nor heard from him since. She asked the professor to help her establish contact with Sao, even enclosing an open letter for her husband in case the professor wished to pass it on.

In Rangoon, Thusandi took advantage of every connection she could muster to find out news about Sao, particularly the news she wanted to hear. The number of astrologers, clairvoyants, relatives of military men, and dubious informants who knocked at her door exceeded that which had come to her in Hsipaw. The better she liked their news about Sao's whereabouts and well-being, the more generous she was with her cash gift. Predicted dates for his release came and went, yet she always had another prediction to rekindle her hopes.

Thusandi also made contact with someone very close to Brigadier Aung Gyi, the second in command; he assured that person during a visit to Pegu that Sao was alive and well. The same message came from the interior minister, U Soe, through a close friend. Thusandi felt hopeful and encouraged again, but not for long. She stayed awake at nights, wondering why she was singled out as the only wife denied contact with her imprisoned husband. Perhaps they were punishing her for defiant behavior after the takeover. Was Sao refusing to confess to crimes he did not commit? Or was he no longer alive? She tossed and turned for hours every night, unable to escape into deep sleep. Thusandi was losing weight, and she found it more and more difficult to make minor decisions concerning daily activities. The problems of double vision, lack of concentration, and difficulties remembering intensified.

It was the wife of the Karen leader, Bo Let Ya, whom she had known for years, who noticed Thusandi's problem and suggested a cure. "Come with me to my meditation master. I guarantee that you'll never regret it."

Thusandi knew instinctively that she should accept the offer.

She was awed by the silence in the room, where at least thirty people sat on the floor, eyes closed, deep in meditation. Walking through the room behind her friend, she stooped low as was customary when passing by meditating Burmese men and women. Some of them looked young enough to be of school age, others old enough to have witnessed the British annexation of Burma. And next to women whose attire suggested considerable wealth sat others in modest cotton clothing. All of them seemed oblivious to the newcomers, absorbed in their search for tranquillity and peace.

The meditation master led them to a separate area of the center. U Winaya was a tall Buddhist monk, wrapped in the orange-yellow robe of his order. Barefoot, his head shaven, he appeared larger than life. His eyes pierced the minds of those who sat before him, uncovering their thoughts and emotions. His face radiated a mixture of compassion and discipline.

Thusandi recognized immediately that he understood her pain, that she did not need to tell him of her suffering. After paying her respects, Thusandi waited until the master addressed her in Burmese.

"You want to learn how to meditate?"

"Yes, I do, but I know nothing about it."

The monk laughed and said, "You don't need to. You'll learn as you practice."

"When may I begin, Sayadaw?"

"Right now," he said.

"But I didn't fast this morning—I ate breakfast."

"That does not matter," he said. "I have no conditions, except that you abstain from alcohol.

"I want you to find a spot in the main room and make yourself comfortable on a mat. You may sit any way you feel comfortable. Then, you must close your eyes and concentrate on breathing rapidly through your nose. Try it now. Can you feel cool air passing your nostrils as you inhale and warm air when you release it?"

He waited till Thusandi tried and nodded affirmatively. Then he continued. "Be aware of when your mind starts wandering or when outside noises distract you. You must gently but firmly dismiss any other thoughts or sensations and return your mind to the breathing process. I will tell you when you should discontinue this. At that point, you must concentrate on any major physical sensation in your body until it goes away."

"What do you mean by that?" Thusandi asked the master.

"You will see," was all he said.

Thusandi slowly got up and backed away from the monk as she was supposed to. She found a spot among the meditating crowd, close to her friend, who was already doing her breathing exercise.

"I don't know what I'm doing, but I might as well give this a try," she said to herself. She closed her eyes and followed the master's instructions. The first few minutes seemed easy, but then Thusandi lost her concentration. Thoughts about Sao entered her mind, and she remembered how he had meditated in their private chapel in Hsipaw. Those were happy memories and she savored them.

"Stop those memories and concentrate on your breathing," Thusandi heard the meditation master say to her in a firm but gentle voice. She wondered how he knew what was going on in her mind.

During her first sitting, Thusandi was told many times to direct her mind toward the tip of her nose. Intermittently, breathing became painful and difficult. But the sayadaw was always beside her when she needed encouragement and guidance, as he was for everyone meditating around her.

After twenty minutes, he told Thusandi to concentrate on a physical sensation in her body. Her back ached terribly, and she had no problem thinking about the spot that hurt most. She didn't know how long it was before that excruciating pain disappeared completely, but it did, simply by the power of concentration. And the sayadaw knew when she had reached that stage.

"You may open your eyes now. Your first sitting is over."

Thusandi opened her eyes in amazement. She looked at her watch and realized that she had spent forty minutes on her first attempt at meditation. She felt tired, yet refreshed, and determined to persevere with her meditation on a daily basis.

Over the following months, while the children were at school, Thusandi meditated under the watchful eyes of U Winaya. After the rapid breathing routine, Thusandi began seeing beautiful colors and shapes, only to be told by U Winaya to stop such visions immediately and concentrate on a physical occurrence. She hesitated to let go of the brilliant blue circles—they raced by her at ever-increasing speed until they changed color. It took more than one reminder by the meditation master to tear Thusandi away from these extraordinary visions.

At some sessions she felt excruciating pain, at others she was aware of sinking into the ground, deeper and deeper until she was buried under its surface. Once, all her limbs fell off her torso, like apples from a tree, except for one hand that remained, growing grotesquely out of all proportions.

Under U Winaya's direction, Thusandi overcame these various sensations and gained a new awareness of her physical existence. Then Thusandi had her first out-of-body experience. Without warning, she moved away from her body, leaving it behind on the floor of the meditation room. As she hovered over the room and observed the physical shell of herself down below, she felt herself cease to exist as a separate entity. An indescribable feeling of harmony and peace came over her.

A few weeks later, when she was meditating, she started to see faces—hundreds of them coming toward her, merging with bodies that marched past her eyes. Initially, they were whole and sound. But as the procession continued, they took on various stages of decomposition until skeletons supporting hollow skulls paraded past her. Thusandi observed the images with amazement, recognizing herself in each of the bodies.

Although her situation had not changed, Thusandi's state of mind was transformed by her meditation. She felt peace again; she had regained her strength and her power to concentrate and to make decisions; and she recognized more clearly what mattered in life and what did not. Thusandi was approaching the point when she could decide on a future course for herself and her daughters.

Nineteen

In spite of abounding predictions that the days of Ne Win's regime were numbered, his army tightened its hold over the country's people and its economy. Large business enterprises and foreign-owned firms were taken over first. Then all banks were nationalized, renamed as people's banks, and numbered. Thusandi's Rangoon bank, which was owned by several Shans, including Sao, became People's Bank No. 20, managed by a lieutenant commander of the Burmese Navy.

Smaller businesses—gas stations, rice mills, oil mills, and saw-mills—were confiscated next, leaving the rightful owners financially ruined. Soon after, all retail shops, even the smallest, were taken over. On her daily drive to the children's school, Thusandi saw incredible scenes: Soldiers walked into little shops of all kinds, took possession of them, physically removed the owners, and exchanged the shop's existing sign with one that read "People's Shop No. 37," or whatever. People in uniforms remained to operate the store, while the previous owners were deprived of their business, their stock, and their opportunity to earn a living. Businessmen and professionals of Indian origin not only lost their businesses and practices, they were deported with nothing but the clothes on their back. One of Thusandi's doctors was deported after his home, his dogs, and his prize orchids were confiscated along with all his belongings. Rumors circulated that all private houses, automobiles, jewelry, and large-denomination bank notes were next on Ne Win's hit list. The government was expected to take over the private practices of all doctors and lawyers, regardless of their nationality; pharmacies had already been confiscated. As the number of ruined entrepreneurs grew, many of them barricaded their houses, hoping to keep the official thieves at bay. They entrusted children and servants with their life savings, sending them daily to banks to exchange large bank notes for small ones without arousing the suspicion of the uniformed bank managers.

Thusandi watched these developments very closely. Her limited financial resources were dwindling, while her obligations remained the same. Many people asked her for help, but she had nobody to whom she could turn for financial support. Sao had never heeded his friends' advice to secure funds in a foreign country. It was against the law, and he never compromised his high ethical standards.

Thusandi maintained regular contact with Hsipaw, but the news was seldom good. The Foundation School had been shut down, the remaining agricultural machinery had been confiscated, and she was unable to gain access to her local investments. Moreover, the new orange crop was expected to be very meager.

It had become clear to Thusandi that she could not wait for Sao in Rangoon indefinitely. She had to start planning for a new life in Europe or the United States, where she could earn a living for herself and her daughters. When Sao could join them, he probably would not be able to work for some time. Her foreign friends, whom she met secretly at various locations, urged her to leave Burma without delay. But her Shan family wanted Thusandi to stay in the country, and she delayed making a decision.

She decided to use the months of waiting constructively, by taking French lessons and enrolling in a typing class. An old man, part Burmese, part Indian, whose little business had been confiscated, had opened a one-room typing school. Her Austrian high school had not taught typing, and Thusandi had always regretted this deficiency. One day she asked Hla Tin, the driver, to take her to the side street in downtown Rangoon where the typing school of Mr. Murti was located. The Mercedes and the MIS spy-jeep parked in a busy street in an impoverished neighborhood. Thusandi climbed dark stairs to Mr. Murti's typing school on the fourth floor. She felt nauseous from the stench rising from the street's open sewers, which a handkerchief drenched in cologne did not neutralize. Thusandi's pace slowed considerably as she approached the fourth floor. For a moment she considered turning back, to avoid ever having to return to these surroundings. When she knocked, old Mr. Murti opened the door and stared at

Thusandi in utmost surprise, as if she were an apparition. She was happy that he did not slam the door in her face. When he had collected himself, she was able to convince him that she was serious about learning how to type and that she would pay him well.

The first lesson began as soon as Thusandi had taken a look around the one-room school and its six old Underwood typewriters. Not a single one of them had letters on the keyboard. Mr. Murti explained that the typewriters were very old and the letters had fallen out of their metal frames. Thusandi soon learned that a soft mass had replaced them: Every time she hit a key, her fingers got stuck in a dark, sticky substance that over the years had replaced the letters—she preferred not to speculate on its origin.

In spite of minor inconveniences, the typing course proved to be a success, at least for Thusandi. Hla Tin, however, reported that the MIS men complained bitterly at having to spend so many hours sitting in such a distasteful street, waiting for the object of their surveillance to learn to type.

In preparation for a return to the West, Thusandi had some dresses made for herself. She wore them occasionally at home, or in the company of her Scandinavian friends, just to get used to Western clothing again. But it was obvious to her that longyi and aingyi were the only sensible things to wear. The ankle-length longyi protected her legs from mosquito bites, and the aingyi could be changed three or four times a day, depending on the effects of heat and humidity on the wearer.

CHRISTMAS IN RANGOON OFFERED the children a wonderful introduction to Santa Claus, stockings, plum pudding, and carols. The English Methodist School put great emphasis on this holiday, involving the girls in exciting activities that were new to them. Thusandi sensed that they might spend their next Christmas in Austria.

On Christmas morning, something happened that left no doubt in Thusandi's mind that she was still in Rangoon. Tawng, her Kachin nanny, surprised them with an eight-pound baby boy, even though nobody had suspected her pregnancy. When Pa Saw discovered the mother and her infant in the servants' quarters at dawn, Tawng was kneeling over the naked infant, trying to choke it. Pa Saw and Thusandi had their hands full assisting an emotionally distraught mother and a newborn whose umbilical cord had yet to be cut.

Thusandi carried the bathed and wrapped baby into the house to call a doctor. She had some explaining to do to her daughters. They had many questions about the baby and its unwed mother, until Mayari remembered what she had learned in school.

"This is a Christmas baby, just like Jesus," she exclaimed, turning to Kennari and to everybody who would listen to her logical explanation. And with that, the matter was closed, at least for the younger generation.

Thusandi, however, was distracted for a few days from her main concerns about Sao and their future. She learned who the father of Tawng's child was, but she never found out why Tawng had attempted infanticide. Everybody wanted to have children, and to take life, any life, went against the belief system of Kachins, Shans, and Burmese alike. The household staff believed that evil spirits had possessed Tawng. Thusandi thought that the unwed mother might have acted out of fear. Tawng became attached to her son, but she did not respond when Thusandi probed as to why she had wanted to kill her own child.

A month after the Christmas baby's arrival, Pa Saw unexpectedly died in her sleep. The sudden death of her trusted nanny shocked Thusandi profoundly. She realized that the extended family around her was disintegrating, that she could not delay a decision about leaving Burma much longer.

Almost two years had passed since Sao's disappearance, and she still had had no word from him or any reliable information as to his whereabouts. Thusandi believed strongly that he would return one day, but she felt more and more doubtful that he wanted her to remain in Burma. She remembered a conversation more than four years ago when Sao had prepared her for such an eventuality. He had just returned from a meeting in Taunggyi, and they were relaxing on their bedroom verandah.

"You must promise me something," he said.

"What is it, my love?" she asked, drawing closer to him as she savored his presence in the cool evening breeze. "I'll promise you almost anything after missing you for two long weeks."

Sao put his arm around her shoulder and held her tight. Instead of responding in a light-hearted tone, he became very serious. "Listen to me and hear me out before you say anything. The political tensions between the Shan states and Burma proper are getting very serious. If one day I don't return home from one of my trips, or if something happens to me, you must leave Hsipaw and go back to Austria with the children. You would not be safe here without me."

Thusandi said nothing for a while. The seriousness with which Sao spoke almost paralyzed her.

"If something like that should ever happen, I would want to look for you first," she said.

"No. It wouldn't do any good. I want you and our daughters to go back to your country and wait for me there. If you don't hear from me for a few years, then you should find somebody who'll take care of you and the children."

She kissed him and said, "Nothing like that is ever going to happen. Please don't worry me with such horrible thoughts."

"Let's hope you are right. But I must have your promise just in case." Sao looked at his wife expectantly.

"Okay, I promise," she said at last.

Thusandi recalled every word from that conversation as if it had occurred yesterday. She had thought hundreds of times about the urgency of Sao's request and her promise to him.

AFTER THUSANDI HAD DECIDED to follow Sao's wish and leave the country, her hopes were raised again. Ne Win declared an impending amnesty. As thousands awaited the release of the detained, Ne Win played a cruel trick on them; he released only convicted criminals from the country's jails to make more room for political prisoners. The leadership of the Stable AFPFL, a party that had previously been close to the army, was arrested along with more students and ethnic minorities. Sources close to Ne Win reported that large-scale releases could be expected on the second anniversary of the takeover. Thusandi waited anxiously, but she also planned to leave for Austria should that date pass without any word from or about Sao.

In the meantime, she continued to press for official news of Sao, sending inquiries, petitions, messengers. Thanks to the discreet assistance of three embassies, she could use diplomatic channels to correspond with U Thant (UN secretary-general), the International Red Cross, and the Austrian ambassador in Karachi. U Thant wrote her that he was certain Sao was in "protective custody." The International Red Cross informed her that the Burmese delegation refused to accept a letter for Ne Win inquiring why Sao was held incommunicado. The Austrian ambassador sent a copy of a letter from Bruno Kreisky, the Austrian foreign minister, to U Thi Han, his Burmese counterpart, asking for Sao's release to Austria. He also forwarded a letter from Professor Hoff, assuring Thusandi that he would personally hand Thusandi's letter for Sao to Ne Win when he visited Rangoon.

Thusandi planned once more to see Ne Win. The day before carrying out this plan, she met secretly with two diplomats. As soon as she joined the two men, she noticed that something other than her own concerns was preoccupying them. She did not have to wait long to hear their news.

"You'll never guess what I saw last night," one of the diplomats said to her.

"Does it have to do with me?" Thusandi asked him.

"Not directly. In a way. It was General Ne Win."

Now he had Thusandi's full attention. Leaning forward, she said, "I'm listening."

"It must have been eleven o'clock. A group of us were enjoying an evening at the Inya Lake Hotel. The band was pretty good and some people were dancing. I was having a drink when, all of a sudden, Ne Win, followed by half a dozen soldiers, stormed into the banquet room."

The young diplomat paused to light a cigarette.

"And . . . what happened?"

"Ne Win looked very upset, and his face was as red as your longyi. With a golf club in his hand, he stormed up to the band and yelled something in Burmese that I couldn't understand."

"And then?"

"He hit the drums with his golf club and ruined them. Then he turned his club on the drummer. But that was not all. An attaché from our embassy hurried over and tried to calm him."

"Did he succeed?"

"On the contrary, Ne Win started attacking the attaché and swinging his golf club at him. He didn't stop until the poor man was on the floor, bleeding. Then he stormed off."

"How badly was the attaché hurt?" the second diplomat asked.

"He had to have eighty stitches on his face, arm, and hand."

"It just shows the violence he is capable of," the second diplomat said, shaking his head.

Thusandi knew then and there that she would not carry out her plan to try and reason with this madman. She would, however, continue to pursue other ways and means to find Sao.

THEN CAME TWO SETS OF conflicting information. A messenger informed her that one of the diplomats needed to see her urgently. Thusandi wasted no time in going to a clandestine meeting place, playing an old trick on the MIS jeep. She had Hla Tin drive her to somebody's house. While her car and the MIS patiently waited for her outside, Thusandi took the rear exit and used a jeep that was waiting for her in the street behind the house.

The diplomat greeted her by waving two envelopes. "I have two important letters for you."

One was from the Austrian Embassy in Karachi, but on the other Thusandi recognized the handwriting of Professor Hoff.

"Is he in town?" she asked.

"Yes, he is, as the special guest of Ne Win."

Thusandi impatiently tore open the envelope and started reading his handwritten letter:

"Dear Inge,

Although I won't be able to see you during this trip, I want to tell you how concerned I am about your well-being. I hope you will not delay your departure for Austria much longer. I can assure you that Sao would want you and the children to be with your parents until he can join you again.

It has not been possible for me to see Sao, but I have good news of him. The general has assured me that Sao is well and that two orderlies have been assigned to take care of all his needs. The physician who looks after Sao was introduced to me, and he testified that Sao is in good shape, both physically and emotionally. The general accepted your letter to your husband and told me that you should expect mail from him soon.

I wanted to send you this information without delay because I can imagine how much it will mean to you. Although this news is very encouraging, I hope to see you in Vienna very soon. Till I see you there, my very best wishes to you and the children.

(signed) Hans Hoff"

Thusandi didn't dare believe her eyes. She read the letter once, twice, and a third time before she felt her eyes filling with tears. Finally, she had received what she had been waiting for since March 1962: the admission by Ne Win himself that Sao was in the hands of the government. And a military doctor verified that statement. Thusandi felt like falling to her knees. But she did not know what to make of the story that two orderlies were looking after Sao; it did not fit the picture.

Without saying a word, she handed the letter to the diplomat, who read it and exclaimed, "This restores some of my faith in Ne Win! I am truly happy for you. Don't you want to see the other letter? Maybe it'll bring more good news."

Thusandi took the second envelope, opening it with less haste than the one from Professor Hoff. As she read the letter from the ambassador, her face expressed disbelief.

"I don't understand this," she said. "The Burmese foreign minister informed Dr. Kreisky, his Austrian counterpart, that Sao was never taken into custody by the Burmese Military Government and that his whereabouts are unknown to them."

"Let me see," the diplomat said. He took the letter from her and read it carefully.

"This is not a good sign," he said. "May I take this with me and make a copy for Professor Hoff?"

"Please do. I'll write to him and send my letter to you tomorrow. Will you be able to forward it?"

Thusandi left abruptly. She needed to be alone with her emotions, to reflect on the guarded happiness she felt. What was the meaning of these two contradictory pieces of information? She wanted to disregard the foreign minister's letter, but such an official statement could not be taken lightly. On the other hand, it seemed impossible that Ne Win would lie to his own psychiatrist.

Thusandi asked Hla Tin to take her to the meditation center. She could not allow herself to be consumed with emotional turmoil. Clarity of mind and a measure of detachment had to be her objectives right now, so her decisions would be the best possible. As expected, meditation restored Thusandi's inner peace. When she opened her eyes, feeling calm and strong, it suddenly became very clear to her that she must leave the country without delay. Thusandi knew from past experience that she needed to take such insights seriously.

She walked across the courtyard to see Daw Khin Myo Chit, a respected Burmese woman writer and a member of the *thakin* party; her small house was always open to visitors. Along with the Thirty Comrades, including Ne Win and Bo Setkya, she had collaborated with the Japanese to oust the British from Burma. Thusandi hoped to find Paula there. Paula was a vibrant and reliable young woman who was well connected in military circles, and she had volunteered her help to Thusandi months ago. When Paula answered the door, Thusandi took it to be a sign that the time to ask for her help had indeed come.

"Can we talk in private, Paula?" Thusandi asked her. She had caught a glimpse inside of a dozen people engaged in an animated discussion with Daw Khin Myo Chit.

"Of course, Elder Sister," Paula said as she tried to extract her slippers from the mound of thongs outside the door.

The two women walked toward the shade of a big banyan tree on the far side of the compound. Thusandi started to speak. "Today, at the end of my meditation, I saw clearly that I must leave Burma and return to my parents in Austria—with the children, of course."

Paula stopped and turned to face Thusandi.

"I am not surprised. Actually, I had expected it some time ago. Is there anything I can do to help?"

"Oh, yes. I hoped you would repeat your offer. I need to know what I should do to get an exit permit for me and my daughters."

"That should be easy for me to find out, Elder Sister. I know exactly where to go," Paula said cheerfully, as if she had just been invited to participate in an exciting adventure.

Thusandi hummed a tune on the way home, feeling confident that she was on the right course, with the right person helping her. She knew her own inquiries would get her nowhere—they never had. It was still a mystery to her why as an Austrian she was not permitted to return to the country of her citizenship without an exit permit.

Sao had always cautioned her not to rush into the acquisition of Burmese citizenship. Now she saw the wisdom of his counsel. Thusandi clearly remembered a conversation she had with U Nu. Asked by him when she would become a Burmese citizen, she replied, "Elder Brother, I think I'll wait for Shan citizenship."

Twenty

IT TOOK PAULA ONLY A FEW DAYS
to gather her information. "Elder Sister," she told Thusandi at the meditation center, "you will be allowed to leave the country if you follow the
proper procedures."

"And the children? What about the children?"

"They can leave only if you can prove that they are Austrian citizens." Paula looked at Thusandi with concern. This was precisely the
answer Thusandi had dreaded. She was painfully aware of the fact that the
children of a Burmese citizen born in the Union of Burma were Burmese
subjects, regardless of their mother's status. However, she was determined.

"Thank you, Paula. I will prove that my daughters are Austrian citizens. And after that, will you help me again?"

Paula looked a bit skeptical, but she refrained from saying anything discouraging. She only said, "You can always count on my help,
Elder Sister."

Thusandi sent her passport to the Austrian Embassy in Karachi and
asked to have her children included on it. Ambassador Kolb's reply was
immediate and negative. Such an action was against Austrian law, and even
if it were done illegally, it would not fool the Burmese authorities. Though
discouraged, Thusandi did not give up. Her next effort was directed to the
Austrian Embassy in Bangkok, which was not in charge of Austrian interests in Burma.

In the meantime, the second anniversary of the military takeover had
passed. A few Burmese students were released from prison; thousands more
remained in jail without due process, without explanation. Sao's letter to
Thusandi, promised to Professor Hoff by Ne Win, never arrived. A colonel

from the Foreign Ministry told Thusandi that he was present when U Thi Han, the foreign minister, asked Ne Win how to respond to the Austrian foreign minister's inquiry about Sao. Ne Win himself instructed U Thi Han to deny that Sao was in the hands of the Burmese military and to state that he was never arrested. Thusandi decided that she had to pursue Sao's freedom from outside Burma—that their hope lay in the United Nations, the International Red Cross, the International Court of Justice, the newly founded Amnesty International, and several concerned governments.

Mayari and Kennari had finished their school year with high honors and great enthusiasm for the English Methodist School. When Thusandi tried to prepare them for the journey to Austria, they were cautiously curious. Mayari, remembering that an Austrian doctor had removed her tonsils when she was three, asked for a written guarantee that this would not happen again. Kennari extracted a promise from Thusandi that she could eat all the chocolate she wanted. And both girls asked if Papa would be waiting for them at the airport in Vienna.

Thusandi proceeded with all possible preparations for their departure. Besides emotional issues, practical matters needed careful attention and the cooperation of relatives and friends. One of the few lawyers still in private practice secretly prepared legal papers for the designated caretakers of the Hsipaw estate. Thusandi preferred not to discuss her plans openly until she had the necessary travel documents. Her three Scandinavian friends provided moral support and helpful suggestions. One of them, Bettan, volunteered the following: "I'm willing to fly to Bangkok and camp out at the Austrian Embassy until they fix up Inge's passport to include the children's names. Of course, you'll all have to look after my family while I'm gone."

This proposal met enthusiastic approval, and Thusandi insisted on assuming financial responsibility for the trip. Due to her diplomatic status, Bettan was able to go within a few days, leaving behind several very nervous friends. It took her only two days in Bangkok to achieve the impossible. She returned with the doctored passport, which included pictures of Mayari and Kennari, lots of official seals, and an entry stating: "The Austrian government hereby certifies that Mayari and Kennari are Austrian citizens."

"How in the world did you do it?" her friends asked Bettan with genuine surprise and admiration.

Mayari (right) and Kennari (left) in Rangoon shortly before escaping to Austria with their mother.

"It wasn't too difficult," she replied. "I was very lucky in finding some unexpected help."

"I just don't know how to thank you . . . I'm so overwhelmed," Thusandi said, holding back tears and pressing the invaluable passport against her chest.

"I'm so happy I could help. And once I tell you the story, you'll see that I had fun in the process." Bettan lit a cigarette and leaned back in the chair, a satisfied smile spreading over her face.

"Don't make us wait any longer. Tell us what happened," Gerd said impatiently.

"I went to the Austrian Embassy straight from the airport, hoping to see Ambassador Mayr-Harting, who is known as a true humanitarian. He wasn't there, so I made my plea to the first secretary. His answer was a loud and unequivocal "no." I appealed to his sense of compassion and chivalry. It didn't work. Then I said I would just stay at the embassy until the ambassador came, or until he changed his mind. I pulled out my book and started reading. When he saw what I was reading, the first secretary recognized which country I was from. He asked me if I knew a certain girl in my home town. I certainly did—she was my cousin. When I told him that, his behavior changed and he became very friendly. He confessed that he had dated my cousin and that he hoped to visit her on his next home leave."

"What an incredible coincidence," Gerd interjected as Bettan paused before continuing.

"Anyway, after that discovery everything was possible, even though my request was highly illegal. It took the first secretary half an hour to get his kind-hearted ambassador's permission to fix the passport to my specifications. Then he took me to my hotel and asked me out to dinner. He had a wonderful time talking about my cousin while I celebrated my success. I would have liked to stay in Bangkok a few more days, but my mission was accomplished."

Thusandi slept with the passport under her pillow for the next few days, considering it her most valuable asset. She realized, though, that any well-trained foreign service official would recognize the entry of her children as improper and endanger their flight from the country. Therefore, she planned a low-key approach to the Immigration Office, expecting it to be staffed by uninformed army personnel rather than career officials, like all the other branches of government. Her first visit to the Immigration Office, housed at the former Rangoon racetrack facilities, proved her suspicion correct. There was not a single civilian among the uniformed officials dealing with long lines of people who wished to leave the country. "Immigration office" was a misnomer; nobody wanted to enter the country.

A lieutenant took Thusandi's application forms, the fees, and her precious passport, promising to forward the paperwork to higher authorities. Yes, she could come back in a few days to inquire about her case, which would be expedited due to the serious illness of her mother in Austria—the official reason she gave for wanting to leave the country. Thusandi returned to the office regularly for five weeks, first every few days, then on a daily basis. She always heard the same answer to her inquiry: "We don't have a decision yet. Come back tomorrow." Cables from her mother's Austrian doctors were added to the official file, but they did not seem to have any impact on the process.

Waiting proved to be another exercise in patience. Supported by her friends and by the discipline of meditation, Thusandi kept her spirits up. The Water Festival came and went, almost as if it were a strange event of little concern to Thusandi. The children, however, took advantage of the festivities to frolic with buckets of water, emptying them everywhere on everybody. These soakings provided welcome relief during the hottest days of the year.

On the ninth of May, on her daily visit to the Immigration Office, Thusandi was ushered into a private office by the lieutenant who usually handled her case. This must be a good sign, she thought as she expectantly looked at the captain across the desk.

"I don't have good news for you, Mahadevi," he said, avoiding eye contact with her.

"What do you mean by that?" Thusandi was stunned.

"The MIS has taken your file away from our offices without any explanation. I'm sorry. There is nothing further we can do."

Thusandi sat, unable to move, overcome by a sense of utter hopelessness. If the MIS is intervening, she thought, they must be aware of the invalid entry in the passport. When she finally looked at the captain, she saw concern and compassion in his eyes. She was touched by this unexpected regard for her.

"Thank you for telling me," she said to the captain. "I realize you did not have to."

Hla Tin drove a very quiet Thusandi back to the house. Within a block of reaching home, she redirected him to the meditation center. After the initial shock had subsided, she determined it was time to ask for Paula's help again. At this point, only Paula could prevail.

Paula did prevail. Two days later, on May 11 at six o'clock, Paula arrived at Thusandi's house, out of breath, on her bicycle. When the two women were alone, Paula handed Thusandi an exit permit.

"Here is your permission to leave with the children, Elder Sister. But you must leave tonight on the weekly Pan Am flight."

"Why tonight?"

"Because a lower-ranking MIS officer gave permission in the absence of Colonel Lwin, who'll be back tomorrow."

"We will leave tonight, Paula, thanks to you. But how did you manage to get this permission for us?"

"Let's just say that a childhood friend with kindness in his heart decided to take a risk."

All of a sudden Thusandi remembered her passport. "Paula, where is it?" Her mood changed from joy to fear.

"I was promised that you'll get it at the airport before you board the plane. So I think you'd better get busy and start packing. I'll come by later and go to the airport with you." With that, Paula left, pedaling away on her bike during one of Rangoon's hottest evenings.

Moments later, the household was turned upside down by feverish activity. Thusandi called the children first and told them that they would be leaving for Austria in four hours. She charged each with packing her most precious possessions into one suitcase. Next, Thusandi had to break the news to her household staff, release them from her services, and hand over sufficient funds for them to return to Hsipaw and to provide for their livelihood. Documents, jewelry, and cash to run the Rangoon house went to a nephew. The suddenness of events took everybody by surprise and did not give Thusandi's extended family a chance to reflect.

When she had a few minutes to herself, Thusandi took a last look at the papers and jewelry she had to leave behind. Diamonds, rubies, and sapphires had been part of her daily wardrobe, and as she placed them neatly into her jewelry box, Thusandi felt she was bidding farewell to good friends. She was tempted to take her ruby engagement ring with her, but she slowly removed it from her finger. Paula had warned her that nobody, diplomats included, was allowed to take any valuables out of the country. Even the wife of an ambassador had been forced to leave her wedding band and engagement ring behind when she left the country. Thusandi then turned her attention to some foreign currency bank notes hidden among her papers. They were left over from previous trips abroad, and under the new regime it was highly illegal to own any of them. Although Thusandi expected to arrive in Vienna without a penny in her pocket, she decided against taking these British pounds and U.S. dollars with her. In the bathroom, she set a match to them and flushed what was left down the toilet.

Packing proved to be incredibly difficult. Their lives had to fit into three suitcases and weigh no more than forty pounds each. The only redeeming factor was the lack of time; it did not allow for indecision and sentimental attachment. What Thusandi found in her closet was not exactly suitable for wearing in Austria. She had a few summer dresses, tailored in Rangoon, but everything else was twelve years old and dated in style and length. The hundreds of longyis would have to stay behind, with all the other belongings that had been important to her.

It was a frightening moment when Thusandi, Mayari, Kennari, and their three suitcases rolled away from their little house in Rangoon. Thusandi closed her eyes as her car sped through the dark tropical night toward the airport. She remembered how nervous she had been when Sao had first taken her to Mingaladon airport almost twelve years ago. On that trip they had been eager to fly north and settle into their new home in Hsipaw. This time, she was anxious to leave her adopted country, with their children, not knowing if Sao would ever come to join them. She smiled when she looked at their beautiful daughters beside her. Their father wished for them to grow up in a stable environment with freedom and opportunity; she planned to fulfill his wishes.

Paula, Bettan, Mabel, and a few Shan relatives came to bid them farewell at Mingaladon airport. Thusandi saw fear in their faces: fear that she and the children might not pass through the various checkpoints successfully and would not be allowed to proceed to freedom. The moment for goodbyes came quickly and allowed for little else except short and tearful embraces.

Two MIS officers escorted Thusandi and the children into a small room, on the way to the gate.

Once inside, the captain said, "We have a few questions."

Thusandi nodded her head while the children, clutching her hands, looked up at the uniformed man with their big, wondering eyes.

"Why do you wish to leave the Union of Burma?"

"My mother is very ill, and she needs me."

"What do you plan to do in Austria?"

"To look after my mother."

"Are you carrying any jewelry, documents, or foreign currency?"

"Only this simple wedding band," she said as she stretched out her left hand. At the last moment she had decided to defy all warnings and wear the golden band Sao had slipped on her finger when they were married.

Then the search began—of the carry-on luggage, her handbag, the children's little travel pouches, even their toys. The two officers searched feverishly, and they looked more and more disappointed when nothing suspicious was found. Soldiers brought the three suitcases for the officers to search. Thusandi's heart almost stopped when she considered that they could have planted something incriminating in her luggage. But nothing was found. After half an hour, the MIS officers seemed satisfied and said, "We will take you to the plane."

Thusandi still had not seen her passport, and time was running out. She held her daughters' hands tightly as she followed the two men. They were led through the gate toward the Pan Am Boeing 707, the only plane bound for Europe that, once a week, stopped in Rangoon. Then, at the foot of the steps leading to the plane, the MIS captain pulled out Thusandi's Austrian passport and handed it to her.

"Thank you," she said, as if she had expected nothing less. The steps leading to the front door of the plane seemed miles long. Thusandi made her daughters climb the stairs in front of her.

Suddenly, on the second step, her feet felt heavy and disconnected from the rest of her body. She could not move and was unable to follow the children.

She could not move her feet. Thusandi felt her heart pounding in her throat and heard her teeth chatter. She did not know what was holding her back, preventing her from proceeding with her flight to freedom. Not Sao, she thought—he wanted her to leave. It flashed through her mind that a part of herself was clinging to her adopted homeland and could not let go. Thusandi closed her eyes and started her meditation practice, standing on the stairs of the plane she had been desperate to board for so many months. With the first breath she took consciously, her inner calm returned, and so did her strength to reach the top of the stairs.

Once Thusandi and her children were seated and buckled in, the doors were shut and the plane began to taxi away from the terminal. As long as they were still on the ground, Thusandi feared a last-minute reversal of her permission to leave. At long last, the pilot revved the engines for take-off. The half-empty plane left the ground and rose very quickly. The captain's voice came over the intercom. "Ladies and gentlemen, we are finally on our way to Calcutta. Our flying time will be approximately two hours. I would like to remind you that we are still in Burmese airspace, subject to their orders."

Thusandi wondered why he said that. Could they still order the plane to turn back? She did not dare believe that they were, at last, on their way to a new and very different life. The children were being showered with gifts by the stewardess: crayons, books, toys, playing cards, flight pins, all treasures that occupied them for a while. This allowed Thusandi's thoughts to return to land—to Sao and the past eleven years she had spent with him. She sensed that this part of her life was over, though she would not admit it to herself or anybody else for years to come. She had to channel her energy toward the future and leave the past behind. Many challenges lay ahead; she was about to return to the West as a single mother with two children. She did not know how she would support them or where they would settle after the initial visit to her parents. She did not even know how she could make a phone call from Vienna airport or pay for transportation without a penny, any penny, in her pocket. Her thoughts were interrupted by another announcement from the captain.

"Ladies and gentlemen, we have just left Burmese airspace."

A spontaneous outburst of clapping filled the cabin of Pan Am flight 001. Thusandi, Mayari, and Kennari joined in. They clapped louder and longer than any other passengers on the flight, though they were not the only ones fleeing Ne Win's police state. Tears began streaming down Thusandi's cheeks, and she made no attempt to stop them. She did not know if they were tears of sorrow or tears of joy; she was overwhelmed by a mixture of deep sadness and rekindled hope.

Epilogue

❖ ❖ ❖ ❖ ❖ ❖ ❖ ❖ ❖ ❖ ❖

THE MILITARY REGIME IN BURMA has never acknowledged its responsibility for the disappearance from custody of Sao Kya Seng more than thirty years ago. Continuous efforts by the author to hold the government of Burma accountable failed. Repeated inquiries into the fate of the Prince of Hsipaw by the governments of Austria, Great Britain, and the United States were met with silence. The United Nations, the International Red Cross, the International Court of Justice, Amnesty International, and other international organizations have been unable to provide assistance to the author in her search for Sao Kya Seng.

Having committed the ultimate human rights violation against the prince, Ne Win and his men have been immune to the consequences of their actions. However, one of their most recent victims, Nobel Peace Prize winner Daw Aung San Suu Kyi, has succeeded in focusing world attention on their crimes against their own people. Only such attention can release the gentle peoples of Burma—be they Shans, Karens, Palaungs, or members of the other ethnic groups—from the oppression that has devastated their lives for the past three decades.

GLOSSARY

AINGYI (AYN-jee). Waist-length blouse, part of Burmese dress for women;
 traditionally fastened by five removable jewelry buttons.

BIRIANI. Indian rice dish prepared with spices and chicken or lamb.

BOHMUGYI. Burmese for "colonel."

BUHENG. Shan district headman.

BUMONG. Shan village headman.

DEWA. Gods from Hindu mythology.

HAW. Residence of Shan ruling prince and family.

HTEE. Jeweled umbrella-shaped metal tip of pagoda.

KADAW. Paying respects to someone of age or status by kneeling, folding
 hands, and bowing three times; may involve offerings.

KHOWLAM. Shan snack of sticky rice cooked in bamboo stick.

KYAT (CHUT). Burmese currency. Exchange rate and value in the fifties
 was approximately six kyats to one U.S. dollar.

LEUN HSAM. Third month of year according to Shan calendar.

LEUN SHEE. Fourth month of year according to Shan calendar.

LONGYI (LOWN-jee). Ankle-length wraparound skirt, or sarong; part of
 Burmese dress for women and men.

MAHADEVI (ma-hah-DAY-vee). "Celestial Princess"; title bestowed on consort by Shan Saopha.

NAT. Supernatural being, or spirit, in Burmese and Shan belief systems.

NGAPI. Fermented, salty fish paste; ingredient in many Burmese dishes.

PANTHE KHOWSOI. Muslim noodle and curry dish.

PONGYI. Ordained Buddhist monk; must have stayed in Sangha, or order
 of monks, for at least ten years.

PUREE. Indian fried bread.

PWE (PWAY). Festival; gathering of people for enjoyment at religious or other occasions. In the Shan states, gambling was an important part of most pwes.

SAHTOO. An expression of gratitude and respect.

SAOPHA (sao-PAH), SAOPHALONG (sao-pa-LONG). Ruling Shan prince, hereditary chief; Sawbwa (SAW-wah) or Sawbwagyi (saw-wah-GEE) in Burmese.

SAOPYIPHA (sao-PEE-pa). Address of Saopha or Saophalong by someone younger.

SAYADAW. Abbot of a major Buddhist teaching monastery.

SAYAMA. Title of nurse or female teacher.

STUPA. Buddhist relic shrine. Also called pagoda or *zedi*.

TANAKA. Cooling makeup paste made from tree bark.

TATMADAW. The Burmese Army.

THAKIN (tah-KIN). Burmese title for a man who is highly respected.

THAMEIN. Traditional saronglike woman's long skirt.

THONAU. Dried fermented soybean cakes, a Shan food staple.

Place Names

BAWGYO (BAWH-joe).
HSIPAW (SEE-paw).
INLE (IN-lay).
KYAUKME (CHOW-may).
SAKANDAR (su-KAHN-dar).
TAUNGGYI (town-JEE).